Index

Chapter One: Jungle Evil

Chapter Two: Finding a Monk

Chapter Three: Getting a Scar

Chapter Four: Departing Phnom Penh

Chapter Five: A Meal Missed

Chapter Six: Forever Pain

Chapter Seven: The Boogie Man

Chapter Eight: Out of the Jungle

Chapter Nine: Going Fishing

Chapter Ten: Finding Her Family

Chapter Eleven: Leaving Cambodia

Foreword

This book is dedicated to the people of Cambodia and to my dear friends who endured unbelievable hardships and still to this day have the emotional scars from traumas suffered in the early years of their lives under the Khmer Rouge and Pol Pot.

For my mother, Jo Hayes, who never stopped believing, that thru my writing, I would someday truly learn to express myself.

A special thanks to Jeanie Calci.

"Do not fear the pain of love; fear a heart that is no longer able to love" Pablito

Prelude

Cars rolled past the gas station at the corner of Harwin and Gessner in Houston. Three sides of the gas station have windows that open on to the busy streets around the station; the fourth side of the gas station was brick.

Turning into the strip shopping center behind the station, a car entered the alley behind the strip center. Turning off the car lights, the car came to a stop. A person got out of the car and begins to tape pieces of cardboard over the license tags of the vehicle.

The driver leaves the vehicle and cautiously walks about a hundred and twenty feet to the east side of the gas station. He stays hidden in the blind spot of the gas station where those inside could not see cars or people approaching from his vantage point. The gas station has a back exit door, because there is a trash dumpster sitting just outside this back exit door. The person waited behind the dumpster, others driving by could not see the person waiting in the shadows. It was just a few minutes before closing time for the gas station, near midnight.

This was just another typical night at the gas station. Vichem had just finished counting all the money in the register and was preparing to lock up the store.

The phone rang. "Hi, I just wanted to know what time you were coming home and if everything was okay?" his wife said to him on the phone.

"Yes, I'm fine. Don't worry so much. I survived in the most dangerous place in the world, with the most dangerous men in the world, at the most dangerous time in history. I'll be okay."

"Do you have your gun with you?" She inquired.

"Yes, I have it here with me." Vichem replied.

"I noticed that you don't have your bullet proof vest with you. It's sitting here on your desk at home. Why didn't you wear it?" She questioned.

"I'll be okay, it's been several weeks and I don't think they were serious about trying to kill me. It was just someone blowing off steam. Everything will be fine." He replied.

"It's only been 29 days and I would feel better if you wore it to work. I don't have a good feeling about this threat and the possibilities." His wife pleaded in a worried tone.

"Okay, I'll go back to wearing the vest tomorrow night. Just so you will not worry." Vichem conceded.

"Hurry home. I would feel better. I don't have a good feeling about the day." She answered.

The date was May 13 and the gas station was located at 9891 Harwin St., a very racially mixed and socially economical area of Houston, Texas.

In his hurry to lock up the gas station and get on his way, Vichem had forgotten his gun under the counter in the store, instead of tucking it in the waistband of his pants, under his shirt. Closing the store at 12 am, he locked the doors and turned off the lights of the store inside as he exited.

He had gathered the nightly deposit and was crossing the parking lot to his nearby parked car.

Hearing the scuffle of footsteps behind him, Vichem turned to see his enemy rapidly approaching, pistol already drawn and pointed at him.

"You!" He screamed at the person.

"Yes, it's taken awhile to find you."

Vichem reached for the gun at his waist but it wasn't there. With a sinking feeling, he realized he had left the gun in the store because of his hurry to get out the door. He knew fighting back was not an option. He decided to try using his quick wit and humor to attempt getting himself out of this situation.

"You can have her; I'll give her to …." Vichem said when the first of nine bullets pierced his head. The other eight bullets followed immediately, striking his other vital organs with deadly accuracy.

The cash from that day's business was over $3,000 dollars' worth of deposits and would be discovered still lying beside his bloodied body.

The City of Houston Police attributed the murder to "a robbery gone badly".

Chapter One- Jungle Evil

Fear and danger permeated the night! Thunnysok could see that the sun was starting to set behind the tall jungle trees - casting a long shadow as she slowly walked the path. Nighttime was when the Khmer Rouge did their killing. Thunnysok knew that it was time to start finding a good tree to sleep in.

During this time of year in Cambodia, it got dark at about 8 pm. Thunnysok did not know how to tell the exact time of day. All she really knew was that she could not sleep on the ground in the jungle. There were too many bugs crawling and too many snakes slithering along the darkened paths. The one she feared the worst, the most dangerous jungle creature, also stalked the grounds at night - the Khmer Rouge.

The best trees in the world for sleeping in were actually here in the Cambodian jungles. The base of these trees were about 30 to 40 feet around and easy to climb. Thunnysok could climb up about three or four branch levels of the tree. There'd still be plenty of room in the joints of the branches to sleep at night and not accidentally roll out of the tree. They were a perfect place to sleep at night for the little girl lost and living in the jungle.

Thunnysok felt hungry. She'd not had anything to eat for days, but that was not unusual in Cambodia. She started searching around some of the hallowed, fallen branches at the base of the trees - hunting for food.

Thunnysok used a stick to lift the fallen branches because she could never really know what was lurking underneath. Carefully she turned the log over and she was happy to see that there were five or six large black beetles starting to scramble for the cover of a nearby bush. She managed to hit one with the stick and then leaped into the bush after a second one. She was able to catch the beetle with both hands. The beetle bit her, but she was used to the pain and discomforts of living in the jungle, the bite of these small creatures did not bother her. Instead her mouth watered at the thought of the joy of eating. Quickly, she stuck the squirming beetle, which was about 4 inches in length, into her mouth and cutting the beetle in half with her teeth she began to chew, savoring the moment. Then she began to eat the remaining half of the beetle, the legs still wiggling. She did not mind that either. The substance was good and would nourish her starving body. This helped ease the painful feeling of hunger gnawing in her stomach.

Thunnysok chewed on the beetle until the only part left was the hard outer shell. She spit the shell out on the ground, grabbed the other beetle and retreated up into the tree. This beetle she would save until later in the night, she knew she would soon be hungry again. This was her nighttime food and she actually feels lucky to have found some on this night. It was not unusual to go days without anything to eat.

Thunnysok was only 7 years old and a mere 45 pounds of nothing but skin and bones. She called herself a monkey and thought of herself as one. She loved being high up in the trees and felt safer up there, off of the jungle floor.

She knew which trees would have the best spots for sleeping and resting. She'd slept in the branches of the trees many nights and had never fallen off. Her favorite spot would be about 20 to 25 feet off the ground. This gave her an excellent panoramic view of the jungle floor below. She would be hidden, by the dense foliage of the tree, from anyone or anything that might be walking below on the condensed jungle floor. If there were any snakes in the trees they would stay higher up, about 40 to 45 feet off the ground. This gave them protection from humans and other larger animals. In the jungle everyone and everything is either hunting or being hunted.

She quickly scrambles up the tree she has chosen to spend the night in, a small knapsack slug over one shoulder. Thunnysok would use her small sack as a pillow. The bag contained all she owned in the world. This consisted of two shirts, one she uses as a makeshift blanket to cover herself with. The second one was for replacing the one she was wearing. She would wash the dirty one she was wearing when she could find water, even a rain puddle would do.

Selecting the best spot in the branches surrounding her, she curls up with her bag substituting for a pillow and attempts to drift off sleep. Not that Thunnysok really ever slept at night, not deep sleep like most people. It was a dangerous world she lived in; and she constantly had to remain alert, listening for danger around her - the sounds of panthers, snakes, monkey's - anything that might bring harm to a little girl living alone in the jungle. She had no family and no friends. There was no person whom she could look to for advice, shelter, protection or comfort. Having survival instinct and faith in God was all she possessed in this lonely time, in the most dangerous place in the world.

This dangerous world she lived in was Cambodia- after the takeover of the Khmer Rouge. Cambodia would later become known to the world as the "killing fields". In reality most of the killing actually occurred in the jungles surrounding the fields. The Khmer Rouge leaders fertilized the soil of the rice paddies with the decomposing bodies of those they had executed. Human life was cheap and there was no place in the world, during this period in history, where life was cheaper than in Cambodia during the reign of the Khmer Rouge and Pol Pot.

Just as Thunnysok began to drift off to sleep, she heard a dreaded sound. There were humans in the jungle! Occasionally it was just villagers trying to travel from one village to the other without being seen by the Khmer Rouge soldiers. Anyone traveling from one village to the other without permission could be tortured or killed. Whole families could be murdered for even the slightest infractions of breaking rules of the great "Angkar". Angkar was the name given to the communist party when the new regime took over the country. No one really knew what it meant or who was behind the great Angkar, but that was the name that the soldiers were always shouting.

Startled, Thunnysok lay very still, frozen, fearing she would be discovered. She could hear the human's walking on the path below her. There must have been 7 or 8 of them, judging by their footsteps and the rustling of the bushes. She was hoping that they would just pass by and keep moving down the path, away from her hiding spot. This was normally what happened. Tonight, Thunnysok was not that lucky.

The footsteps below went about another fifteen feet down the path and then Thunnysok heard a person say. "Here, this is a good spot." Thunnysok realized that they were not moving on. So she decided to take a look at them. She felt her heart drop into her stomach at what she saw below. There were four Khmer Rouges. The first one she saw was a girl who was around 14 years old and a boy about 15 and a second boy around 18 and the oldest one, who was giving the commands, might have been 20 years old. Thunnysok watched as the soldiers dropped the shovels and their back packs.

There were very few soldiers who lived long in the Khmer Rouge Army. Most of the soldiers were forcibly recruited from the poverty stricken rural farm lands and had no education at all.

That was the way that "Angkar" wanted them. Soldiers like these were easy to control, they did not think for themselves, they did not reason, and would kill anyone or anything on command.

Thunnysok could see four Cambodian peasants. Each had their hands tied behind their backs. Two of the prisoners were men who resembled each other. One of them was a younger version of the older one, so Thunnysok assumed they were a father and a son. The other two prisoners were a man and woman who appeared to be in their 30's. Because of the way they were sitting, their postures almost comforting each other, Thunnysok assumed that they were married and had been for a long time.

In Cambodia it was not unusual for marriages to be arranged by the parents of the children at birth. By the time the child reached 14 or 15 years old they were considered ready to marry and for their adult life to commence. Cambodia is a country where marriages were more often for mutual convenience rather than love. Thunnysok could tell that this was not the case. This was a couple who loved each other and had been happy to live together.

Now they were sitting on the ground, blindfolded, with their arms tied behind them. The resigned expressions on their faces revealed that they knew their worst fears were about to be realized.

The two youngest Khmer Rouges went to collect firewood. In no more than 20 to 30 minutes there was a raging bonfire going in the jungle clearing. With the fire on the jungle floor, the light rose about 20 feet, illuminating the clearing. If someone was hiding higher up in the trees, they could observe without being seen. On this night, this just happened to be the case with Thunnysok.

The soldiers untied the father and son and gave each a small shovel and ordered them to start digging. Thunnysok's heart was pounding. She knew this was the beginning of the end and the prisoners were going to be killed. The Khmer Rouge would make the prisoners dig their own graves before killing them. Next they untied the woman's husband and forced him to help dig the grave. The soldier yelled "extra deep! You must dig, extra deep!"

The oldest soldier took out a bottle of something and started to drink it. Thunnysok could not see what the soldier was drinking, but it seemed to make the man much louder and braver. Father and son were digging. A soldier walked over to the father and kicked him in the head which knocked the man to the ground and he fell over in the pit. The son looked like he wanted to help his father, but he knew that it would mean instant death if he did. The son looked toward his father - frozen with fear and hopelessness.

The soldiers were singing and chanting to "Angkar" the mysterious and unknown ruler of the country. Thunnysok wondered, "Who was this ruler who brutalized and killed the peasants - the people of the country?"

Several hours passed and the holes were now deep enough. The soldiers motioned for the men to get out of the holes. They bound their hands behind their backs and then motioned for them to sit on the edge of the pit. It was inevitable that this would be their final destinations! These men knew there was no chance of escaping and no hope of survival even if they tried.

The Khmer people and villagers had been slaves of Pol Pot and his followers since the fall of Cambodia. Most of the Cambodians had been physically, emotionally and mentally abused. They were over worked and most were starving to death; if not already dead from starvation or illness. They were hopeless and lacked the strength or will to fight back.

The Khmer Rouge Army was scattered all over Cambodia. The odd of escaping the soldiers was slim. In situations such as this, people tend to resign themselves to their own death. It was better to die, than to live and be treated like scum from the bottom of the earth. The Khmer Rouge scarcely used their bullets for killing their own people. Bullets were reserved for wars with the Cambodian Soldiers and the Vietnamese soldiers invading Cambodia.

The chosen instrument of death for tonight's executions was to be the sharp, long blades of the soldier's machetes. These were normally used as weapon and for cutting the rice, corn and sugar cane in the fields.

The oldest soldier watched as one of his men swung the machete down on the head of the father. The son winced as watched as his father's body collapse into the grave. Thunnysok clamped her hand over her mouth to hold back her own horrified scream.

There are so many thoughts raging in a person's mind, in those last fleeting moments before one realizes that this really is the end and death is inevitable. There are regrets and there are the good memories, there is the tiniest glimmer of hope for life to continue long past this moment of pain.

"Whack" the machete came down on the head of the son and his body parts fell into the grave which he and his father had just dug. There were no signs of life from either father or son. Both were now collapsed into the shallow grave with severed heads and body parts comingled atop each other.

The camp fire was blazing. Thunnysok watched as the soldiers placed an oversized wok over the fire. It appeared as if they were going to cook a meal for the night. For the husband and wife, it seemed a long, solemn night as they awaited their brutal destiny.

"You! Get out from that grave and come over here now," one of the Khmer Rouge yelled and motioned at the husband who was still digging the grave. The man, exhausted and hopeless climbed out of what was to be his and his wife's grave. He was pulled up by the younger soldier and dragged toward the heated wok that was propped up above the bonfire. He was beaten severely, beaten so badly that he could not stand up. The soldier left him crumpled and bleeding, lying on the ground, while he motioned the other team member to bring the wife over to the fire.

The woman, grief stricken over her husband's abuse, was dragged by her hair to the bonfire from where she had been sitting. With her hands still tied behind her, the team leader ordered "Blindfold her and make him stand." He pointed at the husband "he's going to watch his wife die" he sneered. They blindfolded the wife and dragged her to the other side of the wok. Then the husband was lifted from the ground propped up between the two Khmer Rouge and was positioned directly across from his wife, separated by the burning wok. One of the Khmer Rouge grabbed the woman by her hair and pushed her head over the burning wok as the other took one broad stroke with his machete and partially severed her head into the wok. The blood came spurting out from the severed arteries in her neck and head sizzling as it splashed into the wok, spurting onto the ground, and spraying onto her husband's face. An acrid odor filled the air as the blood and human tissue seared in the wok. The agonized husband watched, horrified as his wife was savagely murdered. The soldiers force him to continue to watch as her liver begins to cook.

A few minutes later, the husband suffers the same fate.

Thunnysok could watch no longer. It was all she could do to keep from crying out at the atrocities she has just witnessed. She buried her face into the rough bark of the tree trying to escape the horrible visions that still danced in her head. Silently she cried. How is a child of seven years old to understand these vicious acts of torture and brutality? How can she to cope when she is all alone in this cruel world? She cried many silent tears - something that she'd been learning to do for the past several years.

Thunnysok felt horrified and guilty that she could not take her eyes off the events on the jungle floor. Yet she could not drag her eyes away from the scene that was unfolding below. The soldier rolled the bodies of the husband and wife over to the edge of the grave. He took the machete and proceeded to cut the livers from of their lifeless bodies. Holding the livers high in the air - a sign of a conqueror killing his victims - the soldier put one of the livers to his mouth and began to eat it.

The female Khmer soldier had not been actively engaged in what was happening and the commander went over to her and made her eat part of the liver. Then he yelled at her and she slowly got up and went over to the two dead bodies where the commander handed her a machete and demanded that she cut off the remainder of the head of the woman. It was not easy for her and it took her several minutes to finally cut through all the flesh, tissues and bone. Both men and women of Khmer Rouge soldiers were equal in cruelty and savageness.

Once the killing was done, they dumped all of the body parts, including the cooked heads, into the grave. They were talking loudly, laughing and proceeding to go about their business.

Thunnysok's heart dropped to the pit of her stomach as she witnessed this dreadful scene. She had witnessed so many deaths, but never seen anything so cruel and this close before. Fighting back her tears and the pain in her heart for these unfortunate folks, she managed to paralyze her emotions. From that day forth, Thunnysok will have no emotions when it comes to death or abuse. Life was lonely, cold, and dark. She trusted no one. The only hope and salvation left in her was by talking to the almighty above. Who that higher being was, she hasn't a clue. But, she spoke and prayed to him in her heart every day. He kept her safe and strong, despite the dangerous journeys of a child, struggling to survive in the jungle, during her country's war.

It was 3am. Tossing and turning in bed, Angela awoke. Try as she may, she could not fall asleep. She got up out of bed and walked into another room of the house. She started crying uncontrollably. After a few minutes she finally fought back her tears. "No!" as she silently demanded of herself. "I will not cry nor will I be weak. Life has brought too many triumphs to be weak now. I must put the past behind me." Angela had resolved to never let anyone see the fear that existed in her. She'd kept most of her emotions locked inside herself and would never let anyone see her in tears. She proceeded to the bathroom to get cleaned up before heading back to bed.

"I have a meeting and need for you to watch Meredith tonight." Angela said. "What time?" her husband responded. "It starts at

7pm and I don't want to be late." Angela added firmly. "I won't be late," Simon responded. "Yeah, yeah, you say that but you were late last week. I just wish I could get you to be more proactive. Besides, you should spend some time with Meredith."

"She'll be asleep by 8pm anyway. So it's not much time."

Simon previously had a great job with an energy company in downtown Houston. The company had downsized, Simon had lost his job. But, finally, last month he was able to find a job with a Dallas based company. This meant he had to fly out of Houston each week to a different location and return home each weekend. Time was precious when Simon returned. Each week, Angela looked forward to going to her cosmetic sales meeting. She saw it as an opportunity to make some extra money and improve her life. Success always seemed to be something that eluded her or existed just slightly beyond her reach.

Recently she had been making more and more efforts to get out of the house. Last year she had quit her corporate job with a major computer company. She noticed repeatedly that her manager seemed to be offering her promotions in an effort to get her to meet for lunch away from the office and her co-workers. Angela knew she was being sexually harassed, but there isn't much a woman can do from within this predominately male work force. She wasn't interested in exchanging sex for a promotion. She never did and she never would. She found it hard to believe that these men just seemed to want to get in her pants.

Angela decided that maybe the answer was to be her own boss. She had purchased a donut shop about a year ago but was finding that it was more than she had bargained for. She was starting to resent how much time it was taking, how little money she made for the effort and how the grease smell never seemed to leave her body. She could never get over the feeling that some of her customers were looking down on her.

Angela tried to put those feelings behind her and hold on to her optimism that she would become successful in America. She would prove to everyone that she could succeed. She wanted to prove to herself, that she was capable of accomplishing the American dream. This thought boosted her hope and made her happy, if even just briefly.

Jon David was working late. Recently he had been working more and more hours at the hotel. Jon had several new employees in his department and one employee was out on medical leave. What started out as a minor operation was well into eight weeks of absence. Having an employee on leave can be harder than having them quit. You can't replace them until the situation is resolved. Jon David had to carry a bigger work load to cover for the employee on leave.

To make matters worse. Jon was starting to feel the strain in his marriage. He had been married for over twenty three years but slowly the marriage was getting worse. Jon knew that it was not a question of if it would end, more like when it would end. Never truly in love with each other, Jon David and Carolina had worked at being happy but happiness always eluded them.

Houston, over the past several years, had added a new baseball stadium, a new basketball center for the Houston Rockets and many additional small restaurants and bars in the downtown area. Revived, downtown Houston had come alive again.

The hotel business had always been a "time intensive" business. Jon David Conner was a Director of Finance, at a large Galleria Houston Hotel. The hotel, which was built with city bond money, had over 500 rooms and was close to the Galleria Shopping Mall.

"Enedina" Jon said to this secretary as he was heading out the door" I am going down to the gift shop to get something for these allergies. It will serve as my "escutcheon".

"Escutcheon?" Enedina replied

"Yes, my shield of protection" Jon replied.

Everyday Jon would try to give Enedina a new word or idea. Enedina's parents had crossed the Rio Grande River some 30 years ago and their children, born in the United States, the children had become American citizens.

Taking the escalator downstairs, Jon walked into the gift shop.

"Hi, Lea" Jon said clearly as he walked into the gift shop.

"Hi, Mr. Conner, I see you are working late again."

"Yes, another late, night...the wife is starting to wonder if I have a girlfriend." about this time Jon could not help but notice the Asian girl in the gift shop. She raised her head and made eye contact as Jon was remarking on his need for a girlfriend.

Jon's eyes caught her eyes. She was obviously very attractive.

"Excuse me, do you work here?" The Asian beauty took a step towards Jon.

"Yes, I do, is there something I can help you with?" Jon responded.

"Yes, I just pulled my car into the garage and as I was coming into the lot, the gate at the entrance raised and then lowered so quickly that it put a dent in the hood. I was wondering if there was anyone that I could talk to about the problem." She inquired.

"The garage is actually owned and operated by a separate company, but I would be glad to take the incident report and pass it on." Jon responded.

"So you're saying there is no way they are going to pay for the damage?" the Asian woman said.

"No, what I am saying is that I can take the information and fill out the report, but I cannot promise that they will pay you for the damages." Jon retorted.

"Well, I don't know if I should even bother. But I have to go to my cosmetic sales meeting and I am late." Angela flipped her hair and started to head out of the gift shop.

"Wait a minute" Jon said..." here is my business card. If you want to fill out that report or need anything else please just give me a call." Jon quickly handed her his business card, doubting that he would ever see her again.

"Thanks" The Asian girl said as she paid the cashier and walked out of the shop.

"You were pretty quick to give her your business card" Lea said with a smile and wink at Jon.

"I was just trying to take care of the guest:" Jon replied with a smile and a returned wink.

1965 Prince Sihanouk of Cambodia had just broken diplomatic relations with the United States thus ending the flow of American financial aid into the country. Prince Sihanouk turned to the People's Republic of China and the Soviet Union for financial support for his country.

In 1966 an agreement was struck between the Prince and the Chinese, allowing the presence of a large scale of 'People Army of Vietnam' (PAVN) troop deployments and logistical bases in the eastern border regions. Sihanouk also agreed to allow the use of the port of Shinanoukville by communist flagged vessels delivering supplies and materials to support the PAVN military effort in Vietnam. These concessions made a sham of Cambodia's neutrality.

Sihanouk started to lose support because of the growing economic crisis developing in Cambodia. Most of the rice production was going to the Vietnamese and there was a strong communist presence in the country. On September 1966 General Lon Nol was elected prime minister of defense and his deputy became Sirik Matak, who was a long time enemy of Prince Sihanouk. Friction was rapidly developing between Lon Nol and Sihanouk

One of Lon Nol's first priorities was to fix the ailing economy by halting the illegal sale of rice to the communist. Soldiers were dispatched to the rice growing areas to forcibly collect the harvest at gunpoint. The farmers were paid only the lowest government price for the rice. There was wide spread unrest, especially in the rice rich Battambang Province. Battambang for many years had the presence of large landowners and there was a great disparity of wealth among the population. The communist still had a strong presence in this region of the country.

"Son, I need you to hook the oxen up, we are going to take the rice to market." His father said to him that morning.

"Yes, father" was the reply from Son Sary, who had just turned 17 years old. Son Sary was the oldest of the three sons and two girls in the Sary family. Vichem Sary had been married for 19 years. As was the custom in Cambodia, the marriage was arranged by both families' parents. With the exchange of two oxen and five chickens, the marriage between Son's father and mother was sealed.

The Sary family was never rich, but was not the poorest either. They lived season to season on the rice they produced in their small fields. Vichem dreamed of purchasing more land and he had his children to help in the fields to produce more rice.

It was 5:30am and the sun had not yet risen over the trees. The trip to the Battambang would take over 2 hours. It was less than 12 miles, but that the roads and paths through the jungle were rough and took a great deal of time to traverse - not to mention the dangers along the way. There were the regular dangers of travel in the countryside, wild animals and snakes. To top it off they would have to watch out for communist patrols and bandits. Lately there had also been rumors of government soldiers in the area. The older Sary wanted to get closer to the city before the sun came up. Then he could sell the rice to a man, whom he knew, for a higher price than what was being offered in the official government purchasing centers in the area.

"Father, I am 17 years old. I am a man."

"Yes, son, you are becoming very much a man."

"I would like to marry." Son Sary said solemnly to his father.

Son's father smiled and then paused for what seemed like an eternity to Son.

"Yes, my son maybe it is time that we put out word to the nearby villages that we are interested in finding a suitable wife for you."

"Dad would you mind if I ..."   Son Sary paused

"Yes, Son, I will let you see her first before I make my decision" the elder Sary interjected.

Son Sary smiled at his father, feeling the appreciation that he may get to have some input into who his bride would be. Son Sary felt joy in his heart - knowing that he would soon have a bride. Finally, there was something to look forward to. Son had worked hard for his father on the family farm. He had enjoyed the closeness of his family.

Chapter Two - Finding a Monk

Thunnysok had been following the river for several weeks - staying within sight of the river but not walking on the exposed ground of its banks. She was careful about not letting anyone see her.

Thunnysok came across a path that lead up from the river and decided to see where it led. She followed it for about 400 yards before she came to a small clearing, which contained what appeared to be a Buddhist temple. There were several houses close to the temple and several monks were gathered outside the temple.

Thunnysok had always been taught that the monks should be respected and could be trusted if she were ever in trouble. Thunnysok decided to go up to the temple and see if they could help her. This was a bold move for a little girl who had learned, even at her young age, not to trust anyone.

"Little grasshopper, what are you doing out here in the jungle?" one monk said to her as she slowly walked towards them. Thunnysok could not speak. She had been alone in the jungle for such a long time with no one to talk to. This had made it very difficult for her speak. Also, under the rule of the Khmer Rouge, one did not speak unless spoken to by the soldiers or commanders. To speak unless spoken to could result in torture, at the very least, or worse it could mean death. To dare to look a soldier directly in the face or to be so bold as to stare at them was inviting one's own death.

"Come with me, little one. I can see that you need food. We do not have much, but what we have we will share with you. There does not seem to be enough food to feed those in the villages anymore." The monk gently took Thunnysok by the hand and guided her into the temple. There, on the floor, were several cooking pots with rice porridge in them.

"Look what I found when I went out fishing today." The monk said to his brethren. They all laughed. Maybe in other parts of the world finding lost children was a big deal, but this was Cambodia during a time when millions of people were displaced. Some disappeared - never to be heard from again. One could never know if they had been killed or relocated. Or, if they had somehow managed to flee the country escaping the atrocities that were being carried out against them by the Khmer Rouge.

After Thunnysok finished her food, the monk showed her a quiet spot, in one of the back rooms, where she could rest until they could find out where she came from. They would have to find out if she had any relatives who were still alive and figure out what to do with her.

"Safe, this is the first time I have felt safe in years" Thunnysok thought to herself. Waking up from the best sleep she'd had in years. "Safe".

"Little one, come, go fishing with me at the river" the monk said to Thunnysok. He extended his hand to her. At first, she just stared at it, but then she slowly reached up and took his hand. Thunnysok and the monk walked back down to the river and sat on the on the bank with their fishing poles trying to catch their dinner.

Thunnysok was proud of herself for catching two fish when the monk had only caught one. She giggled, as he sputtered, amazed that he had been bested by this slip of a girl. Not more than an hour later the two of them, still avidly fishing, heard a truck in the background. Trucks were a bad sound; the only time one heard trucks in Cambodia they were filled with soldiers and military commanders.

"Wait here" the monk said to Thunnysok "hide and under no circumstances are you to come to the temple." The monk started to walk up the river bank toward the temple, when suddenly the monk stopped and turned back toward Thunnysok. He hesitated for a moment and then extending his open arms to her, she ran to embrace him. "I will come back to get you grasshopper, when I am sure it is safe." Hugging her, the monk put her back down on the ground. There was peace in his eyes….and yet there was also sadness for he was certain he would not be coming back to get the child. The monk turned back to the path and slowly headed toward the temple.

Thunnysok hid herself in the thick bushes that grew on the riverbank. Several minutes passed before she heard an all too familiar sound that she knew to dread… machine gun fire… "Bang, bang, bang, bang" could be heard in rapid succession.

She clamped her hands over her ears. She could feel her heart thudding against her chest. Thunnysok wanted to cry, but there were no tears. A few more minutes passed but Thunnysok did not dare to move. The minutes turned into hours and still she did not move from her hiding place. Slowly the sun drifted down to the horizon. As night fell, the sounds of the jungle and the darkness surrounded her and yet the kindly monk still did not come back for her.

Dawn was breaking, Thunnysok decided to go to the temple. Slowly, she crept on her stomach, thru the brush and thickets towards the temple. She did not dare use the path until she was certain it was safe. When she got to the edge of the clearing, near the front of the monastery, she paused. Peeking out from the bush that bordered the clearing, she did not see any monks in the courtyard. The huts that adjacent to the temple were still smoldering. They had all been burned to the ground.

Slowly, Thunnysok crept into the temple. Once inside she found the monks. Their bodies were stacked one on top of the other. Each stack was three bodies high. They all appeared to have bullet wounds to the head. She could see where blood had oozed from the wounds had dried in clumps, their faces frozen with grimaces of fear and horror for all eternity. The temple floor was covered in blood.

Thunnysok looked for her monk. Finally, she found him in the next room, his face was battered and it appeared he had been severely tortured before he was executed by the Khmer Rouge soldiers. Thunnysok lay down on the ground beside the monk. She wedged her body in between the body of her friend and another monk. Exhausted, she fell fast asleep. For one full week Thunnysok stayed in the temple. Finally, the smell of rotting flesh and lack of food forced her back to the river. She had been left with no choice but to continue on her journey.

"Doris, can you tell me what groups we have in house tonight?" Jon asks as he stopped by the catering office that morning. "I can print you out a list if you want to see all of the groups."

"That would be great." Jon responded. "Any group in particular that you are looking for?" Doris inquired.

"No, I was just curious" Jon responded. He didn't really want to say why he was checking, but he thought that it had been a week since he had seen the Asian girl in the gift shop; he was just a bit curious, hoping he might see her again.

"Enedina what time are you leaving tonight?" Jon said. It was late afternoon already.

"Around 7pm." Enedina responded.

"Okay…can you just holler when you leave? I have this habit of getting so engrossed in what I am doing I lose track of the time." Jon said jokingly.

"Is your wife getting still getting upset at you for coming home so late?" Enedina questioned her boss.

Jon and Enedina had grown very close over the past five years of working together. Theirs was more than just a boss – employee relationship. They had learned to listen to each other. Many times they shared intimate details of their personal lives. Yes, office etiquette dictates that fraternizing is a bad idea. But over time, when working so closely, you develop a bond of trust with some employees, Jon rationalized. There wasn't anyone Jon David trusted more than Enedina.

A few hours later, Enedina was ready to leave for the night.

"Okay, Jon, I am heading out" Enedina said as she stuck her head into Jon's office on the second floor of the hotel.

"Hold on, I'll walk you down to the garage" Jon said looking up from the computer screen. "No need to do that. I will be okay." Enedina replied.

A few minutes later Enedina was on her way home to her four children and Jon headed toward the gift shop. As he entered, he waved a "hello" to Lea. He continued past the counter and began slowly browsing down an aisle of the shop. He paused, looking at a couple of items on the shelves along the way. Jon David was trying to appear to be shopping for an item to purchase. In reality, he was hoping to bump into the Asian woman he had seen here last week.

7:15, Jon sighed as he glanced at his watch and decided to head back up to his office and finish some work. He was lost in his own thoughts as he rounded the corner of the banquet hallway and ran headlong into someone. Startled, Jon quickly looked up and suddenly he realized that it was her - the Asian beauty.

"Oh, I am so sorry!" Jon blurted out, embarrassed that he had been so clumsy.

"Well, it seems that every time I come here, I am getting bumped and bruised" The woman replied tersely. But then Jon detected a smile beneath the words.

"Oh, aren't you the guy with the hotel that I talked to last week?" She said.

"Yes, I am. I guess you decided not to fill out that report after all." Jon questioned her.

"Oh, yes, I did intend to. But, I lost your business card." She explained. "Would you mind giving me another one and I will call you."

"Sure, I would be glad to" Jon said smiling as he pulled out a card and slipped it into her hand.

"Jon David Conner, Director of Finance   CPA/MBA" very impressive" she read the card aloud, a smile dancing at the corners of her mouth.

"Not that impressive, I might have set a record for the number of times a student took the exam to finally pass." Jon joked.

"Oh, I doubt that" she quipped and turned to go. "Sorry, but I'm already late for my meeting. I'll give you a call about the report sometime soon."

"I didn't catch your name?" Jon quickly added.

"Angela" she said with a smile.

Jon's breath caught in his throat. She really was a beauty he thought, especially when she smiled.

"Angela S." She said being somewhat mysterious about giving out her complete name.

Jon left with a smile on his face but he was doubtful that Angela would ever really call him.

On the way home, Jon got a call on his cell phone. Looking at the caller identification he could see that it was his wife. He hesitated for a moment, debating on whether or not to answer the phone call.

"Hello" Jon said as he picked up the phone.

"Jon, where are you? Why were you working so late?" his wife began interrogating him.

"I have explained to you a hundred times why I have to work late" he stated sharply.

Jon was starting to notice that he flinched every time his wife walked into the room. For some time, he did not notice that as soon as his wife walked into the room, he would find an excuse within minutes to go to another room in the large house. It was not that Jon was trying to be unkind. It was just his attempt to avoid his wife's jabs. She had a knack for making veiled, negative comments aimed at him. Carolina, for whatever reason and sometime for no reason, was constantly either complaining or trying to get his undivided attention.

"Maybe I don't give her enough attention," Jon thought to himself.

"Do you want to do anything when I get home?" He continued.

"No, I just want to get away from the house. I'm going to get out of the house and spend some alone time." She responded.

"So, the boys are there and not behaving?"

"No, they've gone for a sleepover at their friends house." She said.

"So you're going out alone?" He questioned.

"Yes" Carolina replied with exasperation "all alone!"

"So when I get home, you don't want to go out with me and spend some time together?" Jon mused.

"Yes! Exactly!" Caroline said with enthusiasm.

"Okay, makes sense to me…" Not really, Jon thought.

Son Sary and his father had gone about 2 miles along the jungle path when they heard voices and laughter, someone else was in the jungle! Whoever it was, they were near. Pheng motioned for his son to stop the cart. Quickly, he placed a hand on each of the oxen's snouts in an attempt muzzle them. They stood motionless in the dark for several minutes. The voices did not seem to be moving away from them.

Pheng motioned with his hands to Son urging him to slowly move the animals farther into the jungle on the right of the path. There was a clump of bushes off to one side of the path. If they could get the wagon past them, they could divert to their course to another path and away from the soldiers.

Pheng realized that the longer they stayed in this spot the greater the chances that the oxen would make too much noise and give their location away. There was no keeping these beasts of burden quiet for long. Slowly, father and son moved the animals in the new direction, hoping they could steer their way clear of the dangerous soldiers.

A loud "Crack" was the next sound that pierced the early morning air. One of the wheels of the cart had rolled up and over a fallen tree branch about 6 inches in diameter. The heavy load of rice combined with the weight of the cart had been enough to cause the log to split. That "Crack" was the sound that would haunt Son for the rest of his life.

The voices of the soldiers rapidly approached. They suddenly appeared, guns pointed at the father and son. Pheng and Son found themselves confronted by five government soldiers.

"What are you doing in the early morning with rations of rice?" the sergeant yelled at the Pheng.

"I am taking my harvest of rice to the city to sell." Son's father said.

"What is your name?" The soldier yelled at Son Sary's dad.

"I am Pheng Sary and I am nothing more than a poor farmer, who has been here for years trying to make a living."

"You lie; you are working for the communists." The soldier barked.

"No! No! I am just a local farmer trying to get to market" Son's father pleaded truthfully.

"Where are you from?" The soldier in charge asked.

"I am from the village of Reang Kesei, just two miles up the path." Pheng replied, his head bent down, eyes on the ground.

"Then we will take your rice and confiscate it by government decree" the soldier barked. "We will report that we have claimed it and give you credit for it at the government office." He finished smugly, daring Pheng to argue.

The soldier motioned to the three of his underlings to seize the oxen and cart. However, at the same time the sergeant gave a nod to another of the soldiers signaling him to take the father and son into the jungle. The soldier pointed his gun at the two farmers. The rest of the party started back down the path in the opposite direction with the oxen and cart.

The three men had only gone about 30 yards when Son Sary's father looked pleadingly at his son. His eyes implored him "run, run away." Then, suddenly and without hesitation, Pheng Sary turned and leaped at the soldier as he tried to wrestle the gun away from their captor.

Son Sary turned away and started to run into the jungle as he heard the thud of the soldier's gun firing into his father. He heard his father yelling "Run, Son! Run!" Son did not turn around to look back. He ran. He ran as fast as he could into the dense jungle trees and bushes. He did not stop running until he was sure that no one was following behind him.

Son hid in the jungle for hours and hours. He was afraid to move - afraid to go anywhere. He quarreled with himself, attempting to devise a course of action. "Do I go back and look for father? I know he is dead. Or, do I try to find my way home to warn my mother? What if father had managed to escape? How can I go and tell mother that he is dead unless I am certain? What if the soldiers are still there just waiting for me to come back?" Son argued back and forth with himself trying to decide. If father were here, he would know what to do. But father was not here and now, Son knew, he had to be a man and decide for himself.

Son knew he had to go back and find out what happened to his father. It was midday now and about 6 hours had passed since he had run away and left his father to die. He hung head with guilty shame as he started walking. Son decided he would double back thru the jungle to the place where their paths had crossed with the soldiers.

Once there, Son found his father's dead body collapsed in a pool of blood on the ground. It wasn't until he got closer that he realized the head was missing! To his utter disgust he found there were rats eating away at the corpse of his father. Son ran at them swinging a stick and screaming "Get away!" He was so outraged by the scene it did not occur to him that the soldiers may still be in the vicinity. He watched as the rats quickly scattered.

Son could not bear the thought of the rats coming back to feast on his fathers' corpse. He would carry his body all the way back to the village, no matter how long it took he thought with determination. He struggled, awkwardly, to pick up the body and put it on his shoulder. The corpse had started to stiffen making it difficult to balance the load. He soon realized he would have to come up with another plan. He could only go several feet before his blood and sweat soaked shirt became so slippery that the corpse kept slipping off his shoulder.

Son tried to bury the body, as tears flowed from his eyes. He had no shovel, he had no tools. Everything was gone. Using his hands Son tried to dig into the ground, but he could only go inches before the roots of the plants and trees blocked his efforts.

Son realized that he would have to find some other way to protect the body of his father. He pulled vines from some of the trees and tied them around his father's ankles. He tied a rock, about the size of both of his balled up fists, to the loose end of the vine rope he had fashioned. Next he threw the rock up into the tree as hard as he could. It only took two tries before it looped over one of the trees large branches about 25 feet high. Next he began to pull the vine gently hauling the body of Pheng Sary up into the tree. He heaved the body up until it was suspended about 15 feet from the jungle floor. That would protect the corpse from predators on the ground he thought.

This left about 4 feet of vine from the branch to the bottoms of his fathers' feet. Satisfied that no animals in the tree could reach the corpse he wrapped the vines around the tree several times and then firmly knotted them. He hoped the body would be safe here. It was the best plan he could think, given the circumstances. Son's mind was racing, but clearly, he was in still in shock from today's course of events and how your whole life can change in an instant.

Son realized it was getting late and he needed to get home.

The Chim family lived in Phnom Penh - the capital of Cambodia, which boasted a populace of 1.3 million inhabitants. They lived in what was considered an upscale house with several maids and a nanny to aid with raising the children. There were three boys and two girls in the Chim family. Due to the recent death of Maly Prey, the regular nanny, they had been forced to find a substitute.

The Khmer Rouge troops were hidden in the surrounding countryside, and would lob shells on the city, several times a day. This usually happened around 7am, near lunch time and again in late afternoon. These attacks were intentionally planned to impact during the rush hours to inflict the highest rate of casualties. This was several years before the city fell to the Khmer Rouge on April 17th, 1975.

Thunnysok Chim had always been like a monkey - climbing on furniture and beds. If there was a place to explore and climb, she'd find it. She was very small - barely the size of a monkey at 3 years old.

It was about lunch time when Thunnysok and Botum, her older sister, decided to play a game of hide-and-seek. Botum, who was very clever, hid in a very good place and Thunnysok could not find her. "Ha" her older sister teased as she came out from her hiding place. "You can never find me!" Little Thunnysok, a very competitive 3 year old was determined to find an even better hiding place.

The Chim home had three stories and the girls were playing on the third level of the house. The nanny, busy with Thunnysok's little brother, was relieved that the girls seemed to be keeping themselves occupied

Thunnysok's sister hid her eyes and started to count. "One, two, three…" And Thunnysok rushed into the hallway and over to the ledge which wrapped around the stairwell and curved into a little enclave. "Sister will never find me there." Thunnysok thought to herself. "I will win this time."

When Thunnysok got on the ledge she realized that it was a bit smaller than she'd thought. But Thunnysok was not worried about falling she was just determined to beat her sister. She thought her sister would be so surprised and proud of her. Time was running out so Thunnysok moved fast.

Just as Botum yelled out, "Ten" she heard Thunnysok scream. Running out into the hallway Botum saw Thunnysok, her white knuckles clenched on the ornate light fixture that hung next to the enclave. Paralyzed she watched as Thunnysok, who had lost her balance and her grip on the light fixture, was now falling, tumbling down the three flights of stairs. Thunnysok's arms flailing, desperately groping for something to hold on to as she rolled head over heels down the stairs.

The nanny and the rest of the family, having heard the commotion, came running. And there, in a twisted heap at the bottom of the stairs, was tiny Thunnysok. Her body was broken in several places but the most severe injury was to her neck. She had punctured her throat on the hanging light fixture that she had tried to catch herself with. She was bleeding profusely.

The nanny quickly picked Thunnysok up and ran from the house. She headed toward the hospital, which was in the center of the market district, not too far away. "Help, please help" she cried as she stumbled into the emergency room, gasping for breath. Thunnysok was covered in blood from her neck injury. Nanny had been mindful to keep a firm grip over the wound to slow the bleeding until she could get her charge to the hospital.

Running to the hospital midday was a very dangerous thing to do, but the nanny had no choice. Thunnysok had heard the shell explode as she lost consciousness. That was the first of Thunnysok's many near death experiences. The doctors were able to stop the bleeding quickly. They quickly cleaned and sutured the wound. The cut reached from her chin, all the way down to the base of her throat, stopping at her collar bone. She would carry the scar for the rest of her life. They also set her broken leg and both arms.

Months later, Thunnysok boasted to her sister, "I would have won if I had not fallen."

"Jon, you have an appointment down stairs, but I don't have anything written in your calendar."

"Appointment?" Jon mused "I don't think I have any appointments for today."

"The front desk just called and said that someone is here to meet you." Enedina informed Jon.

"She didn't give her name but they said it is a very attractive Asian woman."

Angela! Jon thought with anticipation as he quickly grabbed his jacket and headed to the elevators.

There, in the lobby, was Angela - all dressed up and looking radiant.

"Hi! I'm a bit surprised that you're here!" Jon quickly said as he extended his hand to greet her.

"Well, you did offer if I was ever in the area...." Angela said with a big smile.

"Did you want to fill out the accident report? I'd be happy to get one, they're right back here." Jon headed behind the desk to get a report.

"Yes, that would be great, but do you have time to get a glass of tea or some coffee?" Angela said with a smile that made it nearly impossible to say no.

"Sure, Angela, I would enjoy that." Jon responded.

Jon picked up a blank report and escorted Angela to the restaurant.

Jon glanced down at the form in his hand as they were walking. He noticed his hand was shaking. "Damn, what's wrong with me" he thought. "Here I am with this beautiful Asian woman that any man would want and desire. And my hand is shaking!" He groaned internally. He hated himself for feeling this way. "I should be more confident than that." Jon cajoled himself as he led her into the restaurant…still surprised to be so nervous.

Angela stopped at the entry way, letting him lead the way. Jon decided on a secluded spot in the corner of the dining room.

"Are you hungry?" Jon said to Angela as they sat down at the table.

"Yes. Starved" She replied, not really hungry but not knowing what else to say.

They ordered from the menu and both seemed to relax, a little more comfortable with each passing moment.

"You are just too smooth." Angela said.

"Smooth!" "What do you mean by that?" Jon said.

"Smooth………." With a smile Angela was mimicking Jon David.

Jon David gave her a puzzled look, but then realized what she was trying to say.

"Oh, are you implying that I might be one of those guys who talks to women so he can get them into bed and have sex with them as quickly as he possible can?"

"Well, that sounds a little harsher than I intended." Angela acknowledged apologetically.

"But, Yes." She continued with a smile.

"Well nothing could be farther from the truth." Jon said surprised they were branching so far off the original topics.

"Oh sure!" Angela responded. "Do you think I am gullible?"

"No, I think just the opposite; you're not naive or gullible. Your eyes are always wide open and looking for a lie." Jon explained.

"Do you blame me, Jon?" Angela said.

"So many men have lied to me that I know better than to trust anything a man says." She continued to explain.

Jon was puzzled by her comment and was thinking about what she had said…

Angela blurted out, "I am not looking to get laid!" She could not believe that she was actually saying this to this man, who is almost a perfect stranger. "Hmmm you are very direct aren't you?" He said laughing out loud.

Angela felt embarrassed that she had been so brazen. "But a girl needs to set things straight from the start. Then there are no misunderstandings." She thought to herself.

"Well I have read that there were certain things that a man wants in a woman…and number one was sex. Do you deny that?" "Did your list have anything else on it?" She said.

"Yes. It said that a man <u>looks</u> for a pretty wife."
"He <u>desires</u> sex, but not necessarily all from her."
 "He <u>wants</u> a partner who likes to do everything he likes to do"
"He <u>needs</u> someone to admire him
"He <u>has to have</u> someone to keep his castle in order. You know the laundry done, the dishes cleaned and the children tended to."

"So do you disagree with those?" he finished with a glimmer in his eyes.

"No not really, I think there is a lot of truth to them."

"Men want to be admired for whatever they do even when it's something stupid."

"So men do want sex?" She seemed to be leading the question.

"Well I think all men have that in the back of their minds. But I think there is a difference between lusting after a woman and wanting her."

"What do you mean?" She questioned him further.

"Well some men feel they have to possess a woman…that is the lusting to have her… and then some men want a woman because they admire the beauty of the woman without feeling like they have to have her or possess her. The key is to know the difference" Jon explained.

"So you don't think men can be truly "in love"?" Angela questioned.

"A man just does not love the same way a woman does. Men learn to cherish the object of his affection. He fears that if he messes up he will lose what he already has." Jon continued to explain to her.

"Okay, Jon, but how does this affect his attitude about sex?"

"Well the act of a guy putting a woman into this puzzle is sex. Men believe that once they have sex with a woman that somehow they do not possess her or own her, they have made her a part of his puzzle. She is in his now and he is a part of hers."

"But it is not truth!" Angela explained.

"Yes, women know that, but remember that men are basically

stupid." Jon chuckled.

"Women know that nothing could be farther from the truth, but men don't. Sometimes I wonder if it goes back to the old caveman mentality, but instead of hitting her over the head. He just tries to screw her." Jon continued.

"Just my point, and damn it, I am not looking to get laid." Angela insisted again. "Better stop saying that, the more you say it I will go to start thinking your projecting… "Screw you" I know what projection means…" Angela responded to Jon's mental prognosis. Jon just smiled, knowing that he would never win this exchange with her.

Jon started to get a more serious look in his eyes." I just think there is more to be appreciated in a woman than just touching her flesh." "Like what? Jon" Angela wanted to know

"Like the complexity that she has inside her. There is nothing in the world more complex than the heart of a woman. The reason she does the things that she does. How she can love so passionately and then hate just as passionately. How she will allow herself to be screwed, sometimes for years, by a man she does not love for the sake of her children. How she can hide in her heart the love she feels for someone else when she feels like she is dying inside." Jon said.

"I could go on and on about the heart and soul of a woman. But I just don't think most men ever take the time to see that side of a woman, much less try to understand the reasons." He said.

"And you do?" Angela gave Jon a very skeptical look.

"One thing I know, no matter how much you think you know about how women think, there is so much more to learn." Jon answered.

"And that is all women are to you, an opportunity to learn and satisfy your intellectual curiosity?"

"No. But I do believe there is a time when we must learn and a time when we must practice and a time we must teach those around us." "So where are you?" He asked.

Chapter Three- Getting a Scar

The sun beat down on Son Sary's forehead as he ran through the jungle towards his house. He expected to see his mother and family outside, busy about their daily chores. Slowing his pace, he realized there was no one around. He was dreading the moment he would have to deliver the news about his fathers' untimely demise. He realized quickly that there something amiss. There was an eerie silence around the farm house.

"Mother" Son yelled as he approached the house. "Mother" he called out again. But there was nothing but silence.

Son ran into the house only to find it was empty. With dread, he looked around the rooms and seeing the disarray he realized his home had been ransacked. Much of the furniture and personal items had been broken or appeared to be missing. Son ran through every room. But he could not find any sign of his missing family members.

Suddenly he was overwhelmed with dread. He felt a sickening feeling in his stomach and his heart was pounding loudly in his ears. He realized that something is terribly wrong. Realizing that his knees were about to buckle, he knelt down on both knees on the floor.

Son slowly surveyed the room around him. This time he paid more attention to the detail of the damages. His gaze landed on a series of bullet holes in the walls that surrounded him. The sun was streaming thru some of the holes on the exterior wall next to him. Son jumped up and ran out to check the damages from the outside of the house. And there, as he rounded the corner of the house, he found his family. They were there, crumpled and bloody in the dust, all of them dead.

"Noooo.... his mind screamed!" He felt as if the world was tipping upside down and spinning out of control. He dropped to the ground where he stood, sobbing aloud. It appeared they had been lined up along the wall of the house and executed.

"How could this be happening?" He felt a sudden rush of guilt. He should be with them. He too, should be dead.

He went back into the house and grabbing a knife he headed back outside to be with his family. There, he would join his family. He would die right there where the rest of his family had fallen.

Son dug the knife into his arm cutting a deep gash. He counted the bodies on the ground as the blood began to flow. There was his mother, his sisters and brothers. But wait! His youngest brother's body was not there. "Maybe he is alive!" Son had new hope. He rushed back inside the house and grabbing a dish towel, he quickly wrapped his bloody arm. Then he went to the kitchen and dug out a stash of hidden food. Mother always kept some food hidden for such emergencies. She would always say "You never know when the rain will come." Now Son understood she had not been referring to it raining outside.

He gathered a few more meager supplies into a knap sack and left his home. He headed down the path past the fields, toward the jungle. There were some obscured caves, not far, where he and his brothers use to play and hide. If Tran was still alive, this is where he would have run to hide.

""Tran! Tran, are you there?" Son yelled as he reached the mouth of the cave. "Son, Son is that you?" Tran cried as he clambered out from his hiding spot and ran to give his big brother a hug. They held each other tightly, both sobbing uncontrollably.

"What happened to our family?" Son questioned.

"The soldiers came looking for you." Tran replied. "They wanted to know where you were. They said that you were a member of the communist party and as such an enemy of the government. Mother kept insisting that you were no communist, just a farmer, but they called her a liar. They said she was just trying to protect you. Then they lined up everyone against the house and shot them. "They killed father too…" Tran continued.

"Yes, I know, Father and I were on the way to the market, when a group of Lon Nol's soldiers captured us. They were ordered to kill us. Father struggled with them to give me a chance to escape. The soldiers' gun went off during the struggle and father was killed. I ran and hid in the jungle. Later, when it was safe, I went back to find his body. Tran, they took his head…it was awful." Son shuddered. "I wrapped him with vines and heaved his body up into a tree until we can go back with shovels to bury him." Son rapidly filled Tran in on all the details of what had happened that day.

"I know" Tran nodded "They brought his head and showed it to mother and the children before they killed them. I was in the field working when I heard the soldiers approaching the house. I kept low and crept up close enough to see and hear as much as I could. When I saw father's head, I knew that things were going to get ugly." Tran admitted. His eyes filled with tears. "I am such a coward. I should have tried to stop them." He said remorsefully as the tears streamed down his cheeks.

Son consoled him, "This was fate - a sad fate. We have to find peace and accept this. There is nothing we could have done to prevent this. The soldiers have guns and we are but mere farmers. If you had shown yourself they would have killed you too. You did the right thing." Son continued.

"Come on Tran" Son said, putting his arm around his younger brother's shoulder as he guided him toward the cave. "It is not safe to go back and bury the bodies" he sighed. The soldiers may come back let's. Let's try to eat a little something and get some sleep. When we are rested we will decide what we should do." Son grabbed his knap sack and they both headed back into the safety of the cave.

Life had begun to change for Angela. Construction on the busy interstate highway required the traffic to be detoured. To her good fortune, the detour redirected traffic to the street in front of her donut shop. Suddenly, the failing shop was flourishing. Angela had owned this shop, located on the western side Houston, Texas

The shop was so busy lately Angela found she was spending more and more time there. She had even gotten better acquainted with most of the area merchants. One in particular, Donald, had really gotten her attention. He owned a business nearby, so he often came into the donut shop. Angela was not sure why she was so attracted to Donald. He was 53 years old and she, 20 years his junior, was 33. He was well over 6'2 and athletically built. He had a loud voice and an engaging smile. Donald was everything that her husband wasn't. He was confident and worldly. Their conversations had been that of friendly acquaintances so far.

Donald always had a blue tooth, hands free device, attached to his ear. He always seemed to be occupied with important business calls. He was a partner in a regeneration and renewable energy sources business in Houston. The new business had several other partners that boasted many years of experience. The idea of renewable energy was a relatively new concept but Donald's business was trying to turn Energy Credits into a commodity.

Donald had lived in several different regions of the world, including Brazil and Italy, and had, at one time, thought of becoming a Buddhist monk. A worldly man, he was fluent in at least four languages, Spanish, English, Portuguese and Italian Having decided that he desired a family while he was living in Italy, he married a lovely Italian woman named Kara, who was 15 years his junior. They'd had three children and now lived in a modest part of west Houston.

Since he had decided to operate his own business, Donald decided to run for a position on the Houston School Board. Currently, he had fallen way behind in the polls. His campaign platform was one of honesty and integrity.

The more she learned about Donald, the more intrigued, and infatuated she became. Angela was married to Simon, but recently she found herself obsessing over Donald. One day after an encounter with him, Angela realized there was no one in the world that she cared for more than Donald. Not her family, not her child, not her business associates or anyone else in the world. Just Donald! The man she felt would rescue her from all her unhappiness in life.

Angela and Simon had been growing farther and farther apart for a long time now. Several months earlier, he had lost his job with a large, local energy company. Each year the company would rank all their employees according to their performance. Everyone in the company got a score. When they needed to increase profits they would "right size' the business by eliminating a percentage of the staff.

Simon lost his job even though he was at the top of his class in mathematics. He had scored in the bottom 10% during the last yearly review from his employer. This had made it a very difficult summer for Angela and Simon financially. They did not have any money coming in, except for the small amount that Angela was able to make in the donut shop.

Maybe some of the resentment Angela felt stemmed from Simon's refusal to help around the house. Even though Simon had plenty of time to help, he preferred to just wander the house in his own little world. He did not engage her in conversation or make any effort to show that he even cared about her. He expected Angela to do the all of the household chores, the dishes, the laundry and the lawn work. On top of all that, he insisted she care for their daughters and maintain a daily 12 hour shift at the donut shop.

Simon was a handsome man, with black hair and nearly 6 feet tall. He bore the scars of his life with a father who was very dominating and abusive. His mother was Vietnamese and had waited on him and his father hand and foot. She was more like a servant than a matriarch. Simon's father was the master of the house. Now Simon was following in his footsteps.

Simon's father, Bill, kept his wife in the house and "protected from the outside world", she had become disillusioned and depressed as shut-ins often do. Simon did not realize how unhappy his mother had grown with her husband.

Simon had started dating Angela when he was a senior at the University of Houston. One day he had just finished his exams for the semester and had called his mom to let her know he was on his way home. "Strange, mom is not home. It's rare for her to go anywhere without my dad." Simon told Angela. "Yes, that is very strange" Angela responded… "But she said some things to me that were strange the last time we visited her."

"What did she say to you?" Simon questioned as Angela seemed to become more concerned. "She said that it was going to be my responsibility to take care of you if something happened to her." Angela responded. "And you didn't think that this was important to tell me?" Simon yelled.

"No, I just thought she meant in the very, distant future. You know, that she was hoping that we marry." Angela replied.
"I just hope she is okay." Simon said as he calmed down.

Simon dropped Angela off at her house "I am sure everything will be okay, don't worry about it Simon." Angela said as she got out of the car. Simon head home, driving faster and faster as he approached his house, he was certain that something had to be wrong. This was anything but normal. Racing into the driveway, he parked his car in the front driveway and dashed into the house. "Mom….. Mom!" Simon called out. "MOM where are you?" But there was no answer. Simon went into the kitchen and found that the evening meal had been prepared. The food was cooked and places at the table were set for him and his father. But the house was silent.

Simon rushed upstairs, but there was no sign of his mother there either. "Strange" Simon thought. His father never wanted her to go anyplace without him. Bill would go out several nights a week to hang out at a bar. But she was expected to stay home.

"Mom's not here" Simon nervously said to Angela when he called her cell phone. "That is strange" Angela replied. Then
Angela heard an agonizing cry from the phone and then a thud as if Simon had dropped his phone. She could faintly hear him crying in the background and then frantically screaming, "Call an ambulance, NOW!" Angela wiped the tears from her own eyes as

she dialed 911 and gave them the address. She rushed from the house as soon as the 911 dispatcher affirmed that an ambulance was in route. Angela jumped into her car and headed for Simons' house. As she opened the front door she heard Simon screaming and weeping..."she's dead, she is dead." Simon's mother had committed suicide.

Simon had never gotten over the loss of his mother. Always asking the question "why" his mother had left him. What had happened that was so awful she would take her own life? Simon felt intensely guilty. He was convinced he had done something, or failed to do something, that had driven his mother to commit such a desperate and final act.

The maternal side of Angela surfaced in the following months. She took care of Simon. Her mother offered Simon a room in their home and Angela had devoted herself to taking care of Simon. What he wanted she provided. They soon became lovers. Angela would sneak into his room at night to take care of all of his needs or just to comfort him in his grief.

After the funeral Angela thought about how unhappy his mother must have become. What gauge is used, she wondered, to determine you have reached your limit and must end your own life? "She was barely 40 years old - a beautiful woman, and now she was gone.

Angela thought about the subservient lifestyle of Simons' mother. It had seemed like she was a prisoner, a slave in her own home. Angela had attributed this to the fact that since Simon's mother was Vietnamese it was customary, it was the culture she was raised in and that she welcomed her role in life. Now, Angela had doubts about her previous notions. It seemed they were totally ill conceived.

In the following years, Angela felt that Simon had never completely recovered from finding his mother hanging in the bathroom with a cord around her neck. And now it truly HAD become her responsibility to take care of Simon.

"Where am I in my life right now?" Jon restated the question by to Angela

"I guess I am a bit confused about life." "I lost someone I loved very deeply and then remarried after less than a year." Jon continued.

"Are you happy?" Angela questioned him.

"No, I can't say that I am really happy. It's not that my wife is a bad woman. There are some couples who just don't necessarily bring out the best in each other."

"What do you mean?'

"Well, when she needs attention she complains in order to get it, and when she complains, I withdrawal. So, we have fallen into this pattern and things just keep getting worse. I find myself staying at work later and later. And, although I love my kids, and want to be with them, I don't really want to be with her anymore. What about you?" Jon brushed the question back to Angela as quickly as possible.

"My husband and I are separated." She continued "Well, he still comes home on the weekends but he took a job out of town as a trial separation."

So you're not living together now as man and wife?" Jon asked discreetly.

"No, I sleep in my daughter's bedroom. We do not have sex…he only comes home every other weekend. The rest of the time he is out of town working on installing computer systems for a company out of Dallas. There are times when I don't even talk to him for weeks." She sadly said.

"I wondered, when I first met you… there seemed to be sadness in your eyes. I am a big believer that the eyes are the window to the soul. And your eyes say that there are many layers to peel away." Jon said.

Angela laughed, "Funny that reminds me of something a guy friend of mine is always saying."

"Really, who is that?" Jon asked

"Oh, no one." She brushed aside the question.

"Do I detect trouble in paradise?" Jon questioned her.

"You mean with my husband?" she asked.

"Yes, there has to be an issue" Jon persisted.

"He is just very selfish, he only thinks of himself. I would leave him but he is incapable of taking care of himself. I feel I am always taking care of him and my daughter; it's as if I have two children, not just one. I just want a man to be a man, a partner and to no longer feel like I am the one who has to take care of everyone and everything."

"Sorry to hear that." Jon offered his condolences - knowing just how hard relationships can be.

"What about your childhood, what was it like?' Jon asked.

"I don't want to talk about it." Angela quickly responded.

"Why?" Jon pushed her for answers.

"It is just too painful." Angela lowered her eyes as she responded.

"You have painful the memories?" Jon continued.

"Yes, can't you see that just bringing up the subject makes me upset?"

"Yes, I see that, I'm sorry it causes you so much pain" Jon said compassionately. But he didn't want to let go of the topic.

"Then why do you ask? Why don't you just respect the fact that I don't like to think about it and don't want to talk about it?"

"I do respect you. But I also know that people who have experienced very severe pain rarely heal completely.

"I think you're wrong." He stated.

"What do you mean, I am wrong?" Angela seemed taken aback by his persistence.

"I believe you dwell on it without even realizing it. I think that you are haunted by your memories. You are haunted by your memories to such a degree that they influence everything in your day to day life." Jon explained.

"Let's say you are at a party, and everyone is laughing and it hits you. You find yourself hoping that no one in the room can see through the curtain that you use to hide your past. It's like a deep, dark closet and you are afraid to let anyone else come in." Jon said confidently.

Most people would never want to know." She scoffed. "Most people are just too shallow to care. Most people do not listen to others. And when they do listen, it is only because they want something from me." Angela said sadly.

"You mean like sex?"

"Yes, isn't that all men want?"

"Well it is important to men but it's not the only thing in the world."

"Often when a woman confides in a man, he will come back and use that information against her as leverage to win a fight or argument. Sometimes, he may use it to control her or the situation. It's becomes too hard to trust men at all." Jon continued in his dialogue about relationships. Jon continued speaking to Angela. "Yes, I don't disagree with you. It's very sad that one of the most important needs of a woman is to be able to communicate and yet she often feels can't confide in her male counterpart. Women want to be able to share what is going in their lives and what they are feeling. Often, the man makes it difficult to do so."

"When someone experiences something traumatic it influences them from that point in time up to the present."

Jon explains further, "Love and pain are similar in this way. Excitement and fun are the same way. Let's say someone goes snow skiing. They have fun…then weeks pass and they have a memory of that trip and it brings back good feelings of that time….well, this past experience still produces many of the same feelings. But what if the event is painful or traumatic, like rape or the death of a loved one? The pain is even more intense if it is a murder or something tragic. Each memory of that event causes the same depth of pain to return. The pain never leaves nor does it necessarily lessen. Pain, deep emotional pain can never leave one's soul unless it is shared, validated and experienced by another individual who understands and loves us. The pain can be like the water in a damn. The walls of damn can hold the water back, but inevitably one of two things will happen. Either some of the water will spill over or the damn will burst."

"But what about seeking help from a psychologist?" Angela questioned.

"I think they can be helpful. I think psychologists are terrific sounding boards. They give people the opportunity to openly speak about things that are very painful in a safe, non-judgmental environment. I think it is harder unburden yourself of your pain when you are paying someone to listen. Deep down inside you realize that they have no emotional investment in you." Jon continued.

Angela seemed confused, "So, you're saying if I pay a psychologist or trade casual sex in exchange for someone to talk to, it doesn't really help to talk?"

"No. I'm saying what really helps more in life is to talk to someone who is emotionally invested in you. You give them your pain. By doing so the pain is released. By sharing your experiences and allowing someone to offer you comfort or even forgiveness, the pain is surrendered to someone else. It is no longer your burden." Jon replied.

"Think of yourself packing a suitcase. You put all your pain, all of your bad memories and old wounds into the suitcase. Now, you have filled the suitcase. The suitcase is very heavy, yet you still carry it along with you. The longer you carry it the heavier it feels. Eventually, you may feel like you just can't go on because of the sheer weight of the suitcase."

"Maybe it's time to set down your suitcase Angela" Jon said with a smile.

That night Son Sary had a dream. In the dream there were two snakes slithering on the ground in the fields - trying to sneak up on the workers. One snake draws back to strike and bites several of the labors and is hacked to pieces by the workers. The other snake is in a park in the middle of a city, and is discovered by a man in a uniform. He is at the park with his children. They plead with him not to kill the snake and convince him to let them take it home. There it lived a long and prosperous life, as their pet.

The next morning Son Sary awoke and told his brother about the dream. This dream was like a vision, which they used to help them determine what they would do next.

"I think the dream is telling us that we need to split up or we will both be killed." Son spoke to Tran. "I think I will go and join the communists and I think you should go to the city. There is a large park in the middle of Phnom Penh and that is where you need to go, Tran."

"What about our family? Shouldn't we tend to our dead before we run away like cowards? Tran said bitterly, unhappy with the thought of leaving his brother.

"No!" Son said emphatically. "We do not dare go back there!" Son shuddered, his dream still fresh in his mind.

"But brother I do not want to go!" Tran argued. "I want to stay with you. Where you go, I will go. If you fight, I will fight. And if you die, I will die at your side." Tran said earnestly.

"Brother, I love you deeply. But now I am sure that our paths must part. This is our fate. It is no longer a matter of choice. You must go." Son continued.

"But how will I find you again?" Tran questioned his brother, fearing they may never see each other again.

"Here, in this cave we will find a hiding place for messages. Son looked around the cave. He found a hole in the wall near the entrance. There was gap in the rocks just big enough to fit his hand. He put a small rock in the hole to make sure it was not a bottomless hole. He reached back in and pulled out the same rock. Satisfied he turned to Tran "Here is a place where you can leave messages for me. This cave will be our safe haven and a way to communicate, just like it is today." Son said turning to bid farewell to Tran.

On that day, the brothers parted in great sorrow.

Jon and Angela found their conversation flowed as if they had known each other for years - each feeling more comfortable as they spoke.

"Jon, do you think I can find happiness?"

"Yes, of course I do. But my question is 'do you know what does happiness looks like to you?" Jon asked the question with emphasis.

"Well, sometimes I think I do." Angela responded sheepishly.

"I mean do you have a clear idea of what happiness looks like?"

"No, I guess I am not completely sure. I was engulfed in pain and very unhappy. The next thing you know, a man walked into my life and brought me happiness."

"What happiness did he bring you?" Jon asked curiously.

"He felt the pain I had been keeping locked inside." Angela said as if this guy preformed some great miracle just for her.

"So did he bring you joy or did he really just share the pain that you were feeling inside?" Jon delved deeper.

"I guess he was sharing the pain I felt inside." Angela said becoming shyer with each question.

"So you think that what brings you happiness is that someone else can feel your deepest pains?" Jon David said.

"Yes, maybe you are right." Angela replied.

"So do you think something is missing in my life, Jon?" Angela said looking straight into Jon David's eyes "You are getting to know me very well. What am I missing?"

"I think you are missing what everyone wants. Everyone wants to feel safe at a very deep emotional level. I believe you want to know that there is someone who cares about the pain you feel. I think you want to be able to share, at a deep emotional level all your fears, your dreams, your pain, your memories and even your body in ways that you have never been able to express." Jon challenged her

"But how can I share what I don't know exists within me? What man will really listen? I get the feeling all they really want is sex and not to hear what I have to say." Angela retorted cynically.

"Men will always want sex. Don't hold that against them." Jon said with a laugh. "But after the issue of sex has been resolved, that's when you can tell whether you have a man who will really listen and validate what you are saying."

"What do you mean by validating?" Angela questioned.

"Validation is the process of you sharing the feelings you have with another and then their ability to listen and take that information about you that allows your feeling to have real meaning to them." Jon explained.

As he was speaking, Angela was amazed that the more Jon spoke, the more attractive he became to her. When he spoke, what was on the inside seemed to radiate from him. She admired the depth of his understanding and the depth of his soul.

Angela found herself more fascinated and longing to continue the conversation. "Funny, how you can know someone and be in the most exotic place in the world, yet that would not matter because you do not feel any connection to them."

"Then there are other's that you look forward to seeing and talking to so you can tell them the even the smallest details of your day. It doesn't matter where you are…you simply enjoy their company." Angela said reflecting on the many exotic cruises she and Simon had taken as their annual vacation. Yet she still found that she wasn't really happy with him. Just a week ago she had come across some pictures of herself and Simon. They had been taken while they were on a cruise. She had noticed how they both looked so stiff, so distant and unhappy.

"Trust me, Angela. I can relate…I always thought that heaven and hell were the same car trip to some place, just with different passengers." Jon continued on the same line of thought.

"What do you mean?" Angela asked.

"Well if you are traveling someplace in the car with someone you don't enjoy being with, the trip is hell. You are constantly arguing, tense and tiptoeing around each other. However, when you are in the car traveling with someone you love - someone who makes you feel special - the miles and hours seem to blur together because you are with them."

"Yes, Jon I do know what you mean. I think I have been missing that. When I am traveling with Simon we hardly ever speak. I find myself in such deep thought the whole trip. Then without realizing it, we have driven several hundred miles and my mind has done nothing but wander the whole time. It's almost like I'm not even there." Angela said.

Jon had noticed Angela rarely looked into his eyes as he spoke. He found it strange that, as he talked, she would not look him in the eyes. Angela instead kept her chin tipped downward, looking at her hands or averted looking off into the distance. Finally, Jon asked her about this habit.

"Angela, I have noticed that you don't look at me when I speak. Is there something wrong? Am I missing something?" Jon had been afraid to mention it, but after a while he had to wonder why she could not look him directly in the eyes.

"Oh, I am sorry, it's just that when I was very young, it was considered disrespectful to look at someone in the eyes. There were situations where you could be severely punished or in serious trouble." Angela said apologetically.

"I see. I wondered why you were having a difficult time with it. I'm sorry" Jon said.

"No, Jon, it's not you. It's me. It's because of the way I was raised, the world I lived in as a child" she said sadly.

Angela looked down at her watch and said "Oh, I didn't realize, we have been talking for two hours. I am so sorry for keeping you so long. I have to let you go and I need to get back to my business."

"I have some things to do." Angela picked up her purse and headed to the door of the restaurant. Jon picked up the check and charged it to the hotel as they headed out together.

"Thank you for lunch and the talk" she said as she pulled her keys from her purse. She opened her cell phone to see how many missed calls she had. "Five missed calls" she grimaced. I guess I had better return them and get back to work. Thank you again…for everything." She turned on her heel and strode away, launching herself back into her busy day.

Jon wanted to ask her for her email or phone or something…but he didn't. A part of him couldn't. What would happen if he opened that door, would it lead to cheating on his wife? Jon had opened that door once before. He knew the damage and problems it could cause the already strained relationship with his wife. It was better just to let her walk away from the restaurant alone that day. Jon continued to watch to see if she would turn back to look, but she never did. She made a straight path for the exit, never hesitating. Then she was gone, sighing Jon returned to his office.

"You have been gone a long time" Enedina said as Jon walked back into the office.

"Yes, I got distracted."

"Well the general manager has been looking for you and wants you to come to his office. I think it's something important. Oh, and Shawna from the sales department wants to know who that beautiful Asian girl was that you were lunching with." She slyly smiled, fishing for details.

"Yeah, that figures," Jon said… grinning as he turned toward the General Manager's office."

Chapter 4- **Departing Phnom Penh**

The first thing Thunnysok noticed was that her father did not go to work that day. He and her mother had locked themselves in their bedroom to talk. The girls were snooping and tried to listen from the next room. Thunnysok, her sisters, Botum could not quite hear their parents conversation. Mother was very concerned about going to the country house. Thunnysok thought it would be fun to go to the country. The family had gone many times before and had loved spending time in the country.

But for some reason, mother and father were upset. Thunnysok knew something was wrong. Especially since mother was crying. Father tried to comfort her saying that everyone would be fine. Mother never cried. She always seemed to be strong and confident.

When father came out, he called the girls together into the living room. There, he gave very serious instructions, "Children, we are leaving our house immediately. We are going to grandfather's farm. I only want you to pack a few articles of old clothing. No toys! We will just being taking only what we must have to survive, a few clothes and some food and water. I want to inspect everything you pack in your bags."

They could tell by the tone in father's voice that this was serious. They knew not to question him or to argue with his instructions. Mother was busy sewing her jewelry into the lining of her clothes. "Thunnysok caught a glimpse of her mother putting a handful of gold coins into a small pouch. When mother saw Thunnysok at the door she, she lay the pouch on the nightstand by her bed and hurried the child off to her own room saying "You must go and pack your things as Father said."

Later, the father even took Nhean, Thunnysok's nine year old brother's gold rimmed glasses away from him, tucking them in his pocket. Then he took all of his uniforms to the oven and burned them.

"Children," he instructed a few minutes later when they were packed and ready to go "When we leave the house, I want you to pretend that you are deaf and mute. If men come and ask questions, I want you to be silent and let them talk, yell or scream. Do not respond, just look down at the ground."

The five children, along with their parents, left the house with backpacks of food and other essential items. Mother, carrying Thunnysok's five month old brother in a makeshift sling that passed over one shoulder and across the front of her, along with a sack of supplies on her other shoulder. They started walking towards Grandfather's farm. The farm was in the province that was north of Phnom Penh. The roads and streets were filling with others who were leaving the city. There were soldiers wearing black, pajama like uniforms, waving their machines guns in the air and cheering. All along the roadside residents were coming out to cheer these troops as they passed.

The Chim family had been walking for about 45 minutes when Mother Chim gasped and clutched at her husband's arm. He looked at her quizzically. "Oh no… the gold, I left the pouch of gold coins on the nightstand." She stuttered, glancing at Thunnysok, but never mentioning she had forgotten it because she had stopped to chide the little girl off to her room to pack.

"But we must have that gold!" Father exclaimed. There was no telling how long they would be in hiding. The eldest son Nhean spoke up immediately suggesting that he go back to retrieve the gold. "I am younger and can go much more quickly Father" he explained when he saw his mother's concerned look.

Father decided the boys could go, as long as they promised to stay together and they must hurry. The rest of the family would slow their pace so the boys could catch up. Father set a meeting place in case they got separated. The boys turned around and headed back to their house. They did not return till 3 hours later.

The family had stopped to wait. What could be taking the boys so long? Finally they saw the boys limping up the road. Mother ran to hug them. "What has happened to my sons?" She asked.

Nhean, gasping for breath, began to explain. "When I got back to the house, I found it was being ransacked. The Khmer Rouge had become looters were stealing everything. What they weren't taking they were smashing! I got so angry I began to scream at them to get out. Two of them turned on me and started beating me. Then they grabbed me and threw me out into the street. They were calling me awful names and they said this was their house now! Worst of all, I couldn't get the bag gold coins. I am sorry Mother, but I failed." He finished hanging his head in shame.

Mother went over to her son and checking his injuries and put her hand on his head.

"My son, do not despair." She continued "It is my fault the gold is lost. I am just glad you are safe. We still have my jewelry, I am sure we will be fine." Mother said with confidence, yet deep inside her concern grew.

The family continued on their journey, along with what now seemed thousands of others who were fleeing the city. There were even cars abandoned along the road.

Occasionally, they saw the bodies of dead soldiers along the side of the road. They appeared to have been killed recently. It was not clear whether they had died fighting or been executed upon surrender.

"Father, when are we going to be there?" Thunnysok asked, dragging her now tired feet.

"I really don't know. Just remember what I told you. Don't say much and don't say anything about grandfather having worked for the government. Many people were upset with anyone who had worked for the government."

"Why, Father?" Thunnysok questioned him further.

"Many bad things have happened in Cambodia, people tend to hold grudges for a long time, sometimes years."

The Cambodian culture had a concept called "Kum". This meant that no matter what it took to get even, that revenge would be exacted, even if it took a lifetime. This influenced a culture where it was common to be polite and acquiescent and then, at the appointed time, murder or carry out an act of vengeance against the offender. This included family grudges where hatred was passed down to the next generation. This strong idea of revenge was the reasoning behind the Khmer Rouge's decision to not only murder their enemies but also the families of their enemies.

There was a crowd of people entering a large field. Father soon realized the road was blocked by soldiers. There were tables with soldiers who had files and information forms for them to fill out. Those who were fleeing that hadn't head off into the fields were stopped at the roadblock. There were lines of evacuees being searched.

Next to the Chim's, another family was being searched. Soldiers emptied the man's bag and found an old military uniform. The soldiers immediately took him aside, tied his hands behind his back and blindfolded him.

Father stepped up to the table and talked to the soldiers. He was ordered to fill out a form detailing what job he had held in the city. On the next form he had to list all of his family members; who had influenced his life; what he wanted out of life; and what education he had. He filled out all of the information correctly.

The sun was starting to go down when Father Chim spotted an old friend whom he had gone to early school with. He was a soldier in the Khmer Rouge army. Vichem Chim was not sure it was him, until their eyes met and a slight smile appeared and then disappeared off of his face. In this Cambodia it was dangerous to be friends with the wrong people. Vichem felt the smile fade from his face and returned to his family.

They were corralled with thousands of other families in a grassy area near the road block. Some tried to make fires, in order to keep warm and ward off snakes and other animals. The families huddled around the fires thru the night. It was peaceful, the war was over. Everyone thought that with the Khmer Rouge victory this day the country would return to a time of peace and prosperity. Maybe the American's would lose the conflict they were waging in Vietnam and cease bombing the country. Peace could return to Cambodia for the first time in many years.

"Father, I have to go facilitate, can you go with me?" Thunnysok said squirming as they all huddled around the fire.

"Me, too" said Botum. "Father please, can you stand guard and keep us safe? You will always protect us."

The three of them walked into cover of the nearby jungle. The girls hid behind some bushes. As father waited, he heard footsteps behind him. And as he turned around he saw his boyhood friend, now a soldier, standing in front of him - his machine gun was slung over his shoulder.

"Met Vi," he said, stepping closer so his voice could not be heard by others. "It is best that no one knows we were childhood friends. These are dangerous times. But, I was happy to see you."

"Yes, I am happy to see you also. I understand it could be could dangerous for you, I could see it in your face." Vichem said agreeing with his old friend.

"Did you confess already?" His friend asks firmly.

"Yes, I'd just finished when I saw you earlier."

"Did you tell the truth? Did you put your real family name and let them know that you worked for the government?"

"Yes, I was honest."

"That is bad, my friend - very bad." The soldier said sadly, shaking his head.

"Why? I thought it would be worse to risk being caught in a lie. Besides, I thought they would need experienced help in rebuilding the government. They are going to need many of the people who are fleeing the city."

"Do you have any idea when the people will be able to return to the city?" Vichem questioned him.

"My friend, they will never be allowed to return. I don't think there will be any cites. The plan is to move everyone to the country and not allow them to return. A whole class of people will be wiped out, and there will be no upper or middle class in Cambodia. If you confessed, they are planning on executing you tomorrow morning. You must leave tonight."

"Execute? They plan to kill everyone who worked for the government and military?"

"Yes, you and your entire family will be executed tomorrow morning. You must leave tonight, in the middle of the night. There are so many refugees it will be hours before they realize that you are not here.

"My friend, you must head due north, through the jungle. When you reach the river follow it to the Sern Tern village. Once you see the edge of the village, cut back into the jungle until you come upon the great lake. I am not sure how many patrols are in that area, but we have many throughout the country."

There is a commander in that area, which I trust. I will try and get word to him to watch for you. He cares about the people of Cambodia."

"Thank you my friend. Thank you. My family is in your debt."

That night Vichem did not sleep. He roused his family and had them ready to go while the moon was still high in the sky. The family quietly headed into the jungle. There were Khmer Rouge guards surrounding them, but the family slipped out of camp separately. Father Chim went first. The children snuck out one by one. Mother Chim waited and made her escape with baby Chim still fast asleep in the sling hanging over his mother's shoulder. They each travelled a few hundred yards into the jungle and huddling together, they waited for the rest of the family members to join them. The process of leaving took over an hour. They quickly headed down a small path through the jungle. Sometimes they'd hear voices, becoming suddenly still until they passed.

Thunnysok's heart pounded each time they stopped - afraid they might be discovered. Although a child may not grasp the gravity of the situation around them, they can sense fear or danger in their parents. Thunnysok could see the fear in her mother's face each time they stopped.

When morning broke, they had only travelled about two miles into the jungle.

Hiking fifteen miles farther, exhausted, they rejoined the road. Surprisingly it was still full of people. Instead of going by way of the river, Vichem decided on a quicker route. They journeyed on for most of the day.

Suddenly, the line stopped. Vichem realized they must have come upon another road block. He was considering taking the family back into the jungle when he realized that there were Khmer Rouge soldiers positioned along the edges of the outlying jungle, to prevent this.

At this particular road block there was a fork in the road. The majority of the refugees were being directed to the right. This was creating quite a traffic jam. As the family approached the fork the Father asked the soldier for permission to go left. He told them that his family farm was to the left and that he and his family had been returning from the market and gotten caught up in the flood of people from the city. The Khmer Rouge cadre asked them to stand aside while he handled the crowd.

Twenty minutes later, with the soldiers busy directing the flow of people to the right, Vichem motioned for his family to go with him as he started to edge away. The Khmer Rouge, in all the confusion, did not realize that the family had simply walked away. Sometimes confusion works to one's disadvantage, but today the confusion obscured the Chim family's escape. Thus, allowing them to continue their journey the family farm.

Thunnysok had great apprehension about the dangers that may lie ahead. But over the next couple of days they finally reached their destination. She enjoyed being with her family. They would talk and laugh. Her father could tell such funny stories. Thunnysok deeply admired and loved her father. He was her hero. To her, it seemed he knew everything and would protect her from anything.

A few weeks later, the family was working in the fields when they saw thirty to forty soldiers coming up the path - all with AK 47 Soviet made machine guns. The commander stepped towards the family and yelled for them to come to the house.

"You have 30 minutes to get your belongings and to get out of this house!" The commander screamed at them. "Angkar now owns this house!" The family farmhouse was the one of the nicer houses in the village. In fact, it was the largest and the only one that was made of brick and mortar instead of wood thatch hut. The house also had a wall around the courtyard. There were two gates - one in the front and one in the back. The Chim family had been one of the richer property owners in the area. They had at least 6 acres of land to farm.

"You have very attractive children." The commander said "especially these two little ones."

Vichem cried out "Take them!" Thunnysok could not believe her ears. Her hero, her father was offering to give her away to this man with guns. "Here, they are yours." Vichem pushed the children toward the commander. But she did not want to go. She could not believe that her father was betraying her. She started to cry and her father scolded "Thunnysok, never cry. You belong to Angkar, not to me. I am no longer your father. You must do what he says. He is your new father!"

And so, she went with them, because Cambodian children were taught to obey their elders from the very earliest age. It was this strict code of obedience, which made Thunnysok find the courage to go with the commander that day. There was no greater fear in her than the fear of leaving her father, mother, brothers and sisters. But, there was something other than the guns, compelling her to go. It was her absolute obedience that propelled her.

"Out! Out of the house all of you! Or we will shoot everyone." They yelled.

Thunnysok's mother frantically grabbing for clothing her and her baby brother. She gave Thunnysok a hug and a kiss on her right cheek....then Thunnysok's mother kissed her on her lower right chin, just were her scar was.

"I am thankful for this scar" Thunnysok's mother said. Thunnysok saw that her mother wanted to cry although she needed to be brave. "If mother can be brave, I can be brave:" Thunnysok thought to herself.

Thunnysok started to grab her little brother. But the commander motioned for one of the soldiers to get the baby. He was only 5 months old. Then he motioned for someone to pick Thunnysok up as well. As they headed to a hut down the road, Thunnysok looked back and could see her mother at the door of the house before they went out the gate with the wall blocking her view. Tear welled up in Thunnysok's eyes. But nobody noticed.

On April 17th, 1975 The Khmer Rouge ended a long civil war in Cambodia. They were able to cross the last body of water on the ferry outside of Phnom Penh. The last government troops abandoned their positions and fled for their homes. Many of the government troops discarded their guns and uniforms along the road back to the city. This day the Khmer Rouge was victories and drove into the city on the backs of tanks and trucks, quickly taking over the key government buildings and businesses. This included the National Bank and all of the radio and television stations.

The Khmer Rouge leader had said publicly there was a list of 27 former leaders of the Lon Nol government that would be executed when the Khmer Rouge took over. However, some of these men, whose names were on the list, did not believe that they would be executed and had remained in the city.

At the time of the takeover by the Khmer Rouge soldiers, Phnom Penh had an estimated 2.5 million Cambodians living and working in the city. Many of these people had fled the countryside to escape the bombing by the United States Air Force. Cambodia, which contained part of the Ho Chi Men trail coming down from Laos, was considered a huge threat to the safety of South Vietnam.

America bombed the Cambodian countryside into submission. All of the villages were abandoned for the safety of the Capital. The Cambodian countryside and farmlands were pummeled with more bombs than those dropped on Germany during all of World War II.

Few people realized that the bombing of the countryside enabled the Khmer Rouge to take control of the countryside - forcing millions of individuals into the city. Then, they divided the city into five sections and controlled the five major roads and other paths around the city.

Individuals who were unfortunate enough to have been separated from their families were forced onto the highways and into following whatever direction the crowds were going. They were not allowed to go any other direction.

The soldiers would break into private homes and tell the families they had only minutes to get their items and get out. Those who resisted were shot immediately. The first day, each of the 27 on the "Death List" who had not yet fled the city was shot immediately. Systematically all of the other government and military men were rounded up and shot. On that first day alone over 800 government officials and military officers were executed.

The killing did not stop there. It was estimated that, over the next couple of days, there were over 15,000 sick and bedridden invalids executed by the Khmer Rouge soldiers. There weren't any orders to execute the invalids. The orders were to get everyone out of the city. Since it was impossible for those who were too sick to walk to join the exodus from the city were executed instead.

The Khmer Rouge soldiers carrying out these orders were 13 to 15 year old boys and girls who had been raised in country and had only known the ways of the Khmer Rouge. To them, the individuals in the city were corrupt and had polluted the country. The inhabitants of the city were bad and evil people. They had no sympathy for these capitalist. The Khmer Rouge had won the war and all of the spoils of the war. They had been better prepared to win a war than they were to rule a country.

House after house residents were ordered to leave at gun point. Cambodians were initially told that it would only be for 3 days. It was for their own safety as the Americans were going to bomb the city. In truth, America was upset that the Khmer Rouge had taken over the city. The refugees were given only moments to make decisions on what to do, where to go and what to take.

They were forced to make quick decisions, under the duress and panic of having guns shoved into their faces. Foolishly, people packed pictures and family history into their cars and other vehicles.

Everyone was ordered to leave the city and head to the countryside. Even thru the second day the five main highways were still crowed with millions of individuals.

Son Sary headed to the countryside around the Tonle Sap. There, Son Sary knew he would be able to find the communists who were in the area. Son Sary's plan was not to find the communists, but to let them find him. He went to an area where he knew they'd had camps before. He setup camp and built a camp fire at night. He did not worry about the government troops because he had nothing that would identify who he was. He had nothing to steal. He was now alone in the world.

After making a fire, Son went to sleep. The next morning he was awakened by the barrel of a gun in his face. He was a bit startled, although he'd expected this. He rose to find five other communist soldiers in his camp.

"Kill him now?" one asks the leader. "No, he is either too stupid or he was trying to find us. No one comes to this area just to camp. He would already be dead by now if he were government and robbed if he were a merchant. We already know all of the locals in the area."

"So, who are you young man – tell us before we cut your liver out?" the leader said. This was a group of boys ranging from 13 to 17 years old. The oldest could not have been more than 20. But in Cambodia, age had nothing to do with how dangerous a person was with a gun or a knife. These boys were dangerous. They would kill or be killed in this battle with the government.

The communists were scattered in the remote jungles around the mountainous Eastern areas. Recently the communist party was receiving much needed supplies and arms from the Viet Cong and North Vietnamese. In return the Cambodian communist party helped with the locals and with logistical support along the

Ho Chi Men Trail, which ran from North Vietnam through Laos into Cambodia and out into South Vietnam.

"I am from the Tonle Sap area, my father was a poor farmer. He and the rest of my family were killed by Lon Nol's men." Son Sary spoke quickly.

Suddenly, Son Sary's world went black as someone from behind thrust a black, cotton, rice sack over his head.

"We will send someone to your village and find out about your family. If what you are saying is not true, then you will not see the light of day ever again. You will die a very painful death."

Son Sary screamed out the name of his village and village leaders who might be able to tell them who he was and what had happened to this father.

"You seem distant tonight" Carolina said to Jon David as they drove to a movie.

"Oh, really? I didn't notice. I guess I was just caught up in my own thoughts." Jon said vaguely with a smile - trying to reassure his wife that everything was fine. But, she pressed him further "Is everything okay at work?"

"Well, not really" Jon said in a matter of fact tone.
"I found out today the hotel is for sale."

"Are you going lose your job?" Carolina asked with a great deal of concern.

"I'm not sure yet." Jon David said calmly.
"Do you know who is going to buy the hotel?" She asked inquisitively.

"No, there is no firm buyer yet. But, I also found out that there is an issue with the convention shared agreement and they are asking us for about an extra 2 million dollars on the contract. I don't believe we owe the money but trying to convince everyone of that is a little bit disconcerting."

"You didn't do anything wrong did you?"

"No…I didn't do anything wrong. But sometimes issues can be more complex than the average person can understand. That is the case with this issue. The problem is that it will be harder to sell the hotel until these issues are resolved."

"Okay, I was just worried. You are being unusually quiet." She reaffirmed to Jon David.

Jon was glad to finally get to the movie. "I cannot get her out of my mind," he thought to himself. He kept replaying, over and over; the conversations that Angela and he had had they were together. "I love the sharing we experience when we talk." He thought to himself. Jon was fascinated by her.

Tran Sary had walked and hitchhiked all the way to Phnom Penh. Tran had no money or food. He had not eaten in almost a week and had grown weaker each day. Tran was doing what Son Sary, his brother, had told him to do. He was heading for the city park, close to the Market District.

Tran could see that families were now living in areas of the park. The population seemed to be growing faster than people could build places to live. Tran sat on the park bench and prayed to the spirit of his brother. Tran was wishing that he had stayed with him. Even if they both did not survive, Tran did not like this feeling. Tran felt that it would have been better to die with his family than to be here in the city, alone.

The sun was descending behind the city skyline. It was getting darker by the minute. Tran looked up and saw a young man in tattered clothes, running with some objects in his hand. There was another man chasing behind him and a woman was standing about 80 yards away. Tran was not sure what was going on. But something told him he needed to help catch this thief. Not sure why and with little regard for himself, Tran tripped the thief who was running with the objects. This allowed his pursuer to catch up and throw himself on top of the thief who was still reeling from being tripped. The thief struggled and tossed his pursue off, jumping up off the ground and leaving the booty where it had dropped he ran away.

"Thank you" the man said as the woman caught up to the both of them and hugged her husband. Then she turned to Tran. "Thank you for helping stop that thief; he just grabbed my jewelry right off my neck! Thank you so much." She exclaimed.
"What is your name?" She inquired.
Tran looked at her sheepishly. "I am Tran."

The woman and man turned and started to leave the park. Tran was happy he was able to help but the hunger in his stomach made a noticeable, loud, rumbling sound embarrassing him.

The couple walked a few yards back in the direction they come from and Tran disappointedly head back to the bench where he had been sitting. Placing his hands on his chin he closed his eyes and wished his older brother was here with him.
"My brother, I need your help." Tran said without realizing that he had actually spoken out loud.

"I am not your brother, but if you are hungry, please come home with us. We will feed you and give you a place to rest. Maybe we can help you find work. It is the least we can do to repay you." Tran looked up to see the face of the man he had helped. Tran's felt relieved and blessed that he had found a good meal and maybe, a nice place to sleep.

"Thank you" Tran said gratefully. "Thank you, I appreciate this very much. I promise to repay this act of kindness, someday"
Tran got up and walked with the man as they headed to toward his wife. Many bad things had happened to him this past week, but at this moment, Tran felt very thankful."

Thunnysok was still alive. The sun had not yet come up over the trees, but the first sign of light seeped into her surroundings. It was time for Thunnysok to get ready for work. As she rushed to pull on her shirt, Thunnysok and Met Maih, her foster mother, headed to the gathering hut for breakfast. The rations of rice had been cut each month and now they were only allowed 5 or 6 oz. of watery rice in the bowl.

Taking the bowl, Thunnysok was always careful to squat on her legs to eat. Since she had lived in the camp she had observed several people who had taken their meal and crossed their legs to eat the food. When someone was sitting with the legs crossed this would signal to the Khmer Rouge that the person was a "new" person. A "new" person was someone like herself that had come from the city.

Thunnysok thought about her Father often, she remembered his instructions clearly "When faced with any problem, do not talk. Pretend that you are mute." Since leaving her family, Thunnysok had spoken very little and not often. Each morning she ate her little ration of food, and got in the line for her work assignments. Some days she would work in the rice field, some days she would clear plants from the banks of the river, which ran next to the camp.

The prisoners had been broken up into separate groups of male and female. Then the children and adults were separated by their ages. Thunnysok was in the youngest age group. Her little brother was left with her foster mother, Met Maih, who was now the wife of the camp commander but even her food rations were cut. She spent that first month with Thunnysok's little brother in the hut and tried to raise him as her own. Her fiancé had been murdered by the Khmer Rouge the week before Phnom Penh had fallen. She had not been allowed to grieve for very long. She was in her early 20's and was very beautiful. The commander had taken her to live with him as his wife. There was no ceremony to become a wife. The Khmer Rouge did not recognize the family unit. When Met Maih was taken by the commander, she knew what was expected of her. Choices in Cambodia were very limited. You did what the Khmer Rouge told you to do or you were killed. There no discussions and you had no rights. There was no disagreement or protest.

The commander did not stay at the camp, because he was a top boss with the Khmer Rouge. He was normally gone visiting other districts. Most nights they were on their own, just Met Maih, Thunnysok and Thunnysok's baby brother. Thunnysok could see her baby brother getting weaker every day. He was not eating anything.

In order to save her little brother, Thunnysok used her voice for the first time, "Met Maih, you must help baby brother. He is getting weaker." Met was surprised and replied, "I am trying Thunnysok. There is no food and he is getting sicker every day from being malnourished."

"Met Maih, he scarcely moves anymore. His eyes open briefly and then he goes right back to sleep. PLEASE do something, he is dying, help my brother." Thunnysok continued to plead with her. Met Maih felt all of the pain, guilt and helplessness of a mother forced to watch her own child slowly starve to death. Thunnysok's brother was only 7 months old.

Thunnysok went into the fields at dawn and worked until sunset. But the whole day, today, Thunnysok had sensed that something was wrong. One cannot leave their job in the fields without the permission of the guards. To ask the guards anything was to risk one's life. Thunnysok had seen a little girl, who was about her own age, who had asked to go to the bathroom and had never returned from the bushes. "Why?" Thunnysok would ask herself. "Were even the little children being murdered?"

Each night the camp soldiers would call everyone together for indoctrination into the ways of the Khmer Rouge and "Angkar." Thunnysok finally got to eat and listen to the Khmer Rouge scream about the American's and the evils of capitalism. Thunnysok found she could not listen, in her mind; she was worrying about her little brother. Finally, around midnight the meeting was over. They were ordered to go back to their huts. Thunnysok walked slowly back to her hut, it was the nicest one in the village, because she was living with the commander. One did not run around the Khmer Rouge. Any quick motions or actions could be interpreted as hostile. But Thunnysok walked quickly to get to the hut that night.

Met Maih did not look at Thunnysok when she entered the hut, but instead turned away and busying herself with something else. Thunnysok walked over to her and grabbed her hand;

turning around Thunnysok looked into her eyes. The look in her eyes told Thunnysok everything. Her little brother was dead. The painful reality of the absolute separation of death came at an early age to Thunnysok. She wanted to die as well. How could death be worse than living separated from those she loved? She felt the pain deeply. Her last remaining link to her family had just disappeared. Everyone was now gone and Thunnysok was alone again.

The following days were a blur, working in the fields or in the river. All the while, there were people dying or being murdered all around her. Such was the life of a four year old. Each night however, the death was more personal with her memories of her little brother. Thunnysok's Mother Chim's last words to Thunnysok were, "Protect your brother and keep him safe." Thunnysok had failed her mother. She had disgraced her mother and had not been able to protect her bother. Her brother was gone and it was all her fault.

Tears flowed each night when she was alone with Met Maih, who would hold her in her arms and try to comfort her. She would cry herself to sleep and then things got worse, she began having nightmares.

Jon was sitting in the General Manager's office talking over the contract negotiations regarding the convention center. "I know these issues could come back to bite us with the ownership group. Greg and Keith are not happy either" said Lon, the general manager of the hotel. He was not a man to joke or kid around. The slightest problem or stressful situation and Lon would commence to berate his employees. "How could this happen? How could anyone be such an idiot" Lon would question.

Jon often turned off his cell phone when entering his office. The executive committee of the hotel had learned that the general manager would use his eyes to convey how disappointed he was if a cell phone accidentally went off in a nearby office or worse while in Lon's office. Lon's focus was always on the small nagging details and that drove everyone around him crazy.

Lon would do this in many ways. No matter what the issue, his reaction was the same. Lon's typical reaction would be just as much disapproval over a $5.00 mistake as they do with a $10,000 one.

Jon's cell phone suddenly went off and he received the "look" from Lon.

"It's Enedina. Let me check and see if it's important." Jon said.

"Hello? What's up?"

"Jon there is a guest at the front desk who wants to see you." Enedina said.

"Do we know who and what it is?" Jon inquired.

"It's your Asian friend." She replied.

"Okay! Let them know I will check on it as soon as possible and get back to them." Jon said loud enough for Lon to hear.

Then in hushed tones "Yes, I will be right there." Jon continued.

"We will have to cover this more later, Jon said as he picked up his notebook. I have some issues to take care of in the Accounting Department."

Jon David went by the front desk and there in the lobby was Angela – dressed nicely and looking very beautiful and radiant. "Hi" she greeted Jon.

"I am sorry. Is it a problem that I just dropped in to see you?"

"No, Angela," Jon reassured her "but instead of going to the restaurant would you mind if we go up to my office? I will introduce you to my staff and we can talk in my office." Jon said steering her in the direction of the elevator.

When they got upstairs Jon took Angela around and introduced her to his staff. "Enedina, can you get us some sodas?" Jon said as they both walked into his office.

"You're not mad I am here, are you?" Angela said looking at him with dark brown eyes and long lashes.

"No, I guess I am just a little bit surprised...pleasantly surprised you showed up." Jon said with a grin.

"I guess I have been thinking about everything we talked about and I just wanted to talk to you again... and I had a question for you." she continued "So, please be honest with me."

"Okay" Jon responded with a confused look.

"I have this "friend" named Donald and he told me that he had a friend in the hotel business, but I cannot remember all the details about which it was and I was wondering if you were being nice to me because you are a friend of Donald's?"

"It might help if I knew his last name." Jon replied.

"Oh, I can't tell you that now. I would rather keep that a secret."

"Well, I know several people named Donald. So can you give me any other clues to help me figure out which one is the Donald that you are speaking of?"

"Donald is older, about 54 and he is 6 feet 2 inches, grey hair. He is loud and has a big smile." She explained to Jon

"Sorry, I don't think I know anyone named Donald that fits that description." Jon replied "What does he do for a living?"

"He owns energy reclamation credits business." Angela said seeming to become frustrated that Jon did not know Donald.

"Well, I have never even heard of a business like that, and I have no clue as to who you are talking about." Jon firmly responded.

"Well, I thought about all the things we talked about and it just reminded me of him. I know he said he had a friend who worked in hotels and I just figured that maybe you were being nice to me for him."

"Let me get this clear. You think I was only being nice to you to either spy on you for some old guy or you think I am just trying to get down your pants?" Jon asked in his more professional of business demeanor.

"Hmmm" Angela said realizing how it all seemed a little crazy.

"Well, I don't know you're Donald and I thought you said you were married to a guy named Simon?" How does Donald fit exactly fit into this entire picture?"

"Hmm well, I fell in love with this man." Angela said in a bold but almost innocent way.

"Okay...maybe I should recap the story so far as I think you have tried to explain to me." You're separated and getting a divorce...but your husband comes home every weekend and you live in separate bedrooms?

"You're in love with a man who is 20 years older than you?"
"And let me guess, he is married as well?"

"Yes, how did you know?" She was surprised that Jon had said that, but was honest in her answer.

"Oh, just a hunch" Jon said flippantly

"Does your separated husband know about this Donald?"

"I told him I wanted a divorce and that I was in love with Donald.

Even my husband likes Donald; Simon thinks he is a great guy."

She continued.

"Sorry, if I don't just believe that." Jon replied.

"Yes, he knows Donald and he respected him. Donald even tried to find him a job when Simon was unemployed." She argued.

"Is your husband happy about getting a divorce?" Jon asked as he became more puzzled by the whole conversation.

"He does not want a divorce and he says that he is going to do whatever it takes to win me back. He does not want to lose me." She said proudly.

"Okay, I guess I am a bit confused then, why exactly is it that you want a divorce from your husband?" Jon was definitely bewildered by her situation.

"For many years he has taken me for granted. He would never help me around the house and he expected me to wait on him hand and foot. He expected me to work a full time job, take care of our baby, and tend to all of his needs. He is just like his father, who expected his mother to take care of everything. I just could not take it anymore." She continued struggling to articulate what it was that was the source of her own unhappiness.
"And besides I am in love with someone else" Angela continued.

"You're still in love with this guy, Donald?" Jon questioned.

"Yes, I still love the old man." She said, using Jon's phrase.

"So how does Donald feel about you?" Jon said.

"He says he "likes" me." She said sarcastically, rolling her eyes upward.

"So you had an affair with an older man, who is married, who has kids, I suppose?"

"Yes, he has three children."

"You tell him that you're in love with him, and he responds with "I like you? Even more amazing you are still in love with this guy…enough to tell your husband that you love him?" Jon said quizzically.

"Yes," She responded.

"You don't think that this all seems a little strange and misdirected?" Jon continued to expose the logic of the whole situation. "So why are you telling me all of this?"

"Well you reminded me of him, and as I said, I thought you might be his friend and I guess there is a part of me that respects you, because you are a nice person?"

"Oh and that is all?" Jon kept pressing. "Are you still seeing him?"

"No, I broke up with him last month and I have not seen him since." She said sadly.

"I just feel like I am breaking apart and close to a nervous breakdown, and I thought maybe you could help, but I can see that I am wrong." Angela said as she started getting up out of her chair.

"Hold on a minute, sit back down" he sighed "let's talk." Jon said. And she sat back down…

Chapter 5 – A Meal Missed

Thunnysok kept her eyes closed. Every part of her body wanted to tense up at this moment, but she had to fight the feeling and force herself to relax. Floating on her back and keeping her eyes closed. "If I open my eyes, I might panic and die" Thunnysok kept telling herself "No, just better to keep them closed."

Thunnysok had been placed in a huge container of water. The lid covering the container had small air holes spaced evenly across the top. The space between the container lid and the water level was only four inches. Not enough space for her to keep her head straight or erect. Thunnysok had to float on her back, in order to be able to breathe the air.

Earlier that morning, Thunnysok was assigned to work in the camp kitchen. The rice for lunch was cooked on a huge pot. The water was boiling and the rice had been added to the make porridge. Once it had been cooked the pot was to be moved to another part of the kitchen. This task had been given to Thunnysok, another girl her own age whom she did not know but had seen in camp through the past year.

"Crack" went the sound of the pot as it hit the ground. The food in the pot went splitting out onto the bamboo floor of the kitchen. The porridge had seeped into the cracks and turned with the dirt beneath it to mud.

The boiling substance covered Thunnysok's arm burning her severely. But, Thunnysok did not cry, no matter how bad the pain. The Khmer Rouge guards came rushing over. "Stupid little girls" the soldier screamed at them. Then he kicked the two girls in their stomachs. The guards might not have been able to kill Thunnysok, but they could push any punishment to extreme limits and be very cruel to her. The protection of being a favored child of the commander only went so far with the camp guards.

"We need to teach all of these villagers a lesson about wasting food" the young cadre said to several soldiers and villagers in the area." Bring me two of those large cooking pots filled with water. Build fire under them." The cadre shouted to two other Khmer

Rouge soldiers.

Within minutes there were two large cooking pots with wood placed underneath them. Thunnysok and the other girl were placed into the cooking pots. Hands tied behind them, the pots were then filled with water. Thunnysok could hear Met Maih yelling something.

Thunnysok looked into the eyes of the other little girl as she was being placed into the cooking pot. As she looked into the face of a little girl, they both knew she was going to die. The little girl's eyes were pleading for help and terrorized by fear. There was nothing Thunnysok could do to stop this brutal act. Thunnysok was helpless. Then the Khmer Rouge soldier lit the fires under the cooking pots. Thunnysok's emotions rapidly changed from guilt and fear to sheer terror and horror.

The fire was lit under the pot containing the other girl. Thunnysok could see the flames from the cracks between the rim of her pot and the lid forced down atop it. At first, there were no screams - just a little girl pleading and begging for her life.

"I will work 24 hours a day!" the little girl screamed at the guards. "I will work very hard every day!" "I will give up my food for a month!" the girl continued.

The water in the pot started to boil and the girl started screaming. The little girl was now shrieking with pain. Thunnysok could not listen; she did not want to listen. She hated herself at this moment.

"Help me, someone help me please" the girl cried out. Over and over she called for her mother. "Mother they are killing me. Help me Mother!" she continued.

The little girl's mother was not far away. She also had three other children. She knew that if she tried to stop the punishment it would mean her death and possibly the deaths of her other children. She turned her back but she was not allowed to even walk away from the pitiful sounds of her daughter dying by the Khmer Rouge soldiers. The screaming continued for ten more minutes. Thunnysok heard every one of her cries for help. She would hear this sound for many years later at night as she would wake from her sleep.

Then there was silence.

Thunnysok expected the flames to be lit under her pot but they were not. She was left in the pot until around midnight. Then she was taken out and sent to her camp mother. Soaking wet and shivering cold, she had chills but no permanent damage. She had not been harmed, with the exception of the mental scars, which were burned into her heart and soul.

Thunnysok had survived the pot of water by relaxing and floating on her back the whole time. She had saved herself by not panicking and not fearing the torture pot she had been placed into. After that day, whenever Thunnysok felt stressed and the pressure of life weighed heavily, she would go swimming and float on her back. What was intended as a torture had turned out to be a lesson on one of the few ways that she could relax and escape the turmoil surrounding her?

The sun glared into Son Sary's eyes as the communist guard took the mask off his head. "The story about your family is confirmed and now you are a member of our army." The leader of the group said. "Here is your first order. Kill that prisoner." Son looked in the direction that the commander was pointing and there, on the ground, was another prisoner also wearing a black hood over his head.

"But do you know what he has ...." Son Sary started to say before. . . "Whack" the rifle butt came down hard against the bottom of his leg. "There is no hesitation in this army!" the commander screamed at Son "Next time, you question an order you will be killed." Son was knocked to the ground and the commander handed him a plastic bag. "Here, use this and do it now!" The commander barked the order at him.

Son, who had just experienced the horror of the murder of his own family, was now forced into the opposite role from victim to executioner. He now was becoming the murderer. He had to take the life of someone else to save his own life.

Revenge was the code of culture in Cambodia. One might never speak of a plan to kill or get revenge but revenge was deeply ingrained. If someone killed your parents or child, it was your obligation to make sure that they paid for it with the death of their parent or child. But this was a total stranger, Son did not understand why he was the enemy and what he had done to kill or harm his family."

Son picked up the plastic bag and walked over to him. He had to take the black bag off of his intended victim. This revealed the terror in the face of the prisoner he was about to murder. First there was the look of surprise as the mask came off and then victim tried to figure out what was going on. Then the look of fear as he realized what was going to happen. His face changed to a look of pleading, then a furtive glance, contemplating an escape and finally, the look of acceptance that death was inescapable.

Son quickly placed the bag over his victims head. He began pulling the strings tighter around the bag and the victims' neck. His victim kicked with his legs but his hands were still tied behind his back. This made it much easier for Son to pull the strings, as the victim kicked Son placed his body on top of his victim. Son did not look at his victim but instead just tried to focus his eyes on the tree. After several minutes the victim stopped kicking and Son looked down into the face of the man he had just murdered. He felt glad it was over.

Slowly Son stood up, covered in sweat and grim, his heart was pounding and his breath had quickened. He could feel adrenaline flowing through his entire body. Son looked directly at the commander. "Good" said the commander. Then he threw Son a long knife. "Now cut his head off."

"I am sorry, Angela. It's just that I am trying to take this all in and understand what you are saying, every conversation we have seems to come back to one man, Donald." Jon said shaking his head slightly.

"Do I think you are a little bit confused about this - Donald?" Jon questioned her rhetorically "Yes, I do," now wondering if Jon David was wasting his time in dealing with someone who'd had an affair with another and that she still loved with him. Donald was the man in Angela's life. He was far more important than anyone else, including her husband, Simon and Jon David.

"I think most men who heard this conversation would be thinking that you are more than just a little crazy." Jon said with a smile trying to soften the fact that he was indicating she was in fact crazy "But I am trying to understand." Jon reaffirmed.

"I don't think Donald ever cared for me, not like I cared for him. I was deeply in love with the man, and thought I wanted to spend the rest of my life with him." Angela continued - trying to get Jon to understand.

"You didn't see it as a problem that he has a wife and three kids" Jon asked.

"Yes, that is why I decided to put my love for him aside and not fight for him. I did not want to be the reason for him leaving his wife and kids." Angela continued trying to explain to Jon

"So you love the guy, have lunch with him a couple of times and then have sex with him and you don't think that would be putting a strain on his marriage?" Jon's questions might have seemed harsh but he always tried to be fair, honest, direct and without judgment. He was just trying to understand the situation.

"I want you to know that I would be the last person in the world to judge you about what you did or didn't do. I was just trying to understand you. I am not even sure monogamy exists in our culture today.

"Angela I am kind of curious. How much time did you really spend with his guy before you decided to have sex with him?" Jon pressed.

"Oh, he came in my shop about 20 times and we talked for a few minutes each time." Angela continued "We went to lunch twice. And we talked on the telephone a couple times." Angela struggled to think of all the times she actually spent with Donald.

"So what I hear is that you might have spent 8 hours of your life with this guy and then jumped into bed with him?"

Angela seemed more reflective than offended by his direct, honesty.

"How long did you see him in a more intimate way?" Jon continued

"Oh, we were only together just a couple of times." Angela said getting a little more embarrassed by the questions.

"So maybe all toll, you have spent 14 to 15 hours of your life with this guy, who is 20 years older, has a wife and kids. And you're ready to dump your husband and chase after him?"

"What do you think?"

"Pretty crazy! Maybe?" Angela asked Jon.

"I am not surprised that you had an affair, I am more surprised you still care so much." Jon said.

"What do you mean?" Angela questioned him.

"What I am saying is. . . Sometimes our lives are like a dry forest, there is no water, and over time the forest becomes so dry that it does not take much for a fire to burn the whole forest. Love is the water. And if you're in a relationship where you don't feel loved, it becomes easier and easier to ignite the flames.

"So maybe the real answer lies in your past?" Jon said.

"Tell me about your background. Normally, in order to understand the choices we make, we must look at what happened in our past? Are you close to your dad and mom?" Jon asked. "My mother and step father live with Simon and me. My father was murdered back in 1993."

"Sorry to hear that." Jon continued, "Were you close to him?"

"No, I hated my father. I was not even speaking to him when he was murdered." Angela said in a very cold matter of fact manner.

"Sorry to hear that, every girl needs her father and the love of her father."

"When I heard that he had been murdered I said, **good**, he was a mean man and he deserved to be dead. The last time I saw him, we were at a wedding reception and we did not speak. I happened to walk to the ladies restroom and there, coming out of the men's bathroom, was my father. We just looked at each other but we did not speak." She continued, almost proudly, that she had been so cold even during a time of utmost joy for a family.

"What brought on all this animosity with your father?"

"He was mean; he never was like a father should be. My mother and father were in a custody battle over my sister, Timm, when dad got murdered."

"My dad was remarried to a woman that he had brought over from Cambodia after the war. He had gotten my mother pregnant with my sister, Timm, about the same time he married this Cambodian woman. Mother had to put up with so much adultery from my real father."

"What happened to your father?" Jon continued pressing forward as long as she would tell him what had happened.

"You are very direct aren't you?" Angela responded. "Well, my dad owned a gas station, down close to Hobby airport. One night he was leaving after closing up, at around 12pm. The reports said that people heard shots fired and that it might have been an attempted robbery. He was murdered. But I think my dad might have had a premonition about his death."

"Why?" Jon asks.

"Dad had been wearing a bullet proof vest for months before the shooting. Then on the day he stopped wearing it, he was murdered." Angela explained.

"That is strange; it doesn't sound like a premonition to me. It sounds more like someone who had threats on his life and decided to take precautions. Sorry. But it doesn't sound like an attempted robbery to me." Jon replied

"I thought it was a little strange too" Angela agreed with Jon "Personally, I thought my step mother did it for insurance money. She became a millionaire with the insurance pay off on my dad's death." Angela continued," She was upset when my dad wanted to go back to my mother."

"That could be a motive for sure." Jon said thoughtfully.

"Yeah, and my father wanted to divorce her and move back in with my mother" Angela said. When he died the FBI even came out and asked us questions because my dad used to work in some government position. But I am not sure exactly what he did."

'FBI only gets involved if a federal crime is committed. So that is really strange." Jon pondered the statements.

"So they think someone in your family might have killed him?" Jon asked.

"No. I think they just had to check. But no one thought my mother did it. She had nothing to gain from killing my father, in spite of everything that had happened between them, my mother still loved him. She really did mourn his death even though they had fought over Timm. My dad could be very stubborn and mean."

"The whole thing seems really strange, sorry to hear that he was murdered and even sorry that you and your dad were not close when he died." Jon said consoling her.

"He was a mean playboy, a cheating, abusive man....and I am not bothered at all by his death."

"Was his murder ever solved?" Jon asked.

"No. No one was ever arrested."

"We did notice the FBI come and take our trash one day."

"So they were investigating your family?" Jon was puzzled by the comments.

"No, I don't think they really thought my mother did it. They were just going through the trash." Angela continued.

"Angela, that means they were investigating your family." Jon felt that maybe Angela did not realize what the implications were of the investigators going through their trash.

"What year and date was he murdered?" Jon asks.

"May 1993. I think. But I am not sure of the exact day. Why, Jon?" Angela wanted to know.

"I am just curious. I have used the Houston Archives many times, in order to go back and read the old news articles relating to things I am researching. I thought I might go look and read up on what happened with your father."

"Oh, okay, whatever floats your boat?" She said smiling.

"Hey, Angela I am glad you came by but I am going to have to get some work done soon. Do you want to exchange emails and we can continue this conversation via email?"

"Great, here is my email" Angela wrote out her email and got up to go. "Jon, I have really enjoyed talking with you again. " Jon saw the look in her face like she wanted to come closer and kiss him, so he slightly moved his eyes to the door, without encouraging her to come nearer.

The communist party in Cambodia was very small in December of 1968. The total communist numbers totaled 3000 to 4000 individuals. They were a mixed batch including men, women, intellectuals and peasants. In the capital of Phnom Penh, in the shadows of the government buildings, the groups of communist were organized in secret cells of 3 individuals. The many different cells were not connected to each other in case any of the cells betrayed its members. The individuals had elaborate schemes for getting messages to the different cells of communist party. Messages were given to one link in the system, to give to another anonymous number in the system. But the communists were able to gain assets or spies in the highest levels of the Sihanouk government. Yet, even this did not keep the communist from getting caught. When the communist spies were caught, they were immediately executed. In one incident, over 45 communists were captured in the capital and executed by the military government.

Throughout the countryside Cambodia the cells worked a little differently. They operated in cells of 10 to 20 men who were not organized with a central command. Some parts of the country had strong leadership and others were weaker. In the far north eastern region were the Montagnards. They were a tribal group who traced their heritage more closely to the Laos Montagnards. In this region, the communist controlled most of the mountainous countryside.

The government began with efforts to seal the villages off from the outside world and the communist from using each village. The communist fled into the jungles chased by the government troops - trying to eliminate them. The government wanted to cut off the communists from access to guns in the cities and towns.

The war between the government and the communists was brutal. There was no policy of taking prisoners. When one side captured another, those captured were immediately executed. The government even offered rewards for the heads of the communist. At times, whole truckloads of heads were brought into the bases and camps for payment. This practice often led to innocent individuals being murdered just for the bounty on their heads. The beheadings of innocent villagers' helped the growth of the communist party in the countryside by inspiring great fear.

Son Sary was one of the leading communist cadres in the area around Battambang. The communists did not try to hold the land, but rather they would strike a small target and then retreat into the jungle.

"We keep waiting for our leaders to give us the order to attack and then there is nothing. We must attack. We must show that we are not afraid to take the battle to the government. I want revenge, I need revenge" Son Sary continued talking to the other men around the camp fire. "The camp at Bay Damram is only a 5 mile walk! We could attack that army base in two hours' time. Now! Now is the time to act!" Son Sary was now second in command of this small group of men.

Most of the young men were ready for a fight. That night 22 young men walked through the moon lit jungle to attack the base. However, the attack did not go as Son Sary and the soldiers had hoped.

Instead of inflicting damage on the base, the communist left with two men killed and several more wounded in the battle. They had been more unlucky that had it been a case of not being organized. When the communist approached the base, the soldiers had put cow bells in the field with strings stretched across the fields. The noise alerted the soldiers and the element of surprise was lost for the communist.

Months later, Son Sary was promoted as a commander in the area around Battambang after the last commander was captured by soldiers and executed.

Two hours after Angela left Jon's office he received an email. Jon started to read.

Dear Donald

I hope you are doing well and I miss you tremendously. I meet today with your friend in the hotel business and found him very delightful. I enjoyed the time and think he is a great guy. I know you put him up to meeting with me but that is okay I still love you. When I was leaving I was tempted to kiss him and test him to see if he would admit you had put him up to meeting and getting to know me.

Yours forever,

Angela

Jon could not believe what he was reading. Here was an email from Angela to Donald, about him indicating he knew Donald. Jon thought that Angela was delusional.

"Is this a passion of the mind" Jon thought to himself? "The mind creates a safe, pleasant image and then holds on to that image even the face of adverse reality. Obviously Angela's image of Donald was so strong that she could not face the truth of her relationship with him. What trauma had this girl faced that she could not clearly grasp reality? Slowly Jon thought about his answer and then responded.

Angela, this is not Donald. This is Jon David Conner. I am sorry you think I might know this Donald person. But I do not. I am very sorry that this person hurt you, but I am in no way connected to him.

 Jon

A few minutes passed and there came a return email from Angela

Sorry. I guess I just wanted you to be someone or something that you are not.
Angela

"Sorry if you are disappointed that I am not someone else. Sorry, I am happy with who I am as a person, because in self-acceptance there is a far more consistent love to be found."

Jon David stopping to ponder, Jon finally decided Angela had to be just little nuts.

Chapter 6 – Forever Pain

Today, Thunnysok was assigned to a work group of twenty young girls who were to clean the shoots of water, which fed into the rice paddles. The water shoot ran along a narrow, swift river. The girls had to clean the plant life debris that was attaching itself to the shoots and clogging the waters flow. The little girls had worked all that morning. They had to be very careful because the river currents were rapid and had risen due to the heavy rainfall. Most of the younger Cambodian girls did not know how to swim.

In the late afternoon, Thunnysok was starting to day dream of going home. She had been growing more tired and ill. Reaching down to gather some plants Thunnysok heard a loud splash behind her. Turning around Thunnysok could see Thay's head going under the surface of the water as she fell into an underwater hole. Thay was able to pop her head back up and gasp for air. The water current started to carry her close to Thunnysok who turned and reached out to grab her as the current carried her down river. Thunnysok grabbed at her hand but Thay's head went back under the water.

Two Khmer Rouge soldiers saw what was happening and came running towards the two girls. Firing his gun into the air and screaming at Thunnysok the soldier said "Let her go, let go!" Thay's head popped back up out of the water and she saw Thunnysok's eyes. Thunnysok heard the soldiers screaming at her and the shots that were fired into the sky. Then, she just let go of Thays' hand, as she watched the terror in Thay's face. Several feet away, Thay went under the water again, and this time, the girl did not surface again.

Thunnysok had killed Thay. Maybe not with her own hands or a weapon, but Thay's fragile life hung in Thunnysok's hands and she had let her down. Thunnysok had let her die that day in the river.

The soldiers came back, about an hour later, carrying her body.

They gave Thunnysok a shovel and pointed out where they wanted it buried. The soldiers got several other girls to help Thunnysok and they finished up around dark.

When Thunnysok came into the hut that night, she was called into the front area by Ma Maih and three soldiers. One of the soldiers had a large cane in his hand. Thunnysok knew she was going to get a beating.

"Hands on the table" the soldier said to Thunnysok. Thunnysok bent over touching her hands on the table. Bracing herself with her small feet spread several feet apart. "Whack" the cane struck her on her tiny butt. Thunnysok refused to cry and then came more "whack" again and again and again... Thunnysok could feel the pain on her body but the pain that she felt on the inside was much greater. She closed her eyes as she was beaten. All she could see was the face of Thay as she released her hand. This beating, Thunnysok was glad to receive, because she felt like it was part of her karma for letting go. This time Thunnysok needed this pain, this hurt, this punishment.

AngelaDonutShop@yahoo.com

Jon,

I thought I would tell you more about what life my life was like as a child. Since you ask and wanted to know. I did not have many boyfriends in Middle School or High School. I was only one of a few Asians in my school. I was a real loner. There were many white guys who liked me, but I was not allowed to go out with them. My parents were very protective of me and my two sisters. My mother worked cleaning houses all day, and at night, had odd jobs to support us. So we were left alone most of the time.

Jondavidconner@yahoo.com

"Did you have a steady boyfriend at all?"

AngelaDonutShop@yahoo.com

Yes, I had one steady boyfriend in high school. He went to my church and we knew each other for over a year before we started dating seriously, or as you would say, messing around. He loved me very much and I loved him completely. He asks me to move with him to Tulsa, Oklahoma, so he could attend a small airplane pilot training school program.

"We kept our relationship a secret. But when our parents find out, they all got upset and made us break up. My father and mother did not like my boyfriend's family. His parents did not like my family. Our families broke us up but he still asked me to go with him to Tulsa. But I could not go against the wishes of my family.

Jondavidconner@yahoo.com

So this was your first real relationship?

AngelaDonutShop@yahoo.com

Jon, I wanted to remind you of something ...that no matter how much we email and get together, you are not going to get down my pants!

Jondavidconner@yahoo.com

Yes, Angela you keep reminding me. Why you think I want to have sex with you is beyond me. The last time I checked, I don't think I've ever asked you for anything.

AngelaDonutShop@yahoo.com

You haven't, I just want you to know the answer when you do ask me.

Jondavidconner@yahoo.com

Thanks I will remember that Angela.

AngelaDonutShop@yahoo.com

Yes, before that I had some guy friends, but nothing serious. I had many guys who had crushes on me, but I was just too much of a tomboy. I had my hair cut real short. All the girls hated me. I think they were jealous of me because they thought I was going to steal their boyfriends.

My step dad was so cruel to me. He beat me, and started calling me a whore and slut. He did everything he could to dishonor me and make me feel guilty about what happened.
It was the hardest thing I ever had to endure on top of losing my boyfriend. I wanted to die.

Jondavidconner@yahoo.com

That was very serious. Sorry to hear it. That is just an over exaggeration isn't it - that you wanted to die?

AngelaDonutShop@yahoo.com

No, Jon it is not an exaggeration. That night I took a whole bottle of Tylenol and tried to overdose on them. I called my boyfriend, said good-bye to him and then hung up. He called my best friend and told her that he was worried about me and was afraid that I might try to commit suicide so she came over.

I was upstairs when Nina came to the door. My step father would not let her into the house at first. But Nina insisted and would not go away. She argued with my step dad and told him that she had to see me. It took her a long time, but finally he let her into the house. She came upstairs and there I was, on the bed, almost dead.

She got them to take me to the hospital.

My step dad told them it would be better that I die than to dishonor the family as I was. He just wanted them to let me die.

They told me that I would have died if they had not gotten me to the hospital when they did. My step father did not even come to see me at first. It took years for him to feel any guilt about his behavior that night.

Jondavidconner@yahoo.com

That is pretty serious if you loved your boyfriend so much that you wanted to die when you lost him. I guess I am surprised that your step dad was so mean to you. It's hard for me to believe a parent could be that way.

AngelaDonutShop@yahoo.com

I think up until a year or two ago he would still ask about me and occasionally call me. I got the feeling that he was not happy in his current marriage and he would call and see how Simon and I were doing. I think he wanted to get back with me, but I never told him that Simon and I were having problems.
He was the most loving boyfriend. And I really did love him deeply. I am sure he still loves me just the same.

Jondavidconner@yahoo.com

I am sure he did.

Around 6pm that night, Jon looked into his email in-box and counted up all the emails from Angela that day. There were 120 emails in his in-box. Jon thought to himself, I wonder how long and how much of the day it takes to write all those emails.

Work seemed to be getting busier and there were more stresses developing at home. How was Jon to keep up? Each day became more stressful. Yet, Jon realized that the one thing he enjoyed most was each new email or call from Angela.

Prince Sihanouk visited Moscow in March, 1970. While he was out of his country, the Defense Minister and his buddies staged a coup against the absent Prince. On March 18th, 1970 they took overthrew the government and Prince Sihanouk was now viewed as an enemy of the government.

 Prince Sihanouk immediately formed a resistance group with the support of Vietnam, which they called, FUNK - Front United National of Kampuchea. Cambodia was now a nation with three separate political forces involved in a civil war. There were those who were loyal to Prince Sihanouk, the Lon Nol and the central government which was support by the United States of America.

In April of 1970 the United States and the South Vietnamese government invaded Cambodia with 30,000 US troops and 40,000 South Vietnamese troops. The invasion lasted two months and reached as far as Svay Rieng and Kompong Cham.

They destroyed great quantities of North Vietnamese supplies and weapons. However, the short term benefits were offset by long term, disastrous results. The Lon Nol government lost more support in the countryside because of their connection with the South Vietnamese and the US. In effect, the communists were now spread around the countryside and were gaining more support with the common people.

The Lon Nol government was anti Vietnamese and proceeded to eliminate the Vietnamese who lived in Cambodia. In one instance, a village of 3000 people was destroyed - everyone killed.

Within two months after the Lon Nol took over the government Vietnamese were ordered into concentration camps or were massacred. They had been ordered out of the country, and by the end of 1970, over 25,000 of them had left Cambodia to return to Vietnam. After the invasion by the Americans and South Vietnamese, the US met their two month deadline to leave the country, but the South Vietnamese stayed to terrorize the countryside - raping the women, burning the villages, killing innocent peasants, and stealing all the cattle.

The age of reason had ended in Cambodia and the seed of the tragedies created by the Khmer Rouge was abetted during the early days of 1970. There was no taking of prisoners in these conflicts. Anyone taken prisoner was considered an enemy and was executed, including 26 western journalists who were captured by the Khmer Rouge.

Son Sary was proud of his next assignment, he was ordered to go into Laos and meet with Pol Pot, the leader of the Khmer

Rouge. Son took three men with him and traveled my foot into the mountainous regions of northeastern Cambodia. Then they crossed the border of Laos and headed to camp 13, located on the Ho Chi Min trail.

Son Sary and the men had been traveling for over a month when they finally neared camp 13. To Son, the camp was just a mark on the map. The men moved slowly during the days and even slower during the night.

During one night's march, Son Sary gave the hand sign to stop. The men stopped immediately and crouched down with machine guns ready to shoot. Son pointed at the red smoke rising slowly into the sky in the distance. Not sure exactly what it meant, Son decided that the smoke in the sky could not be a good sign. He decided to detour deeper into the jungle and take a route around the trail. Then high in the sky he heard a distant sound. It was B-52 bombers flying overhead. Immediately Son and the other men began running. They could see the bombs dropping, coming closer and closer and getting louder and louder. The blasting sound from the bombs was terrifying. They destroyed everything around them.

The bombs created huge craters where they destroyed the landscape, huts and any animals or people within 200 yards of each of the 2000 pound bombs.

As Son Sary and his men ran from the blasts, one bomb hit close enough to kill one of them. Son dove behind a fallen tree, using it to shield him from the force of the blast. He soon discovered the flying debris and shrapnel from the explosion had killed the rest of his men. The B-52's were moving away now, as they headed down the Ho Chi Minh path. Son left the bodies of his comrades on the ground hidden in the underbrush. As he continued down the path, he realized that he had temporarily lost his hearing due to being so near the explosions.

Son did not even hear the Viet Cong walk up behind him, but they were there as he turned around. Before Son Sary could fire his weapon, a Viet Cong clubbed him in the head sending him crashing to the ground.

It must have been several hours later when Son Sary woke up

in an underground tunnel. Camp 13 was all underground.

"Glad to see that they did not kill you, Son" Pol Pot said to Son Sary with a grin on his face.

"What?" Son Sary said, he had still not regained his hearing completely.

"I said they should have killed you, you lazy worthless, commander, allowing yourself to get caught by the Viet Cong." Pol Pot repeated a little louder as a little smile come over his face.

"Get up Son, you have to see this maze of tunnels" Pol said with amazement and as Son got up and they started down the tunnel. The first level of the complex was 30 feet under the ground. As they went deeper into the cave complex, every additional 12 foot descended to three additional levels. There were supply rooms, meeting rooms, recreational areas, hospitals, arms stashes, and command centers on each level. The tunnels and caves were big enough to hold over 1000 men. During the bombing they would go to the deepest levels of the tunnels. Here they had rooms that afforded four separate escape tunnels. If one of the passageways were destroyed they would not be trapped. There was very little chance that the American bombers could destroy this underground fort.

Heading back to the central command room, Son Sary met Pol Pot's wife. She had made the month long journey down from Hanoi to join her husband. She was staring into the cup of water on the table when all the sudden she started screaming, "They have poisoned the water! They are trying to prison us!" Pol Pot rushed to his wife and tried to calm her but she was screaming uncontrollably.

"She is not well, Son" Pol Said. "We will start the journey back once she is feeling better."

That night, Pol Pot's wife passed away. Son was never really sure exactly what happened to her. Whether she had been poisoned or had a mental breakdown and died. The next day they cremated her body and put her ashes in a jar. She would be making the journey back…just not quite how they had expected.

Tran Sary had become a close friend of the Chim's since that day in the Phnom Penh Park. Vichem Chim had taken Tran into their home, and had also found him different odd jobs around the city. The Chim family was very well connected in Cambodia. Vichem's father was head of what can be compared to the Central Intelligence Agency in the United States.

The Chim family lived in a very affluent area of the city. Vichem worked for the Cambodian Navy and was in control of the distribution of money for soldiers and supplies. His father, worked for the national police, which was responsible for the internal security of the country. This was a powerful position within the government. Death could be inflicted by command of the elder Chim to anyone who opposed him. Father Chim had a license to kill most anyone that was deemed a danger to the government.

Just in the past year there had been two assassination attempts on the senior Chim's life.

Once he had survived, only because the assassin given the assignment to kill him lacked the courage to carry out his mission. The assassin had failed because the idea of killing someone and the reality of killing them proved to be much different. It was much harder to do when it came time to pull the trigger.

Father Chim did not discover this until much later. Upon interrogation a prisoner, who revealed that an attempt had been made but the assassin had failed. During further questioning he discovered the assassin had been waiting on the street one night when Chim had been entering his limousine. Though he had Chim in his sights, he had failed to pull the trigger. He had hesitated too long and had missed his opportunity.

The elder Chim's connections in government and politics helped his family maneuver around almost any need in the city. Tran got a good job in the government with the Interior Department, acting as a courier for the government - delivering documents and papers to other departments. After 6 months of living with the Chim family Tran was able to get himself an apartment. It was close to the Chim home. Tran dropped by often to visit the children and talk to Vichem. Tran found himself loving the family that had taken him in.

Several more months went by and Tran met a young Cambodia woman of humble origins and mild beauty. Soon they were married and settled into the capital city.

It was early in the morning and there seemed to be something different going on in the camp. The first thing Thunnysok noticed was that the guards gathering into small groups. Then several of the Khmer Rouge soldiers went to their huts, at first they did not seem to be concerned about guarding the several hundred people who were still in the camp.

Soon, five horse drawn wagons pulled up in front of the huts, and the Khmer Rouge started piling supplies into them. Then several of the men got into the wagons.

Mitt Maih came to the field where Thunnysok was and motioned for her to come with her. They climbed into the wagon with several soldiers and the other women who lived with them. Thunnysok was the only child. Mitt Maih seemed very concerned and wanted Thunnysok to get in the last wagon. Within minutes the wagons were leaving the camp. This was very different for Thunnysok since she had not left the camp since coming there several years ago.

After much yelling between them, several of the guards went over to the field, where the remainder of the men, women and children were working. They raised their AK 47 machine guns and commenced firing on the workers. Thunnysok watched as the spray of bullets killed or severely wounded all of them. Then the guard turned and headed for the wagon without checking to see if they were all indeed dead.

"The Vietnamese are coming! The Vietnamese are coming" Thunnysok could hear them yelling. "We must leave before the

Vietnamese get here."

Since Vietnam was to their east, they took the road heading west. Several hours went by as they lumbered down the dirt road thru the Cambodian countryside. The wagons continued through the night and the heat of the next day.

The second night, just as it was getting dark, Thunnysok noticed the last wagon was getting farther and farther behind the rest of the wagons. Mitt Maih leaned close to Thunnysok and whispered in her ear. "Take your bag and pretend you have to get off the wagon to pee. There is a hut over there in the jungle. The woman who lives there used to know my husband who was murdered by the Khmer Rouge. Go to her and tell her I sent you. Maybe she will help you. We did not have orders to leave the camp so the other members of the Khmer Rouge might kill us if the Vietnamese don't. Your chances of survival are better if you go to her." Mitt Maih said with tears welling up in her eyes. She had come to love Thunnysok. Even in the worst of places and at the worst of times, love can grow between two people.

Thunnysok did not want to go. Mitt Maih was the only person that she knew. She was the only one who had cared for her these past couple of years. Thunnysok's world had become one of the harshest of realities - one where even the smallest misstep or ill-chosen word could lead to terrible consequences. She had grown to depend on Mitt Maih completely.

Mitt Maih hugged Thunnysok and looked into her sad face. As the wagon rounded the bend in the road; Thunnysok turned and jumped off the wagon. She ducked in the bushes and watched as the wagons continued on without her. She started to feel very lost and alone. She thought to herself "it seems like everyone I love always leaves me - if not by death, they just give me away!"

And cry she did. "I am alone, all alone in this world!" Thunnysok cried out loud. Then, as tears dripped down her cheeks, she sat down on the porch of the run down cottage to wait for the owner to return home. She hid her little pack of clothes, which were wrapped in scarf-like material, underneath the three stepped ladder of the house. She waited all night and the next day for someone to come home. Then, finally she fell asleep on the front porch.

The next evening the lady and her five children retuned to the cottage. They had heard the wagons the night before and had run into the jungle and waited until they were sure everyone had gone from the area. The woman's husband had been a three star general in the Cambodian military and was one of the first to be killed by the Khmer Rouge, in April of 1975. The woman and her children had been sent to this cottage to hide from the Khmer Rouge.

"Mother she is alive," the elder boy said as he poked Thunnysok with a stick. "She is alive."

"What are you doing here girl?" "Are you Khmer Rouge?" "Are you a spy?" The lady said in a very angry voice. Thunnysok did not speak. Even now she was slow to speak or did not speak at all. She was fearful she would say the wrong thing.

"What do we do with her, Mother?" the boys asked.

The lady did not want to kill her, but did not trust her either. The lives of her children depended on her, not on this scanty little girl who had showed up on her porch.

"Bind her hands and tie her to the pole" the Mother said pointing to the center pole in the middle of the cottage. The boys grabbed Thunnysok. "Whack" the eldest boy hit Thunnysok in the face and then punched her in the stomach. Then they drug Thunnysok into the cottage and tied her arms around the pole that went from the ground to the roof.

Thunnysok was surprised and angered by this treatment. She had expected to find help. Instead she had found more torture and cruelty. With her hands tied to the pole all she could do was sit on the ground. Occasionally she would stand up to stretch her legs. The five children of the cottage were all cruel, coming over to pinch her or hit her with sticks and curse at her.

This abuse continued for ten days. During this time, her new captors did not give Thunnysok any food. They made a cruel game of giving her water. They would pour the water on Thunnysok's head and let it roll down her face affording her only a chance of catching a few drops of the precious liquid. Her severe dehydration was causing her muscles to cramp, and her heart beat and breathing became more rapid.

Since ten days had passed.

Thunnysok was too young to know that these were all signs of dehydration, but she realized that she had to get away. "I have to go outside to pee and if you don't let me I will just start peeing and pooping on myself" Thunnysok finally said. Surprised that she had finally spoken, the Mother said, "Let her go outside. You have five minutes to take care of your business and then you must come back into the hut again."

One of the boys untied her and she went out into the noise of the dark jungle night. Most people would have been afraid of the jungle but not Thunnysok. She was accustomed to it. Running behind a bush, Thunnysok turned to see if the woman in the house was watching her. Then Thunnysok snuck around to the front of the house and pulled her clothes from their hiding place. She quickly turned and ran into the jungle as fast as she could.

She felt very weak and confused and had no sense of direction. But she prayed to her ancestors for help. Not sure she was even heading towards the river; she stumbled and fell face first into the water. She was so glad to have found water that she decided she would stay close to the river from now on.

AngelaDonutShop@yahoo.com

I just wanted to say I was sorry for what happened today.
I guess I just kind of freaked out when you started to give me a hug. I thought you were going to kiss me. I am sorry, I just couldn't. I am still so much in love with Donald that the thought of kissing anyone else just freaked me out. I have always warned you that there is no way you are ever going to get down my pants.

Jon David Conner read the new email as soon as he got back to the hotel. He had meet Angela for lunch at Café Abode in the Galleria Area of Houston. Jon and Angela had been having lunch together at least once a week over the past several months.

That day after having a nice lunch and conversation Jon had walked Angela out to her SUV and in one of those awkward moments while saying good bye Jon had started to kiss her on the top of her head and Angela had thought that Jon was going to give her a kiss on the lips. She had let out a little yelp and jumped into her vehicle as if she had seen a ghost.

Jondavidconner@yahoo.com

You are starting to drive me crazy with this "down your pants" conversation. I don't know why you keep bringing up something that I have never asked for or suggested.

In fact, this whole Donald obsession is really starring to bother me. I thought you were trying to get over this guy and I am more than willing to help you. But if you're still seeing Donald, I am just not sure I want to be a part of your life at all.

No guy wants to hear about another guy! Or how great he is and what a wonderful guy he was! Or how fantastic the affair was! And then you turn around saying you hate the idea of sex and you aren't attracted to me, but you are still sending several hundred emails a day or calling me 10 to 20 times a day!
 Do you realize just how nuts you seem compared to the average person?

AngelaDonutShop@yahoo.com

Sorry☹

Jondavidconner@yahoo.com

You know, sometimes I think you must have really been traumatized during childhood. The way you react to physical touch, you seem to be so turned off by the topic of sex. Yet the next moment you are throwing it in my face without rhyme or reason.

Sometimes it makes me think you must have suffered physical or sexual abuse. Have you?

AngelaDonutShop@yahoo.com

NO!!!!!!!!!!!!!

Jondavidconner@yahoo.com

Hmm, that was a little too emphatic. I am not so sure that you are telling the truth.

AngelaDonutShop@yahoo.com

I am sorry, it's just that when I get close to you I start remembering Donald and thinking about him. He has been the only man who has ever really gotten to me. I have had so many men try to seduce me, but Donald is the only one I have ever fallen for. I am still in love with him. I even told Donald last week about you and that you and I talk all the time and email"

Jondavidconner@yahoo.com

Really what did he say?

AngelaDonutShop@yahoo.com

He said be careful. He doesn't want me to end up having another affair with some other white guy. He said we had both agreed to be good and remain faithful to our spouses. Of course this is after we had already blown it ourselves. You know, I ask him if he had ever cheated on his wife with anyone else and his answer kind of shocked me....he said that "he had never fallen off his horse before." Can you believe that? He referred to our affair as falling off a horse?

Jondavidconner@yahoo.com

Yes, I am surprised that he would describe your relationship like falling off a horse. But, I am even more surprised that you saw Donald last week. So, are you telling me that you are still getting together with him?

AngelaDonutShop@yahoo.com

That is none of your business!

Jondavidconner@yahoo.com

"Angela you have made it my business, on the basis that you email me over 100 times a day and call me 10 to 20 times a day. You ask for my help and encouragement to help you get over this guy, Donald. You want help getting along better with your husband and then when I ask you a question that is very relevant to the time you and I spend together, you tell me that it's none of my business!!!
Don't email or call me again! Bye!

AngelaDonutShop@yahoo.com

FINE, I won't!!

"Jon, you seem like you are just going deeper and deeper into your own little world" Carolina said. "What do you mean?" Jon responded. "You have not said a single word to me, the whole night except hello when you walked in the door" complained Carolina.

"Sorry, I guess I didn't really notice" Jon said while apologizing to her "It's just all the stuff going on at work. My boss and I don't really get along that well. I have a shortage of employees. Then there is the sale of the hotel, and now this whole contract dispute at the convention center next to the hotel! I guess my mind is racing and my mouth is forgetting to verbalize what is going on inside."

"Jon, I know you have a lot to deal with but I need you to focus on me. I am getting tired of you having your head up in the clouds. You are just no fun. I need someone who will give me the love and attention I need." She continued.

"Okay, do you want to hear all the details that are bothering me, do you really want me to open up and share?" Jon retorted to her.

"No, not really, it's very boring. I want you to ask me how my day went and how the kids are doing in my kindergarten class. I want to be able to talk to you about my day. I just don't think you are interested in my day."

"I am interested. I guess I didn't realize how much I wasn't communicating…" Jon was trying to explain. "It's not just me you're ignoring. It's our kids too." Carolina interrupted him.

"Okay, I will work on it" Jon promised.

Jon woke up at 2am and went downstairs, restless and tossing and turning every few minutes. He could not help but to log on and check his email. And there, sent only a few minutes earlier was an email from Angela.

AngelaDonutShop@yahoo.com

You were right.

I was raped. I realize that you and I may never speak again and I just wanted to let you know that you were right. I didn't want to admit it when we first met. But yes, I was raped.

To Angela's amazement a response came back while she was still there at her computer.

Jondavidconner@yahoo.com

I am sorry to hear that happened to you. But I am not surprised. Can you tell me exactly what happened?

AngelaDonutShop@yahoo.com

I was sixteen years old and my step father's nephew came down to stay with us for the summer. He was a year older than me and was very strong. He was a wrestler in school. Apparently he was a very good one. Remember, I only weighed about 89 lbs wet. One day when my family was all at work, we started just playing around, teasing and having fun with each other. Then he was tickling me and making me laugh. We were on the couch and he was on top of me. Then he stopped tickling me and started trying to kiss me instead. I told him, "Stop! Stop!" but he wouldn't.

He became fierce like a lion just trying to get a kiss from me, and then he reached down and pulled my pants off and I kept saying "No! Stop! Please don't!" but he forced himself inside me and there was nothing I could do. He was done and it was over before I fully realized what was happening. Then he had the nerve to want to kiss me again! Like we had just made love, when the truth was he had just raped me. I was hurt, both physically and emotionally. At first I blamed myself. Then I tried to tell my mother and step father but they neither of them wanted to believe me. In fact, my step father just kept calling me a liar and a whore.

Even the next summer my father still thought this guy was someone I should have married. He came down and tried to give me an engagement ring and I took it and threw it at him. I was not going to let my parents arrange any marriage to anyone and especially to someone who had already disrespected me like that.

Later, he went into the military. I am sure he was running away from the things he had done. I am sure he felt guilty for what he had done to me. I think his brother had put him up to it. He was thinking that this is how you treat a woman you are in love with - just take her, make her your possession.

Jondavidconner@yahoo.com

I am sure it had to be terrible. However, I am not surprised. I'd thought that maybe you had dealt with some traumatic experience like rape or death. You seem to have too many issues, which seem to have come from your past.

I just cannot imagine that you suffered a rape and then your family did not help you or believe you.

AngelaDonutShop@yahoo.com

Yes, I felt the same way, I was very distraught over the rape. Not exactly how a woman wants her first sexual experience to be. And yet it happens to so many women.

"Jon what are you doing up so late" Carolina said as she walked down the stairs and into the den.

"Oh, just checking my emails from work." Jon said as he hurriedly tried to close down the computer screen. But she got there quicker than he'd expected and saw the name on the screen of the emails? "Is Angela one of your staff or hotel employees?"

"Well, that is not exactly one of my employees" Jon said awkwardly.

"Who is it, that you feel so inclined to email back this early in the morning?"

"I had some other emails that I was responding to then I saw one from this person who had been at the hotel and had a accident in the garage and I had tried to help her, it really wasn't much of anything" Jon lied convincingly.

"Oh really, then you don't mind if I read it?" Carolina asked sarcastically.

"Well, actually I do, a little" Jon replied surprised she had asked.

"That is not really fair, Jon, I just want you to take as much of an interest in me as you do in WORK!

"That's not fair; I ask you all the time what is going on with your kids and the school. I make an effort all the time to find out, trust me, I bet I can name more of your children in your class and teachers in your school than you can name at my job" Jon replied.

"NO. You don't!" Carolina said raising her voice.

"Well, its early in the morning, I don't really want to get into this argument just now, maybe we can talk about it more this weekend." Jon said walking to the front living room and turning his back on Carolina.

"Just sleep on the couch, you are always retreating anyway." Carolina shot back as she started back up the stairs, heading back to her room.

Jon lay down on the couch and started to think about the conversation and everything that was going on around him and why this Asian woman was starting to consume all of his thoughts.

Jon was starting to realize that he and Angela could talk about anything. Every topic seemed to be open for discussion. For every conversation there could be a decent discussion of the merits and yet both were very non-judgmental of what the other person believed.

"It just seems that the deeper I go in any conversation, she can follow and listen to what I have to say. I really value that she responds to each comment. There seems to be a real pattern in the way we speak and listen" Jon thought to himself as he turned over and tried to get some sleep. The mornings always seem to come early.

The country of Cambodia was the most heavily bombed country in the history of mankind. The bombing started years earlier than most Americans were officially made aware, while President Lyndon Johnson was president. Then the bombing's escalated under Richard Millhouse Nixon in the 70's.

Throughout the Cambodian bombings, the United States dropped over 2,756,941 tons of bombs on over 113,716 sites during 230,516 sorties throughout the country. Many of these bombing by the United States were nothing more than destroyed the crops and villages in the countryside.

One estimate of the number of people who died is upwards of 250,000 men, women and children. The huge numbers of casualties was a large contrast to the actual number of Khmer Rouge soldiers, which were about three to five thousand soldiers during this time period.

Ten percent of the flights over the country had no specific mission. Targets were listed as unknown or not listed at all. They were just indiscriminate bombings of the Cambodian lands and people. Henry Kissinger had promised Congress that the United States Air Force would not bomb any more than 30 meters into Cambodia. But this was never the case, as the US Air Force dropped bombs throughout all of the Cambodian countryside. The only place that was safe from bombardments was the major cities. The peasants fled the countryside and sought shelter in the cities. Each bomb destroyed everything within a radius of 500 to 1500 meters from point of impact.

Richard Nixon told Henry Kissinger, after the failed invasion on the ground "The Air Force has to go in there and I mean really go in there" ....he wanted everything that could fly to go in there and bomb the hell out of them. "There is no limitation "the number of missions" or "how many bombers you can send".

Kissinger replied "The problem is, Mr. President, that the Air Force is designed to fight an air battle against the Soviet Union. They are not designed for this war. In fact, they are not designed for any war we are likely to have to fight in Cambodia."

A few minutes later, Kissinger got on the phone with Alexander Haig, the commander over the war. "Nixon wants a massive bombing campaign in Cambodia. He doesn't want to hear any excuses. It's an order; it's to be carried out. Take anything that flies and bomb anything that moves. You got that?" And when Kissinger hung up the phone, hundreds of thousands of the poorest farmers and peasants in the world would die in the bomb blasts of the US Air Force.

When the Khmer Rouge took over Phnom Penh on April 17th, 1975 they went to every house and person telling them that they had to leave the city. Many of these people went willingly into the countryside. This resulted in the exodus of over half a million people out of the city. The Khmer Rouge told the citizens that they only had to leave for three days. They feared the Americans were going to bomb the city. This lie was believable to the citizens of the city because everyone hated the Americans and had seen the annihilation with the bombings of their entire country. The lie kept the people quiet as they headed, unknowingly, to their deaths. This would not be the last lie that the Khmer Rouge would perpetrate, in order to get the people to willingly go to their deaths.

Son Sary saw the planes dropping their bombs in the distant sky of the Kandal Province, southwest of the city of Phnom Penh. Although, he was miles away, he could not help but be angry, because he knew there were villages within several meters of the area. "Come down here and fight me!" Son Sary screamed at the bombers that were flying as high as 35,000 feet in the sky above him. He turned to his 12 men, "Come, we need to get to the village as quickly as possible." Marching on, all the soldiers quicken their pace to keep up with their young commander.

The group was heading toward the village which was close to where the bombs had fallen. As they got closer they came across huge craters in the ground and huge patches of jungle that had been destroyed by the bombs. About two hours later the soldiers came through the jungle brush into the village. Many huts had been reduced to rubble. There were craters where there had once been fields and livestock.

Stunned, the villagers that had survived were walking around, as if in some trace, not able to grasp what had just happened. Other villagers were busy trying to find family members who might have survived. However, most were just gathering body parts from the debris and piling them into one huge pile. There were piles of bloodied arms, legs, torsos, and heads. All of them torn apart by the destructive impact of the huge bombs.

Out of the three hundred people who had lived in the village, there were over 100 dead or dying. Another 75 of the villagers had severe injuries. Most of the bodies of those who had been killed were literally blown into oblivion - into pieces so small they could not even be buried.

Son Sary and his men walked up to a cluster of villagers and offered them assistance. The soldiers gave them their food and water, and they tried to help those with injuries.

That night, his men made a fire in the center of the village and called everyone to gather around the fire. "This is the result of Lon Nol and the Americans who support his government." Son Sary said in a somber voice "This is happening all over Cambodia. The Americans bomb the villages and fields and destroy everything. All of Cambodia has been bombed" he said somberly.

"This will continue as long as General Lon Nol is in power and aided by his American allies. This is why we fight. This is our country and it's being destroyed by the Vietnamese and Americans. Join me in this fight for freedom – in this fight to end the government of Lon Nol" his voice rising fervently.

"But what can we the villagers do to help?" one of the elders asked.

"Give me your sons and daughters, so they may fight" Son Sary replied.

"You might was well take our children and let them die in battle because the bombing will kill them anyway" The villager said.

Son Sary turned and walked away from the fire only to return moments later with a dead baby in his arms. Son Sary dropped the baby in front of the villager who had spoken to him. Son said to him, "They are already dying. The enemy is killing your babies and your children. Fight! Fight them! Avenge your children."

"Feed us, support the Khmer Rouge, and when you tend to us you are supporting your children as well."

The next day Son Sary left with 3 boys and 2 girls who ranged in ages from 9 to 13.

"We are winning the hearts and souls of the countryside people" Son Sary said smiling to his unit of soldiers.

"Let the American's continue to bomb us" he jeered arrogantly.

Chapter Seven – The Boogie Man

Even in the darkest hours, in the most dangerous places in the world, children will find a way to play games and try to have fun. For this is the nature of childhood. For Thunnysok, it was that time in the late hours of the night and early morning when she would sneak out of the huts with several other children to talk and play in the dark.

"Tonight lets meet after the adults have all gone to sleep" Thunnysok said to her friend. "Let the other girls know, we will meet. Tomorrow is the day of rest. So it will not matter how late we stay up and play tonight." "Okay" her friend replied, "I will meet you next to the wagons by the river."

Thunnysok was restless as she first dozed off to sleep. She woke when she heard a sound. She slowly realized that night had come. It should be close to time to meet the other girls, she thought. It was hard to tell exactly what time it was, because there were no watches or clocks. Tonight, the moon was hidden behind the clouds. There was not a trace of moonlight, the night was very dark.

Thunnysok crept out of the hut and went down to the river where she had arranged to meet the other girls. Thunnysok started to play by herself with a few sticks as she waited. Still unaware of the time Thunnysok kept herself busy tossing pebbles into the water. She started to wonder if maybe the other girls had fallen completely asleep. The girls were exhausted from working the fields for 12 hours a day, and they had all had grown weaker with the passing of time. But here, in the night, they found their freedom. Here, playing in the dark they did not have to worry about angering a soldier and fear instant death.

Thunnysok loved the nights. Most of the Khmers feared the night because it was the time when the soldiers would come and get people out of their huts and take them off into the jungles to kill them. But Thunnysok thought if she was outside, she was so small that she could hide from whatever came and she would blend into the night.

The hours passed, and the longer Thunnysok waited, the more she realized that no one was coming. The clouds would break apart in the night sky and occasionally the moon would shine through and then hide again. Thunnysok was in front of the wagon, sitting on a tree stump, when she heard a noise coming from the jungle - the rattling of bushes about 40 feet away . . . and it was coming closer.

Thunnysok quickly crawled under the wagon and slowly backed herself up near the side of the river bank. She moved as quietly as she could because the sounds kept coming closer and closer. The moon was behind the clouds so she could not see what was approaching. The noise was unusual. She could hear the footsteps, but also the sound of something being dragged across the ground.

Thunnysok was becoming more and more frightened. She kept thinking "maybe the intruder sees me" or "maybe they know I am here". But there was no change in the pace, as the noise came towards her. Thunnysok was pushing her body flat to the ground. Wishing she were invisible and praying for the clouds to part and cast some light her surroundings.

Thunnysok realized that the noise was now only a couple of feet from her hiding place. Just at that moment the clouds parted and she saw her fears were not unfounded. There was a man walking, she could only see him from the waist down. In one hand he had a machete; it had blood on the blade. In the other hand he had a large, clear plastic bag. The bag contained his victims severed, bleeding heads.

Thunnysok was close enough to see the faces, lifeless eyes peering out of the bag. They were all lumped together in the bag as he dragged it behind him. Thunnysok buried her face into the ground. She did not cry, but she was filled with terror. After the dark stranger was long gone, Thunnysok returned to her hut. She did not sleep that night nor did she sleep the next several nights. Haunted by the faces in bag, she kept seeing them in her nightmares.

Jon David looked at the caller id and the name always seemed to put at least a moment of dread into his mind. "Lon calling" Jon picked up the phone and pretended that the call could have been from anyone.

"Accounting, Jon speaking" Jon barked firmly into the phone answering the call.

"Jon, can you come to my office so we can discuss this whole situation with Keith and Greg on a conference call? They are still very concerned about the whole issue with the office building. They are concerned that it might hold up the sale of the hotel. There is grumbling that maybe it's your fault – which, in fact, you are to blame."

"What? I am to blame for what?" Jon David said in disbelief.

"They believe that –well, that maybe there is something you should have done differently. That maybe you did not catch the errors soon enough, maybe you didn't do your job well enough?"

"I can't believe they'd think that." Jon retorted.

"You know how these corporate guys can be, looking for a scapegoat at the first sign of any trouble. This financial issue is too complicated for anyone to understand except for maybe a C.P.A. who has a Master's of Business Administration in Finance. "

"Oh great, now there is a financial battle that even the guys who are supposed to be on my side don't understand."

"That's about right" Lon said.

"Well there are three ways to interpret that contract, and I am sure that they have been mistaken this whole time in how they have been looking at this problem and errors in the method used for billing the hotel.

"Save it, Jon, there is no way I am going to understand the issues. You're going to have to find a way to convince corporate, they barely grasp what you are trying to say."

"Great, looks like I am stacking the odds against myself." Jon said

"You know I will back you up as much as I can but it would be best if you provide documentation to support your arguments." Lon continued.

After the phone call Jon felt depressed about the whole situation. It's strange how easily one can misunderstand or misinterpret things. If you cannot give clear, concise answers in way that they will understand, you can bet the battle is lost.

Jon had good reasons not to really trust or like his boss. Lon possessed the same negativity as him of his wife. It was oddly interesting how they both had exactly the same birthdays. Jon wondered if there was something about the stars lining up, on a particular day, to make a certain type of personality in everyone born at that time.

Jon contemplated why his boss was so negative. Lon's father, whom he had idolized, had been a soldier on the Bataan Death March. He had spent the rest of the World War II in a Japanese prison camp. In June of 1942 the American's lost the Philippines. 72,000 American's and Pilipino soldiers were captured and marched to prison camps farther north. Along the way, one in every four soldiers was murdered by their captors. The soldiers were beheaded, starved, denied water, shot, ran over by trucks and often bayoneted just for the sport of the Japanese soldiers.

Life for the next three years was quite an ordeal for his dad. Only 3 out of 10 soldiers who entered the Japanese camps survived. Men who entered at a strong 150 lbs were rarely more than 96 and 98 lbs by the end of their imprisonment.

Lon's dad survived the war but he never spoke about the terrible things that happened to him. He drank heavily and was abusive to those around him. Men of this era did not try to resolve the things that happened. They kept it deep inside and internalized it.

Lon had one son who was just entering college at the University of Texas. But his birth, eighteen years earlier, had not come without a price. His wife had to go to the hospital and have a blood transfusion during the birth. This had resulted in her catching the HIV virus. For the last eighteen years, Lon and his wife had to deal with the HIV virus and medical issues related to it. Sex was difficult and medical expenses were high.

Maybe those were all good reasons for Lon to have a negative personality. Jon had heard, a month earlier, that there had been more bad news in Lon's life. His sister and his mother had both, within one month, developed cancer and were battling for their own survival.

With every negative or inappropriate comment he made, Jon tried to remind himself of the overwhelming problems that dwelt within the heart of this man. And this made his behavior understandable, even though it was difficult to bear.

"Simon is moving back to Houston. He found a job working as a wireless system administrator for a large hospital complex." Angela said as she sat down to have lunch with Jon at Erwans.

"Good, maybe that will keep you from running around and having lunch with all these men that are just trying to get down your pants, little crazy Asian chick." Jon retorted.

"Boy, you are being a little cocky today." Angela replied.

"Maybe, but I decided why do I care so much? Whenever we get with each other all you do is talk about Donald and what a wonderful man he was and how you can't believe you had an affair with him."

"You believe he was in love with you? However, I believe that he was just making you his little Asian sex kitten. I think that he never had any intention of leaving his wife. You fell for him deeply and it's really sad that you cannot get over him, but that's the part that really confuses me."

"Maybe I am a little crazy, but I know that I love the man." Angela defended herself.

"Oh, please, your idea of love and mine are so completely different. So tell me what your master plan was just in case

Donald really did love you?" Jon asked snidely.

"Well, I guess he would have had to divorce his wife. I would have divorced Simon. I would live alone for a while and he would have lived alone for a while. Then we would have gotten a place together. Maybe even, sometime down the road we would have another child together."

"Well, have you thought about the fact that you don't even have a job that is making a steady income – After you sold the donut shop?

Simon would only have to give you 20% of his 6 figure income for child support - that in Texas you are not going to get alimony - which Donald would have to pay 30% of his meager income for child support and lose half of his business? So did Donald ever even say that he wanted to move in with you?"

"Yes, one time when we were together he said, "Wouldn't it be nice if we could get a place together and do this all the time?" Angela said.

"Look, if I was you, I would never trust a guy before sex, during sex or immediately after sex. What they say can be just about the moment." Jon said.

"You're just jealous of him!" Angela said.

"No, I am not jealous of him. I might be a little envious, but not jealous." Jon replied.

"What do you mean? What is the difference?" Angela asked innocently.

"Jealous means he has what I want, that he possesses some object or person that I might desire to possess or have. First of all, Donald does not have a right to you...Simon does. Second, envious is more a feeling of desiring something the other person has... this might be true. I guess there is a part of me, which wishes that you cared about me the way you care about Donald. There is a part of me that wishes you and I had done things together, that you have done with Donald. So I think you would describe my feelings as closer to envy and not jealously.

They finished lunch and paid the bill. Reluctantly and slowly has he hated to leave and enjoyed the time with her.

"Do you have to hurry back to work?" Angela inquired.

"No, not really, it's Friday and Lon has gone to Dallas for the weekend. Why?"

"I am not ready to go. I was thinking maybe we can go over the Galleria and sit by the water fountains."

"Okay. We can finish this conversation over there. I will follow you in my car."

How quickly today's friends become tomorrow's enemies. Vietnam had helped supply and arm the Khmer Rouge for many years through the civil war. South Vietnam was falling at the same time the Khmer Rouge was taking over Phnom Penh. Their relationship held for about a year. The Vietnamese government turned to the Soviet Union for international and material support, and the Khmer Rouge government turned to China.

Vietnam had over one million Chinese nationals living in the country. The Vietnamese government saw all of them as a potential economic power block and as such, a potential threat to the stability of their government.

Vietnam started the nationalization of the assets of the Chinese who were living in Vietnam. With all their possessions taken by the government, over 250,000 Chinese overseas nationals were forced into "floating coffins" little boats to flee the country, due to a master plan designed by Le Duan.

Hundreds of thousands of Vietnamese took to small boats, in order to flee to Thailand, Indonesia and Malaysia. Those who fled had to endure pirates along the way who would stop the boats and strip searches all the passengers. Valuables like gold, and silver and diamonds were hid in body cavities. However, when pirates found those individuals hiding valuables they would occasionally shoot one or two of them, in order to encourage the others to reveal their valuables.

Trinh Le, a cute, long haired, little 8 year old Vietnamese girl, was awoken from her sleep. Trinh originally lived in a nice house in Saigon during the war. Several years earlier her family had been forced to move to a small house in the countryside.

"Get your bag, it's time to go." Trinh's mother said. There were 6 people in the Lee family, Mother, Father, Trinh, her older sister and two little brothers. The family walked several miles on a path to get to the river. Once there, the family paid the captain of the boat to take them to Thailand. There were 102 Vietnamese people waiting to board the 38 foot boat. It was anchored next to the dock, was a small fishing boat about to disembark smuggling Vietnamese out of the country.

Trinh hoped it would be a short journey. There was no room below deck for the people to get out of the weather. That night it started to rain, and Trinh was already feeling the chill in her bones as she put her bag between her and her sister. To her right sat a five year old girl with her parents. Trinh noticed that she was already coughing and she tried to keep her head turned away from her. As the boat drifted toward the center of the river, the lights along the river bank got dimmer. Several of the men had paddled the boat away from the river bank before the captain started the motors.

As dawn was breaking, the boat reached the open waters of the China Sea. The morning was beautiful and Trinh was excited and yet scared to be leaving her country. Much had changed since the American's had fled Vietnam after losing the war. The country had changed much and it seemed it was for the worst to Trinh.

"The first night on the boat was not bad." Trinh thought to herself. The captain did not head to the Gulf of Thailand. He was concerned the conflict was heating up between Vietnam and Cambodia and would result in the Cambodian government sending more patrols out into the waters, and endanger the passengers on the boats. Also, the pirates were worse along the coast of Thailand than in any other part of the China Sea.

On the second night, the weather changed. A storm came up and the waves washed up over the sides the small boat. There was no protection from the cold water. The rain continued for the next two days. Trinh became colder and colder, as she huddled with her parents. The next morning, as the skies cleared, Trinh notice that the coughing of the girl beside her had stopped coughing. Her body was leaning against Trinh and she tried to give her a gentle nudge to move over more. Space was very limited. Trinh looked and saw the girl's eyes looking at her, glazed over in a blank stare. The little girl was dead. Her mother started to cry, as she was crying the captain came up to see what was going on. "The girl must go. We must get rid of the body." The captain ordered. The mother was crying bitterly, as the captain picked up the lifeless body of the girl and simply threw her over the side of the boat. Space could not be wasted, especially space for someone who had perished on the journey. Trinh could not help but cry for the little girl. How her little body made such a small splash in the water and then quickly went over the waves. Trinh noticed the fins of the fish following behind the boat and suddenly realized that they were sharks.

The boat headed for Indonesia. Hope mixed with anxiety inside Trinh as her parents said they should be landing in Indonesia in less than a day. Already 7 people had died on the trip; all who perished were quickly thrown over the side of the boat. Early the next morning, there was commotion on the boat. The captain and crew were scurrying around the boat speaking very quickly to each other. Trinh could see the fear and anxiety in their faces and they kept pointing off into the distance at an object.

"Mommy, what is happening, why is the captain so afraid" Trinh said feeling her own fear welling up inside her.

"Pirates" mommy said. "Stay put, I will be back in a minute"

Moments later her mother returned from below deck, there in her hands was a pale of human excrement. "Put this on!" Mom commanded her.

"No mommy this is nasty." Trinh said "don't make me"

Without wasting any time, her father and mother started to wipe the human excrement all over her body. Smelling and stinking was only opportunity for her and her sister to survive.

It took almost an hour for the pirate boat to catch up with them. There really was not much chance that they could outrun these pirates. There were ten armed men on the other boats speaking a language that Trinh did not understand. Then they started a search of the boat and all the people on it. They made each person strip off all their clothes. Everyone was exposed to the nakedness' of everyone else around. No one was allowed even one piece of clothing to cover their bodies as they were searched for jewelry and other valuables.

Due to the odor permeating from the excrement on their bodies, Trinh and her sister were quickly passed over in the pirates search.

The whole experience was over in less than an hour. But as the pirate boat started to leave, they took four of the girls that were on the boat, ranging from 10 to 15 years old. One parent tried to stop them and was quickly shot in the head by the pirate. Mothers wept as their daughters were taken by the pirates. They know that they would never see their innocent little girls again. Pirates had taken the girls to use them for sex. Once they had tired of them. Then the pirates would either kill them or worse …sell them into prostitution.

Trinh would spend the next two years of her life living in a refugee camp in one tent with 17 other people, before being sponsored to come to America. Trinh was always afraid of the guards who patrolled the fences around the camp.

Years would pass before Trinh Le would recover from the memories she had coming to America.

"All Chams must be destroyed as a national identity" Mok said to Son Sary.

Mok had brought word of the movement to pacifism of the

Chams.

"There are many of them. There are estimates that there are 500,000 to a million but no one is really sure." Son Sary replied.

'The central committee has decided they are too unreliable and that they need to be destroyed and broken up and scattered across all the parts of Cambodia.' Mok continued.

"You will get help from the North West commander and the North Commander." Mok explained.

"Good, I will need them. They are a very tight group of people and they will not be broken easy"

"I have enclosed the plans that Pol Pot would like to see implemented. They are all in this directive." Mok said, handing Son Sary the papers. "Remember, these are dangerous times, one has to look over their shoulder for both internal and external enemies."

The Chams were a mix of Muslim and Hindu peoples who practiced Brahmanism - a religion predating the Hindu's. They are perhaps the oldest and least known people of Indochina. They are inheritors of a proud tradition, which was the first Indian originated Kingdom in Indochina with its founding predating the Cambodian rise of about 550 A.D.

Our earliest records of Champa are Chinese, dating from 192 A.D. In these dynastic annals the people of Lin-yi, or Champa, are described as having 'dark skin, deep-set eyes, turned up noses and frizzy hair' traits which are still often recognizable in the modern descendants of the Chams even today. The annalist records that the Chams dress "in a single piece of cotton or silk wrapped about the body". They wear their hair in a bun on the top of their head, and they pierce their ears in order to wear small metal rings. They are very clean. They wash themselves several times each day, wear perfume, and rub their bodies with a lotion made of camphor and musk".

The origin of the Chams, like that of most peoples, are somewhat lost in the records of time, but are closely linked with the islands of the Malay-Indonesian and the Philippines. Legend says that they migrated by sea from the Indonesian Archipelago and settled in what is now central Vietnam.

Cham's prosperity was based on maritime trade. Their principal exports seem to have been slaves (mainly prisoners of war) and sandalwood. Sandalwood was an important product for religious practices in the burning of bodies. One ritual of the Chams was on the first anniversary of the death of a Cham. They would dig up the body and have a ceremony, which included cremating the body. The ashes would then be reburied in the grave.

Much of their wealth seems to have been used for building "Cham Towers" which were made of exquisitely decorated brick-and-sandstone. There are many Cham temples and towers scattered throughout coastal southern Vietnam and in several other areas of Cambodia

In 1471 the outnumbered Chams suffered a terrible defeat at the hands of the Vietnamese. 60,000 of their soldiers were reportedly killed, and another 60,000 carried into captivity. Champa was reduced to a small sliver of territory in the region of Nha Trang in present day Vietnam. The king and many of his subjects fled to neighboring Cambodia rather than submitting to the Vietnamese conquest in 1712. Large Cham communities were established in Cambodia along the Mekong Delta and the Boeng Tonle Sap or Great Lake regions of Cambodia.

In 1972 the Khmer Rouge controlled most of the region around the Tonle Sap and the Mekong Delta. The Chams were ordered to stop wearing Islamic dress and baggy cotton trousers and start wearing the black Khmer Rouge pants and tops. They were also forced to stop wearing the upswing hairstyles and jewelry.

In November 1973 the Chams rebelled. Many of the leaders were chased into the jungle and executed after being tortured to reveal their organizations. Over 200,000 Chams were moved into areas controlled by the Khmer Rouge in the east of Cambodia. There the Chams were forced to work the land, though they been the best fishermen in the country. They struggled to keep their own identities and beliefs during these years of forced labor.

Thunnysok found herself getting very restless. She was sitting in a small hut with 15 other children, listening to a teacher talk about different subjects. Thunnysok found it difficult to concentrate on what was being taught. This was the first time Thunnysok had ever been in a class room. No matter how small it was, this school stuff was boring and hard on the mind.

The hut was several feet off the ground and open on three sides. The children were sitting on the floor with their writing boards. This was all very new to Thunnysok, she had been sent here to become a real woman, to be educated.

Thunnysok was now close to eight years old, but in Cambodia the time was more measured by the seasons of rain and harvest instead of the year, months and days. Thunnysok tried to listen to what the man was saying, but it was no use. She was wiggling and turning and needed to go. The teacher had her back to the class and Thunnysok slowly slipped out of the side of the hut. She quietly crawled under the hut to the side that had a wall; then she headed out into the woods - making her escape from the school to blessed freedom.

Thunnysok loved the water and knew exactly where she wanted to go. She had seen children playing down by the Tonle Sap Island, along the beaches that dotted the lake. This would only take about a half an hour to get to.

Thunnysok found several children playing down by the water. She had been warned not to play with these children because they were Chams. The children were considered dangerous by most of the Khmer Rouge. The Chams lived by themselves and never married outside of their own groups. But, Thunnysok could tell that they were friendly. So Thunnysok joined them and it was not long before they were all playing together.

"What is that over there?" Thunnysok pointed as she asked her new friends.

"That is a Cham tower; built many hundreds of years ago." said a little boy.

"No one ever goes in the tower. It is forbidden. Anyone who goes in the tower will die and so no one enters." The boy continued.

"I am not afraid" Thunnysok replied, defiant as always. This was the Thunnysok who had survived in the jungle for the past half year on her own, who had been tortured and beaten, who had worked from dawn to late night. Thunnysok was a little girl who had seen a lot of death and many horrible things. Nothing was going to scare her anymore….let alone a silly tower where superstition could control those who feared it.

"There are mystical spirits that live in the towers." The boy continued genuinely concerned for his new friend.

"I tell you I am not afraid and I want to go see what is inside the tower." Thunnysok continue even more stubbornly. "I must go and see what is inside. You can all stay here if you want to, but I am going." Thunnysok's was determined. Others had already told her about the tower with the same superstitious awe that these little children were displaying but she was not going to let it stop her. Thunnysok headed towards the Cham tower.

The boy grabbed her arm, trying to stop her.

"Let go!" Thunnysok broke free and stomped her feet into the sand as she headed towards the tower.

"You won't be able to get in." The boy yelled insistently.

Thunnysok approached the tower, which was about 50 feet tall. What wonderful designs and decorations on the outside of the tower, Thunnysok thought as she studied it.

The two doors leading at the entrance were shut tight. Thunnysok tried pulling on them and pushing on them. But they did not open. She walked around the tower and came back to the front of the tower. She could not find any other entrance.

There was a sudden gust of wind and to her utter amazement, the doors to the tower slowly opened. It was like magic all by themselves they just opened. It was as if someone or something was beckoning her. Slowly, she entered the tower. Inside it was pitch black. There was only a slight glimmer of light coming from the third floor. As her eyes adjusted to the darkness, Thunnysok realized that there was a stairwell leading up to the top of the tower. She took one cautious step after another, making sure that the stairwell was solid. When just as she was about half way up, a bird flew out from the dark fluttering past her...

Thunnysok woke up, three days later, surrounded by the villagers. The villagers were chanting ancient prayers for her safe return from the dead. There were no bumps on her head; there were no cuts or scrapes that indicated she had fallen. Thunnysok had just blacked out and was not sure why or where she had gone, but they told her how close to death she had come.

"Do you have to hurry back?" Angela said after they had received the check from the restaurant.

"No, I think I have enough time if you want to do something else. What did you have in mind?" Jon said, smiling, like most men would.

"You can get that little grin off your face. You're not getting down my pants." Angela responded.

"Shame, I am thinking that I have already spent a lot more time with you than Donald ever has and yet he found a way!" Jon pressed.

"Yes, I was attracted to him." Angela said responding in her usually direct way.

"Ouch!" Jon said. "You do have a knack for putting a man back in his place." Jon finished with a jab.

"I was thinking of us going to the fountains over by the Galleria. It's a beautiful day and it might be nice to sit out on the benches." Angela finished.

"Great. Let's go."

Several minutes later, they were in the parking lot next to the Galleria in Houston. The shopping complex was one of the largest in the southwest. Located next to the Williams Tower, a 52 story building and at the base there was a small park and a large set of waterfalls.

The next couple of hours flew by as they walked around the waterfalls and sat on the bench.

"I know you want me, you're just trying to figure out how to get me." Angela said confidently.

"The first week, I saw you; I had this strange sensation that you and I would become close friends. Almost as if I already knew most of what you were dealing with and what was happening to you. I had to ask myself if I was willing to be part of someone's life even if it would never lead to a sexual relationship. Somehow, I already knew that if I did not break off the communication early we would be somehow involved with each other for the rest of our lives in some capacity. Maybe not as lovers, maybe not just as friends, I really don't know. But I have news for you; I am not really interested in having just an affair with you. Personally, I think it would be the worst thing in the world for you. When we first started talking, you were in the process of having a nervous breakdown. You were facing deep depression and adrift in such a hopeless emotional state. I have seen many improvements in you, and the last thing you need is to be having another "Donald" type of relationship."

I consider what you and I have as an emotional affair. Donald was both an emotional and physical affair. But Donald isn't really the issue. The question is why you had an affair to begin with. What needs were not filled in your relationship with Simon?"

"I don't know. I have not really thought about it." She answered.

"Don't get me wrong... I am attracted to you. You are an incredible and beautiful woman. But I am not interested in having a sexual affair with a married woman. What I have truly sought in my life is a much deeper love. I find that I want the kind of love that brings two individuals to a place where they can feel the pain and joy inside each other. Sex should be the last act of two hearts growing closer together, not the first." Jon stated in a serious tone.

"I had that with Donald" Angela interjected.

"Well, Angela that is where you and I keep disagreeing. And it seems to be the only area that we disagree on… I believe Donald never really loved you. You just choose to believe that he did." Jon said with exasperation.

"Let me explain how I see love. Think of a man being like a fire on a cold night. You come close to the fire and you feel the warmth of his love. If you come too close to the fire, you find that the fire will burn you. This is what happened to you with Donald, you came very close, very quickly and not only felt the warmth of the fire, but the burning pain of being consumed by the fire."

"Too far away from the fire and a woman does not feel the love or warmth of the man. This is similar to what happened with you and Simon. For whatever reason, you grew apart from your husband. Whether it is the many conflicts you two have engaged in or the arguments or maybe even the resentment that you feel towards him. You did grow apart from him." Jon continued.

"When a woman is neglected and has grown apart from the fire of her husband. She is more apt to indulge in affairs and relationships with others who make her radiate with passion. You were like a forest of neglect, when Donald came along. You were a dry forest, full of needs and ready to be consumed by the lightning bolt." Jon finished.

"Maybe, I am just not sure what to say." Angela said almost expressionless.

Jon and Angela were sitting on the bench, so close their knees were touching. Jon looking into her eyes, he desperately wanted to kiss her, just to take her in this moment of overwhelming frustration. Yet, he also felt the desire to protect her. Jon was desperately fighting his own feelings, being so close to such a beautiful woman and wanting to help and protect her and the desire to want to be closer to her both emotionally and physically.

"It's just that as you and I get closer….I find myself reaching back to Donald, to grab hold of this image of him and I together. I almost feel like I am cheating on Donald by being here with you."

Angela continued.

"You can be so exasperating! I guess I am just so sick of hearing about Donald and what a great guy he is . . . blah, blah, blah!" Jon said "The last thing a guy wants to hear about is how great some other guy is!" Jon added "let's go!"

They got up from the bench and started walking towards the parking garage. Angela walked about two feet ahead of Jon and he suddenly reached down and swatted her on the butt.

"Ouch! What the crap did you do that for?" Angela turned - shocked that he had hit her.

"You're just so frustrating!!!"

"That is a free one. Next time I will kick your ass white boy." She laughed coyly.

"Yeah right, you are just a crazy Asian." Jon replied as they both got into their own cars.

Tran Sary had enjoyed the last couple of years, in spite of all the worries and concerns, which had surrounded the city of Phnom Penh. He had a job with the government, in a very small capacity, of delivering messages and packages to different branches of the government's Information Ministry.

He had been able to afford a modest apartment, and had even married a young woman who had also fled to the city from the countryside. Their families had actually known each other, but sadly, her family had been killed by an American bomb dropped near their home.

Tran Sary had become a father, to baby boy who was a little over a year old. He worried because the city was bombed several times a day. Aside from this, he still could find much joy in his humble, but simple life in the city.

Late in the day, Tran had been getting ready to make his last delivery. He had just locked up his motorcycle and was getting ready to lift the satchel full of packages, when a guy ran up to the motorcycle and grabbed the bag from him. Tran was shocked as the thief was now running into a nearby alley.

Tran started running after him, not taking time to think about the dangers. As the thief ran down the dark alley, suddenly dropped the package, and continued running out into the next street.

Tran was relieved as he reached down to pick up the bag, until he realized that there was a group of people standing behind him.

"Hello brother" Son Sary said to his younger brother as he stepped out from the shadows.

Tran could not believe his eyes…as he adjusted them to find this was truly his own brother, whom he had not seen in years.

They embraced. Then Tran stepped back to question him with excitement. "How did you find me?"

"We have spies all over the city. I sent some to find out where you were and how you were doing. It is very dangerous for me to be here in the city, I can only stay a few minutes. There are men tracking down our spies to kill them.

"Why did you come?" Tran inquired.

"I wanted to warn you, the city is going to fall. Our troops will take it over; you will want to make sure you are on the road leading back to the province that we grew up in. We are going to empty the cities and everyone is to be evacuated to the countryside. You need to make sure you are on the correct route out of town so that you end up on highway 6 when the evacuation begins.

"Everyone will have to leave?" Tran questioned.

"Yes, they will move all 1.8 million civilians out into the countryside."

"When is this going to happen?" Tran continued.

"The evacuation will start as soon as the city surrenders. I see signs that the Lon Nol's forces cannot hold out much longer."

"If I know where you are headed, I will give you a name to use." As he spoke, Son handed him a piece of paper with a name written on it. "Hopefully the soldiers will realize who it is and contact me. The problem is that the Khmer Rouge armies are vastly different, depending on the commander in charge. If you find that you have nowhere else to turn, I want you to return to hide in our cave. I will try and leave some supplies in the cave for you." Son Sary continued.

"Thank you dear brother" Tran said.

"Brother there is a family that helped me when I first came to the city, is there a way to help them as well?" Tran questioned him.

"Yes, use the password but also, have them head for our province" Son replied.

"What is the name of the family?" He continued.

"They are the Chim family." Tran said.

"Oh, I have heard of the elder Chim, the one that was connected to the security service. He was a cruel man and killed many of our spies in the city." Son said vehemently.

"It will be dangerous, but I will try to help them." Son Sary continued.

"Cambodia has seen some very dark days with the bombings and wars; the people are tired. I am not sure it's ever going to end. My heart breaks for the people of Cambodia. There are many good Khmer Rouge soldiers but, there are also just as many bad. A power struggle is still being waged inside the organization. I fear if some of the individuals are able to gain control, then woe be it to the people of Cambodia." Son Sary said with a somber face, sensing the foreboding future.

"Did you know I have a wife and son?" Tran Sary said.

"Nueon; now is 13 months old." Son Sary said with a slight smile on his face. "We have very good spies in the city."

"I must be going." Son Sary said as he hugged his brother one last time, realizing that in Cambodia, every goodbye could be the last one.

"Goodbye, my brother" Tran said with a tear in his eye. Tran was wishing that his brother did not have to leave but he knew that if someone saw them together they could all be killed, including the rest of his family.

Carolina walked into the bedroom, Jon was watching television. Jon was watching The History Channel. Carolina put away some clothes and was standing in the bathroom when Jon got up and headed downstairs.

"Where are you going?" Carolina said to him.

"Oh, I am just going downstairs to watch television and do a few odd chores."

"Jon, do you realize that every time I come into the room, you find some excuse to leave?" Carolina continued as she followed him.

"You think so? I didn't really notice that." Jon replied.

"Yes, I keep noticing that you make up an excuse to leave." Carolina said.

"Well, I guess the truth is I'm afraid that you are going to find something to complain about. I don't think you realize how negative you can be. You think the things you are complaining about are small and inconsequential, but me, I think differently. Your small comments do hurt and you just never seem to let them go.

"Give me an example" Carolina said.

"Well, let's take the prayer. You and I used to get up in the mornings to pray together and then I realized that you were making negative comments about the way I prayed. Now you even make negative comments about the way I walk, eat, talk, dress, speak, don't speak, think, money, jobs, about everything!" He threw his hands up in exasperation. "My point is that you never stop."

"I am not that bad!" Carolina protested "You're exaggerating"

"No, I am not exaggerating. Carolina, last week I decided to keep track of the comments you made." Jon proudly announced his survey.

"You made a list?" Carolina continued her protest.

"I didn't make a list, but I did keep track of all the positive and negative comments for the weekend. Starting on Friday when I got home until Sunday night. Do you want to know how bad it was?"

"I'm sure I was just terrible!" Carolina said sarcastically.

"You made one positive comment out of one hundred and fifty seven. The other one hundred and fifty six comments were either negative comments or just out right insults!" Jon said.

Jon was spending most of his life trying to avoided negativity and confrontation.

Jon thought to himself that one of biggest mistakes people make is thinking that negative comments do not matter. The truth is that sometimes the small comments do more damage than the big ones.

"I think we need to see a marriage counselor. I will look for one and make an appointment, if you are willing to go with me?" Carolina remarked in a slight sarcastic tone.

"That is exactly what I am talking about. You can't even discuss going to a marriage counselor without making some sarcastic little quip." Jon said getting more frustrated.

"Your right, I am sorry" Carolina said, realizing how frustrated Jon was getting.

"Just remember that someone always pays the price for forgiveness and no matter how many times you say you're sorry, I have to pay the price of that forgiveness." Jon quickly responded. "I am just not sure I want to keep paying the price."

Chapter 8 - Out of the Jungle

Thunnysok had survived being alone in the jungle for months. During that time she had witnessed many atrocities. She continued her journey, heading north along the river and by some miracle, she seemed to be heading in the right direction. Thunnysok went there to find food. She had decided to cross over to the west bank of the river.

Finding a place that was shallow and broad, where the current was not too swift, Thunnysok started to wade across. But as she crossed she realized it was deeper than it had looked. Thunnysok had to swim. As she struggled to swim, she was suddenly hit by what seemed to be a log floating in the river. As she pushed it away she realized that it was the dead body of a woman. Panicking, Thunnysok tried to swim away from it, but was hit by another floating body, then another and another. . . It was hard for her to swim through the cluster of bodies floating down the river. Finally she reached a spot she could stand up and walk. She felt sick to her stomach as she turned around and saw hundreds of dead bodies floating down the river. Many looked as if they had been dead for a long time as the smell of rotting corpses drifted up to her nostrils. Thunnysok wanted to cry for them, but she was numb. She couldn't feel sorrow or sadness. She had become desensitized by the death that surrounded her young life.

Dripping as she came out of the water, she continued to walk around a bend in the river. Here she saw a small house, which was elevated on 4 foot stilts. This was common in this area due to the seasonal flooding. Along the edge of the river she saw an elderly man fishing. As Thunnysok watched, he caught a large fish. She could see the excitement in his face as he pulled the fish onto the bank of the river. The man yelled to his wife, who Thunnysok now realized was right behind him, washing clothes in the river water. They appeared to be friendly and Thunnysok felt the pains of deep hunger. She found herself drawn to them. Thunnysok had a great mistrust of strangers but she decided to take a chance on these two. Slowly, she walked closer, within about 10 feet of the man. He turned around realizing the little girl watching him.

"Hello, I didn't see you standing here." The man said.

Thunnysok did not talk. Always fearful of saying something that would spark a beating, she kept quiet.

"Are you hungry?" The man questioned her. "Why of course you are. You are nothing but skin and bones already." He observed.

"Do you live nearby?" He continued. But Thunnysok did not say anything. She just stood . . . looking at them.

"Do you have a family? Are you lost?" The woman asked as she approached Thunnysok and then she stopped. The woman was standing several feet away from her, she held out a hand toward Thunnysok. The woman understands that it is best to let those who have been wild, freely come to you, such as with wild animals. Even in the animal world trust is a huge factor. For several minutes Thunnysok just stood, staring at the old lady, and then she slowly walked towards her and wrapped her skinny fingers around the old ladies' hand.

"Come into the house and I will get you some food, you are just skin and bones." She said as she led her up the ladder to the hut.

After she had eaten and she went to the corner of the hut and lay down on a mat on the floor. She was sound asleep within moments. The lady looked at her and noticed the scar on her chin. She went out to tell her husband about the scar.

"Do you think it could be her?" He asked his wife.

"Maybe but we should try to get word to her grandparents tomorrow." She said.

Thunnysok woke up early the next morning and went fishing with the old man. Then she helped him work in the fields. Later that afternoon, he told her that he had to run an errand and would be back in a couple of hours.

The fish they had caught were still in the bucket and Thunnysok decided to cook them. Without asking for help, Thunnysok started the fire in the cooking area. She had observed the man using the flints and decided that she could build a fire herself. She didn't realize that the wind was blowing towards the wood hut. Thunnysok wanted to make sure the fire was large enough for cooking, so she kept adding wood. The wind picked up and some of the sparks blew into the grass next to the hut. Thunnysok was trying and put the flames out, but they were quickly spreading towards the hut.

The old lady came to the door of the hut and screamed as she saw the flames approaching the dwelling. She rushed down the ladder and started to beat the flames down. The flames appeared to be gaining on heading to the hut. All of the sudden a bucket of water, containing the fish, flew thru the air in front of Thunnysok dousing her and the flames. It was the old man. With all three of them beating the flames they were able to extinguish the fire.

"What happened little girl?" the man angrily questioned her.

"I was going to cook you dinner, I wanted you to know how thankful I am for you taking me in and feeding me." Thunnysok said with tears in her eyes.

The elderly couple could not stay angry with her. This little stray had come out of the jungle to join them. "Stay with us." The old man said. "We can look for your parents later." But sadly, there are many orphans in this world and many who will never find their families even if they are still alive. Let's go in and remember, Thunnysok, no more cooking without my wife to help you." The old man chided.

Thunnysok was sorry that she had almost burnt down the hut, when all she really wanted to do was something kind for this family. She would try to help in the fields and with the chores. On days when she was left alone, Thunnysok would wander off into the jungle. She would go out during the day and sometimes late at night. Restless, she would wander the surrounding jungle, always looking for something but never really sure what it was that she was searching for.

Occasionally, the elderly couple, realizing Thunnysok had wandered away would search for her in the jungle. It was never easy to find her. It was only when she stepped out from her hiding place that they would discover her. But they were never too mad at this little one who roamed the jungles. A restless spirit lived inside of her.

"The baby is sick. He has a fever. The fever has lasted for two days and he is throwing up and becoming dehydrated." Tran Sary's wife said in a very concerned voice. "I must get him to the hospital." The hospitals were overflowing with patients that are not being treated. Medicine is in short supply and many of the French and English doctors and nurses have fled." Tran told his wife.

"We will take him to the hospital." Tran reassured his wife "we will see what they can do to help him." Tran continued "And I will let Mr. Chim know, he has many good contacts and always seems to be able to find things that are needed. I am sure he will help." Tran could see the hope return to his wife. "Let's go" she agreed. "But you realize that if the Khmer Rouge takes control of the city we will need to leave. We will need to get out very quickly, so keep everything packed and ready."

The hospitals of Phnom Penh were crowded; there were over twenty thousand patients crowded into the various hospitals. Many had to be turned away if they did not have any money or were not in critical condition.

The city was corrupt, yet that was normal. It had been the way for years. The businesses were corrupt, the government was corrupt and the military on both sides were corrupt. Corruption was simply a way of life.

Their baby was admitted with a call from the Father Chim to the local doctor. "I will stay here with the baby and we will take turns and sleep in the waiting room" Tran told his wife. "If there is any sign of danger from outside I will send word." Tran said to comfort to his wife.

The baby was given a bed and Tran's wife stayed by his side as the fever continued to worsen. The doctors were unsure what was wrong the boy.

It was the first of April. The Cambodian New Year was only two weeks away. The city was eerily normal in the weeks leading up to the fall of the Cambodia. People went to work. People avoided travel during the parts of the day that the shelling came from the surrounding countryside but even this was less frequent lately.

The following two weeks passed very quickly as Tran and his wife cared for their baby and Tran went to his job each day. Everyone knew the war could not last much longer. The civil war had lasted for over ten years, depending on when you believed it had commenced. However, the war had almost become a part of everyday life. The first sign of the fall was the stream of men were running back into the city; many in uniforms and many partially naked as they stripped off their uniforms, trying to find civilian clothes. These men even resorted to grabbing clothes that were hanging out to dry on clothes lines. This was followed by the trucks loaded with the Khmer Rouge soldiers. People came running out of their houses to cheer the Khmer Rouge soldiers. Many of soldiers were teenagers or even younger.

Tran was at the hospital when the troops entered the city. "I must go and get our things and so we can leave the city." Tran told his wife.

"How can we leave the hospital with the baby so sick? The heat will kill our baby." She tearfully said to Tran

"There is a place in the countryside that might be safe if we can get to it. Maybe my brother can help us. But it's important that we head to his military sector."

"Yes, husband, but hurry" she said as he hugged her. Tran Sary gave his wife a kiss as he looked into her eyes and he saw the fear and concern.

"I will return" Tran said turning quickly to leave and trying not to think about leaving his wife at his moment. Running down the stairs and out the building Tran got on his motorcycle and returned to their apartment. The items that he needed were already packed in back packs and waiting in the corner of the apartment. Tran grabbed the packs and headed back to the hospital. The hospital was only 20 minutes away by motorcycle.

Khmer Rouge propaganda published a list of men who would be tried and executed when they took over. There were only seven names on the list. Then the closer the date of the takeover came the list had started to grow. On the day of the takeover of the city there were over six hundred names of individuals on the list.

Within hours of the takeover men whose names were on the list were taken to the former Information Ministry and shot. These included military officers, generals, politician and city officials. Over a thousand men were dead within hours of the Khmer Rouge taking over the city. The cheering crowds were replaced by a massive wave of people streaming out of the city. Many wanted to get out of the city and back to their country homes, and some were just fleeing the Khmer Rouge.

Quickly the Khmer Rouge took control of all the government buildings and communications outlets in the city. They started broadcasting that the city was going to be bombed by the US Air Force and that everyone needed to flee the city, and that they would be allowed to return in three days' time.

Tran was heading back to the hospital when he saw a road block ahead. Knowing many of the back streets and roads, he veered into the alley and went around the road block.
Realizing just how dangerous the Khmer Rouge were, Tran got off the motorcycle and cut through a building pushing the bike and then getting back on to it as he kept trying to bypass the roadblocks on each street corner.

It was growing more dangerous by the hour, Tran started picking up speed. Rounding a corner into the street Tran ran right into a squad of Khmer Rouge soldiers. AK 47 pointed at him as he came to an abrupt stop and tipping the bike over on its side and into a skid. Tran fell to the pavement. He looked up to find the machine guns pointed at his face. Instantly, Tran heard the machine guns firing and turning his head he saw several people falling to the ground. It appeared they had been lined up against the wall of the building.

"Angkar needs your motorcycle" the soldier said to Tran in a very polite way. This was the Cambodian way, politely speaking to someone else and then murdering them. Never be misled by how politely a Cambodian speaks to you. Understand that it is what is in their heart that matters most.

Tran got up and leaned the bike towards the soldier. The soldier politely handed Tran the bag that was on the motorcycle.

More and more crowds of people streamed out into the roads around the capital. The 20 minute ride by motorcycle turned into a six hour hike back to the hospital. There was Khmer Rouge soldiers posted at the front doors of the hospital. Tran went to the back of the hospital. There were guards on these doors as well. Tran walked to the side of the building and saw a window to the basement. Tran busted the window and climbed in.

Immediately, he fell on a pile of bloody corpses. He quickly picked himself up and stepped over the bodies. He heard the sound of machine gun fire in distant parts of the hospital. There seemed to be systematic shooting going from one part of the hospital spreading to other parts. He heard the screams of women and then they would go silent, leaving only the sound of machine gun fire.

Tran made his way to the room where he had left his wife and baby, hiding behind dead bodies as the soldiers came down the hall. Tran's stomach was in knots, fearing that something had happened to his wife and child.

As he entered the room, he saw the corpses of the nurses, doctors and his wife's bloody body on the hospital bed. She had been shot by the soldiers. Her body was shielding the body of their son. Tran could see the bullets had passed through her body and into small and fragile body of their son.

Why had he left them? Why had he not stayed behind to make sure they were safe? Trans mind racing as his tears flowing.

Tran dropped to his knees and cried silently, hitting his chest overwhelmed with guilt and anger for not being there to protect them. Had he done things differently, he may have saved this woman and child that he loved so dearly.

Tran got up and took several mattresses from the beds around the room, stacking them around the bodies of his son and wife. He set fire to the mattresses. Turning with a groan of agony he left the room. The mattresses burned slowly for several minutes and then exploded into flames. Tran was in the street when he turned and saw the hospital engulfed in flames and several soldiers running in to put out the fire. This was the only burial that his wife and child would get.

Tran was numb as he joined the flock of people in the roads. There was a solid mass of people streaming out of the city. An hour later, Tran snapped out of his walking trance realizing he needed to take the highway his brother had told him to take. It was too late, the Khmer Rouge were not allowing people to change course on their sojourn out of town. Tran was supposed to be on the highway heading towards Kampong Cham and the great lake, but instead, he was being directed to the Eastern Zone towards Vietnam.

"What does it matter now?" Tran thought to himself as he walked along. He was ready to die.

Son Sary might have been able to look for his brother during the fall of Phnom Penh had he not been given a temporary assignment to the Cambodian Island of Koh Tang. The Khmer Rouge now had several American swift boats in their fleet of national defense.

"Go to Koh Tang and prepare the defenses there" Mok said to Son Sary on the short wave radio "When?" Son questioned. "Immediately" came the response. "We think the South Vietnamese government is going to fall to the North. We want to make sure they do not claim the island of Koh Tang. We will fight if they try and take the island. We want you to go and prepare the defenses. It should only take you about a month. Then you will return to your district." Mok continued. "I will send a dispatch with specific orders, but we want an underground island defense, which uses the natural defenses of the terrain to prevent any landings on the island." Mok said hatefully.

Son took a swift boat down the Mekong River to the island, 60 miles south of the Cambodian coastline. Its 7.5 square mile surface was mainly covered by jungle growth. The north end of the island gained elevation and rose to several hundred feet. The middle of it was narrower than the wide South end.

Son Sary immediately set to work improving the island defenses. He used the northern heights of the island as a central base and used the Viet Cong tactic of tunnel defenses on the island. Then Son Sarys' troops constructed a series of tunnels and caves around the highest areas. They used tunnels to get to an even broader line of defensive farther down the hill. Son Sary realized that there were only two places where the enemy could land on the island - on the East and West beach areas, and he had his mortars dug into caves on the sides of the hill where they could be pointed at these areas. He also had a line of tunnels dug right to the edge of these landing areas. There were two hundred Khmer Rouge soldiers on the island, but there was a plan to reduce the number of troops if the threat from the Vietnamese decreased.

May 13th, 1975.

"Randy" The Commanding Officer needs to see you in his office. We have another emergency situation" said Buck, a fellow soldier and friend of his.

Randall Austin was the commander of the 2nd Battalion, 9th Marines which was currently at a base in Okinawa. Two weeks earlier, he had been in Saigon helping the evacuation of the United States embassy during the last days of the Vietnam War. The United States had been in Vietnam for the last ten years. Ironically, the 9th Marines had been the first troops sent to Vietnam in 1965. These troops were the first in and the last out of the country. Now they had been moved to Okinawa for some training and rest after the fall of the South Vietnamese Capital on April 30th, 1975.

Walking into his commanders' office and closing the door. His commander began "Have a seat, Randy, we have a situation and orders have come down from the President himself."

"Yes, sir, what's the situation?" Randy pressed him.

"Yesterday, a US flag ship, the SS Mayaguez was boarded and captured by the new Khmer Rouge government in the Democratic Kampuchea." The Commander explained.

"Democratic Kampuchea?" Randy was puzzled.

"Cambodia. They just changed the name a couple of days ago.

A surveillance aircraft P-3 has determined that the ship has been taken and anchored off a small island called Koh Tang, which is 60 miles south of the main port of Kampong Som. The President considers this an act of "Piracy" and wants to take the ship and crew back." The Commander continued.

"No chance it can be done diplomatically?" Lieutenant-Colonel Austin asked.

"No, this Khmer Rouge are a nasty bunch. They've pretty much murdered everyone in the hospitals and city that refused to leave. There are estimates that upwards of twenty thousand people being executed and murdered in the first couple of days of the takeover of Phnom Penh." The Commander replied grimly.

"That's pretty bad; even by the standards of the Viet Cong force used when they took over Saigon." Randy responded.

When the capital city of Saigon fell to the Communists, some government officials were executed. Civilians were sent to re-education camps to change their political views on the government.

As the two men were discussing the situation a messenger knocked and entered the office.

"We just got a message that one of the helicopters on its way to U Tapao Air Force Base in Thailand crashed."

"How many dead?" The commander asked.

"Twenty three" He responded.

"Hope this isn't any indication of the luck we are going to have on this mission." He grimaced.

"I need you to get your men, all 600 of them, over to the air base in Thailand. From there some will land on the USS Holt. The Holt can move in beside the Mayaguez and board her under fire from the guns on the desk of the destroyer." The Commander ordered.

"We haven't done that in a while, board another ship under attack." Randy replied.
"One hundred and fifty years I guess?" Randy continued.

"Close, one hundred and forty nine years ago, in 1826. I had to look it up." The commander continued.

"Here is the plan. The Holt will pull up alongside the Mayaguez, using the superior firepower of the cannons and machine guns on the deck, force the Khmer Rouge below deck. Once that is accomplished, we take control on deck and use tear gas to flush them out by dropping the canisters in the air ducks. I can't imagine it taking more than an hour or two to take control of the entire ship. Issue your men gas masks and have them practice as soon as you get to the air base so they are ready to go first thing tomorrow. You will need to recon Koh Tang island as you are flying to Thailand."

"We're on our way." Randy responded to the commander.

"Good luck son." The Commander replied.

The helicopter veered off course and headed away from the Koh Tang Island coast. The pilot, trying not to get too close, in an effort to maintain stealth and not be seen or heard by the occupants of the island. From this altitude they were able to see that the only feasible landing places were the east beach and the west beach.

PFC Gary Hall, LCPL Joseph Hargrove and Pvt. Danny G. Marshall were a three man machine gun team that was attached to the 2nd Battalion, 9th Marine Unit.

"Having seen how hairy things went in Saigon I am not too

excited about going back into action so quickly. We probably have to go back into Vietnam and get some of the people that we left behind." PFC Hall said to Danny.

"I overheard one of the brass say we were heading to Thailand." Hargrove added to the conversation of his buddies.

"Yes, but Thailand could just be a closer jumping off point to go into Vietnam or even worse, Cambodia … scuttlebutt is things have gotten pretty bad for the journalist and foreigners in that country. Maybe we will have to go in and get them out of Phnom Penh or something." Hall continued.

"Well if we do I can't imagine that a bunch of teenage boys and girls running around in pajamas can be all that tough at fighting." Hargrove added.

"They must be doing something right to have taken over the whole country. From what I've heard we bombed the hell out of them, even worse than we did in Germany during World War II. Damn! They must at least know how to dig deep holes." Marshall joked with a nervous laugh.

"I don't like to start off with a helicopter crashing before we even get into the mission. That gives me a bad feeling, like a sign that maybe we shouldn't be doing it." PFC Hall said shaking his head slightly.

"Whatever the mission is, I heard that the President called the shots on this one personally." Hargrove said.

"Gerald Ford, himself" Hall said. "Well he is a new President but I think he'll be a damn good one. So this mission must be important."

"This might be your last chance to win a medal before going home." Hargrove said to Hall.

"Not sure I need a medal, I'll just be glad to get home to those American girls." Hall added with a boyish smile.

Early on May 14th, four swift Khmer Rouge boats left the island heading back to the port of Kampong Som, just about a four hour boat ride away.

"We have to stop them. They might have the crew of the ship on board. Stop those swift boats!" The Commander barked.

"What do you want to do?"

"Send the fighter bombers, the F-111a's and the AC -130 Specters to stop them. Tell them to shoot across the bows of the boats. Don't sink them; just try to get them to turn around."

"What if they don't stop, sir?" The officer asked his commander.

"Give them every chance in the world, and then sink them." He replied grimly.

After an hour of engaging in the attack, using the 40mm cannon and the 105 howitzers, three of the gunboats turned back. The defiant fourth boat continued its course to the island of Kampong Som. The Air Force sent F-111a, F-4d's and A-7d aircraft shooting live rounds and dropping riot control gas on the boat…to no avail.

"Our attack is not stopping the fourth boat sir. What are our orders?"

"Sink her." The Commander sighed.

A few minutes later, an A-7d aircraft used 20mm cannon fire and 2.75 rockets and blew the swift boat out of the water. There were no survivors.

"Sir, there is a fishing boat now leaving the island. It's flying a Thai flag. The boat is big enough to hold a 40 man crew. Do we engage?

"Tell the air force to keep firing across the bow and dropping bombs close to the boat, but don't sink her. Whatever you do, don't let one of those bombs land on the boat." The commander cautioned.

On board the Thai fishing boat, was actually the crew of the Mayaguez. However, the Khmer Rouge had them tied up down below. They had boarded under the cover of darkness and close to the jungle loading dock.

The journey was harrowing. The air force would fly down very low to the boat and drop bombs just within 50 meters of the boat. Water from the explosions would hit those of the crew that were top side. After several hours of bombing, the Thai boat still would not stop.

"Sir, they will not stop under our fire. Do you want us to sink her?"

"No, let her go. Obviously they know we are not going to sink her. Let her go. They are flying under the Thailand flag and it might cause an international incident. Let the boat go." The commander said with disappointment.

"Listen up, guys." The mission will be organized into several groups. A unit of 57 Marines from Delta Company will go to the USS Harold Holt they are assigned the task of securing the Mayaguez. A unit comprised of the Gulf and Echo companies will conduct the combat assault in eight helicopters to seize and hold Koh Tang."

"We will be divided into three groups. A helicopter with troops will be landing on the east beach, which will be a smaller holding force to keep troops from the north and south ends from joining with each other. There will be one small force on the west beach responsible for holding any movement of troops from the south moving up to the west beach unloading and loading areas. The main force will land on the central west beach and move in full force to the north part of the island. If there is no resistance, the forces on the East beach will cross the island joining our troops on the west beach. This force will be hitting any enemies in the rear that might be pinning down the troops on west beach. Then we will extract from the West beach landing zone." The commanding office said.

"You are an idiot!!" I should have you shot!" Son Sary shouted at the captain of the swift boat unit.

"What were you thinking - giving the American's an excuse to invade Cambodia?"

"Take the prisoners and put them on boat, take them to Kampong Som and release them on a boat set them adrift out in the ocean. We don't want to be holding the crew and giving the American's an excuse to invade."

"Get out of here before I have you shot!" Son Sary yelled.
"Then get the men ready for a fight, the American's are coming, I can feel it." He barked.

That night Son Sary readied the Khmer Rouge soldiers for battle. Knowing that the American's would come to the island, he was hoping to get the crew of the ship off his island and adrift off the coast of Cambodia before the American forces could come up with a plan to get rescue them. He was prepared to use what men he had to do his best to defend the island.

"Make sure we have machine guns and RPG's close to the beaches. If it was me, that's where I would land if I wanted to invade this island" Son Said to Tum, his assistant, as he handed him the orders to give to the other cadres.

On May 15th, at 6am, the first phase of the attack on the Mayaguez was completed. The ship was boarded and after an hour of fighting, the ship was secured. There were no remaining crew members. The Khmer Rouge had lost 23 men because none had surrendered. They expected death as a consequence of surrender, much like the Japanese had during World War II. This was the code of warriors.

May 15th, 6:15 eight helicopters of the assault force approached the island of Koh Tang and immediately encountered intense resistance. Automatic weapons fire and rocket propelled grenades from the Khmer Rouge forces were running out onto the beach to fire their weapons. They were getting the closest range possible even though they were more likely to get shot from the machine guns on the helicopters. Showing no fear, the Khmer Rouge kept coming closer to the helicopters attempting to down them before they could unload any troops.

"Get your men to the beach give up your cover to get close enough. Shoot down those helicopters!" Son Sary barked at his number two.

"The key to this battle is to stay close to the enemy. Do not let them bomb the hell out of us. If they create any distance then we will be blown to pieces. We have only two options; hide in the caves or get so close that they can't bomb us." Son Sary continued yelling.

A CH-53 was approaching east beach landing zone when it was hit by a self-propelled grenade to the blades of the engine. The helicopter was close enough to the ground to make a safe landing and off load its crew of twenty marines. They immediately spread out around the other landing helicopters and set up a defense perimeter. However, the CH-53 was out of action and could not be used to get the troops off the island.

"Sir, we're hit!" An RPG had hit the chopper. "We are going down!" the pilot screamed at the men in the helicopter.

The CH-53 was about 100 feet in the air and coming down quickly. Hitting the water hard and breaking up, several of the men trying to jump out before the chopper hit the water. Under 100 feet of water, someone might have a decent chance of surviving. The dangers of a chopper crash are many, hitting the water and blacking out, the blades of the helicopter cutting and slicing men up, explosion on impact . . .

The air traffic controller realized that he needed to get out and take the radio equipment with him. The equipment was waterproof and would float in the ocean. Hitting the water from about 20 feet up, he went under the water but was able to get back to the surface. About thirty yards away was his equipment. He swam to it, unhooked the line and started directing the fighter jets to their island targets.

A second Ch-53 in the east beach sector was shot down by two RPG's, it exploded and crashed fifty meters off shore. A pilot, five marines, and two navy corpsmen were killed instantly. Another Marine drowned while swimming from the wreckage. And three more were killed by gunfire as they tried to reach the beach. A tenth Marine died clinging to the burning wreckage. The surviving ten marines and three Air Force crewmen were forced to swim for four hours before being picked up by the gig of the arriving USS Henry B. Wilson.

On the western beach of the island, the first section of two CH-53 helicopters came in at 6:30am. They landed safely but came under heavy fire while delivering Marine troops, destroying an engine. It managed to take off, being protected by suppressive fire from the second CH-53, and ditched a mile off shore where all but one of the crew was picked up. The second CH -53 was damaged so severely that it turned back with its Marines still aboard and crash landed on the Thailand coast, where its passengers were picked up and returned to U Tapao.

Two other sections of the first wave, consisting of the remaining four helicopters, eventually landed all of their Marines on the island. This occurred between 6:30 and 9:30 A.M. They required heavy supporting fire from an AC 130 gunship to afford them a successful landing. 81 marines landed on the west beach under command of an Executive Officer and 29 Marines of the Battalion Command Post and Mortar Platoon landed a kilometer to the southwest, 130 Marines had finally reached Koh Tang, in three isolated pockets and in very close proximity to the Khmer Rouge troops.

Even though the troops were split into three separate pockets they were able to communicate with each other and coordinate use of their 81mm mortars as fire support for the contingents. They devised a makeshift communications network for controlling air strikes on the enemy positions on the island.

What had seemed like a winning plan was now proving to be a very awkward situation. Instead of finding a few defenders who were lightly armed, there were overwhelming enemy numbers that were heavily armed and well trained.

"Get on the radio and tell them to set those sailors free." Son Sary could feel his heart racing as he realized he was in for the fight of his life on this little island. "If we are not holding the American crew they will have no reason to invade the island or continue this battle." Son yelled at Tum. "You must make them release the crew and alert the Americans that they have been released." He shouted emphatically.

"Make sure the men are below ground any time we pick up aircraft in the area. Go below ground until the coast is clear and then return to the surface. I can assure you the American's are doing the same thing on the beaches." Son Sary continued to bark orders into the radio.

Several hours of heavy fighting continued, the Marines were pinned down on the beach and the Khmer Rouge pushed towards their foothold. Son Sary was determined to keep those Marines pinned down on the beaches.

Hall, Hargrove and Marshall were off loaded from the helicopter. They ran to a cluster of trees on the edge of the jungle. Facing the jungle they set up the machine gun and started to pump rounds into the surrounding trees and undergrowth. The jungle is very misleading. It's difficult to tell from what direction the enemy is coming and from where the shots are coming. One cannot see very far through the profuse jungle undergrowth. Bullets were flying through the air and coming dangerously close to the three men's heads. One was forced to stay close to the trees and ground.

"Damn, I can't see a thing in this thick jungle." Hall exclaimed to Hargrove as they were reloading the machine gun. "Me either." They could be hiding behind any of these trees and then I see bullets coming from one direction, we fire there and they are gone. I know I had to have hit them but then they are right back to firing again in a few minutes!"

"Brass is on the line. They say the rest of the men are not coming. They have ordered them back to U Takeo in Thailand."

"What the hell!" Austin exclaimed.

"Get the General on the phone. I don't think they can understand what the hell is going on here." LC Austin said urgently.

A few minutes passed before Austin was able to get Central Command on the phone.

"Austin, we think the mission is successful and it would be better to not send any more men to the island. The crew of the ship has been located off the Thailand coast and they are all safe. Mission successful, let's bring your boys home."

Another attempt to extricate the Marines on the east beach was made at 14:15 hours but was repulsed by heavy machine gun fire and RPG fire. One of the two helicopters had fuel line damage but was able to make it onto the USS Coral Sea. The repair crews went to work immediately on the helicopter and had it back in service by 17:00. At 16:00, Forward Air Control Craft arrived and took over the rescue of the East beach. More rescue attempts were made on the East beach and the third one was finally successful. The 3rd Platoon force had suffered one Marine and one helicopter crewman wounded besides those who had been killed in the crash off shore.

The three remaining helicopters were joined by a fourth out of Nakhon Phanom base. This force immediately began to withdraw the remaining 202 Marines on the island. The extraction was supported by AC-130 gunships and fire from the naval gunfire from the USS Henry B. Wilson positioned off shore. The first load of 41 marines were lifted out at 16:30 by the only operable CH-53 and flown to the USS Coral Sea. They were followed by 53 men who'd been taken aboard the helicopter with the repaired fuel line. When a new HH-53 arrived from the Nakhon Phanom and picked up a load of 34 men, the remaining Marines on Koh Tang came under intense attack. The USS Coral Sea was a thirty minute round trip, so the pilot decided to deliver his Marines to the nearby USS Henry. B. Wilson in complete darkness while hovering over the ship with only its front wheels touching down. The HH53 immediately returned to pick up 40 more.

"The damn perimeter is getting smaller and smaller and the Khmer Rouge soldier's keep coming and getting closer and closer to overrunning the withdrawal" the executive office in charge said into the radio.

"Keep your machine guns where they can cross fire and cover the helicopters way out. I think we can get down to three and then pull the middle one. We will use the machine guns on the helicopter to cover the other two positions leaving. We are going to need lots of fighter cover to keep the perimeter safe while we pull those last two machine guns off the island."

The time was nearing 20:00. The island was totally dark with the exception of the trace of bullets flying through the air.

"Sir we have the dead body of Ashton Olney. It's going to be hard to carry it out to the helicopter. It was left about twenty meters out from the where the perimeter was a couple of hours ago and in the dark it's going to be hard to find it behind the enemy lines."

"Then leave it behind." The CO ordered.

"Sir, are you sure, marines never leave bodies behind." LC Austin questioned.

"Are you telling me I should let the risk the remaining battalion just to retrieve one dead Marine? I am not going to send more men to their death on this island! Let the Khmer Rouge have their worthless piece of shit, island! Let's get the hell off it!" he barked.

Several minutes later, the last helicopter landed to pick up the remaining men. There was support from the jet fighters that were bombing the island, and from a second helicopter that was spreading bullets across the dark jungle floor. Any time there was machine gun fire from the jungle the gunners on the helicopters would return deadly fire.

"Major, you go 100 yards north and I will go 100 yards south and make one final sweep before we fly out."

"Okay, we have about two minute's tops to get the hell out of here. So hurry it up."

The two Majors made one final sweep of the island, dodging bullets as they run. Then they returned to the helicopter. "Okay, Major let's get this chopper off the ground. "

"Radio the Air Force, tell them we are off the island and tell them we need an air strike. Leave this island with the biggest damn bomb they have."

Several minutes later as the chopper headed back to the USS Coral Sea they saw a huge ball of fire as the BLU-bomb exploded on the island. The BLU was 15,000 lbs., the largest non-nuclear weapon in the United States Arsenal at the time.

"Sure is a beautiful sight." The chopper pilot said.

"Yes, as long as you're nowhere near it when it goes off. I am glad we have it and they don't." His co-pilot nodded.

"Yeah, me too!" the pilot agreed.

With that, the helicopter headed to the USS Coral Sea. In less than an hour they were unloading the men and materials and heading for the rest area. The Major reported to the Command Center for debriefing, "Shit! There were not any crew of the Mayaguez on the island and I lost a lot of good men!"
"Well there were far more Khmer Rouge soldier's on that island than intelligence thought there was, and they were far more prepared than even I expected."

Hall, Hargrove and Marshall had been focused on keeping the Khmer Rouge soldier's at bay from the marine perimeter. They kept firing until their machine gun was out of ammunition and then started to load it up and retreat closer to the perimeter. In the dark overgrowth of the island, the men had headed in the wrong direction. Instead of heading closer to the perimeter they were heading away from the beach area.

When they realized there was no longer any machine gun fire coming from the beach or the jungle. There was nothing but silence. The natural noise of the jungle returned.
"Shit, I don't hear the choppers" Hargrove said.

"I don't hear anything and the radio has been dead for hours. One of the Khmer Rouge bullets disabled the radio earlier." Hall said to the small group.

"Leave the machine gun; it's not going to do us any good at this point. We still have our side arms. If they have left us surely they'll realize it and come back and get us."

"Shit, they'd better come back and get us. I don't think I want to be hiding out on this island for several years." With a small nervous laugh, the men realized their situation was very grave.

"Let's see if we can make it back to the beach area"

"How are we going to do that?" Hall said.

"Well, let's go this way" he said pointing west. "We're bound to come to the beach eventually, we're on an island! If they do come back for us, they are going to come back to the rendezvous coordinates."

The men started through the jungle, stopping several times because they could hear the Khmer Rouge soldier's.

"I hear a fighter coming back" Marshall said quietly.

"Shit!" With that the three men were blown backwards by the effects of the bomb that had just impacted over ¾ of a mile away.

"You okay?" a minute later Marshall picking himself off the jungle floor.

"They just bombed the island, a good bye present from the US Air Force."

"Don't they know we are still here?"

"Obviously not."

"We were left behind. Maybe they will figure out that we are not on the helicopters. Don't give up hope. We still need to get back to the rendezvous coordinates."

"Damn, I hope there are no more Air Force gifts."

"We don't have a choice, let's get going."

An hour later they stopped.

"I can hear the ocean now. Let's get close enough to see the water and then we can follow it around to the beach. It shouldn't take us more than a couple of hours to get back to the pickup point." Marshall told the other two men.

The major sat in the debriefing room with the other military staff when another Major entered into the room and sadly said, "I have got some bad news. We are missing three men from the mission."

"Who?"

"Hall, Hargrove and Marshall" he replied.

'Good soldiers, we have to organize a rescue mission and get them out of there. You and I checked the perimeter and there wasn't anyone there. Maybe they got lost in the jungle. Maybe they were captured or worse…killed."

"Shit and we dropped that bomb on the site. We may have killed our own men."

"I will get Central Command on the phone. Get orders to go back. You start organizing the plan to rescue them."

"Sir we have some men missing on the island, I need permission to return and get them." The Major said speaking on the telephone to Central Command.

"Permission denied, we've already lost too many men on this mission. After the mission commenced we found out that the crew of the SS Mayaguez was already in the middle of the ocean when we attacked. The President and no one else on his staff are willing to reinvade this island and cause an international incident. It's only been several weeks since Saigon fell and we don't want a bigger embarrassment than it already is!"

"I repeat, mission accomplished, permission to return denied!"

"You realize you might have just condemned my men to a death sentence." The Major said sternly.

"Yes, Major, I realize that. It happens in war." Central signed off.

Several hours later, Hall, Hargrove and Marshall made it back to the beach. They stayed in the jungle tree line hidden from view by the dense foliage.

"Man I'm getting thirsty; do you have any more water?" Hall said to Marshall.

"No I am out as well." Marshall said harshly.

"You two stay here and I will go look for some water." Marshall said.

When morning broke, the two men still in the jungle tree line could see Khmer Rouge gathering the bodies of the men who had died in the conflict. They started to stack them up in rows and seemed to be making a list of the dead.

The hours passed and the body count increased. There were over 70 corpses on the beach when the final count was taken.

"He hasn't returned from looking for water. Do you think Marshall's been captured?" Hargrove asked.

"I don't know, but I think we are going to have to surrender. We will never survive without water and food on this island and it's just a matter of time before they capture us. This island is too small to escape capture." Hall said to Hargrove

"Okay, but we only tell them Name, Rank and Serial Number." Hargrove responded.

Taking a deep breath, the two men stepped out from the tree

line. The Khmer Rouge soldier's hearing the rustling from the jungle turned around, guns aimed at them. The two surrendering soldiers raised their hands high in the air. The Khmer Rouge soldiers gathered around them and pushed them in the direction of the commander, Son Sary.

The two men were forced to kneel on the sand where they could see all of the dead bodies. Son Sary took out his pistol and walked behind the two men. Son Sary fired one bullet into each of the men's heads. They both fell forward, face down into the beach sand.

Marshall having not found any water returned to the hiding spot just in time to see the execution of his two buddies. He immediately moved deeper into the jungle to hide. After a couple of days realizing that without food and water he was going to die as well. One night he was close to the Khmer Rouge camp and saw some supplies on one of the boats that had brought supplies to the island. He crept forward to get some water and was drinking it. He did not notice the Khmer Rouge soldier who came up behind him. They fired shots into him before he even knew they were there. Death was instant.

The Marines never tried to rescue the three missing men. Their names appear today on the Vietnam Memorial. Theirs were the three last names added to the Memorial in Washington D.C. They are gone but not completely forgotten today as they were that fateful day.

"Alright, who wants to start tonight's dialog? Jon? Carolina?" Peggy asked Jon David and Carolina as the weekly marriage counseling session started.

"Okay, first, let's start with the appreciations. What exactly did the other person do to help make it a better week?" Peggy said as she was backtracking on her comments.

"Jon, you want to go first?" Peggy asked.

"Sure, there are many things that I appreciate about what Carolina does. She works, keeps a great house, and runs the family, cooks. All of those things I really do appreciate."

"That's good" Peggy praised him.

"And you Carolina, what do you appreciate about Jon?" Peggy said now looking at Carolina.

"Well, he works hard, takes the boys to school, takes care of the lawn, spends times with the kids, goes to church, takes me out on the weekends and gets up early so we can to pray together." Carolina acknowledged.

"Anything else he does that is positive?" Peggy said still looking at Carolina.

"He does many things positive and he is a great father." Carolina continued.

"Jon, how does that make you feel, when you hear that?" Peggy said turning to Jon David.

"Great, I really enjoy hearing positive comments and statements from her, it's very important to me." Jon said solemnly.

"Jon, do you want to go first listing things you would like to see Carolina do better or improvements she could make?" Peggy continued.

"No, I'll pass and let her go first." Jon replied.

"Okay, Carolina what do you want to discuss this week?" Peggy said again turning to Carolina and noticing that Jon was taking a deep sigh.

"Jon, you're not supposed to do that." Peggy said sternly to him.

"Do what?" Jon asks her.

"Sigh, you're sending nonverbal signals that you're not really listening but instead tuning out what Carolina is getting ready to say." Peggy said in a professional tone.

"Okay, okay…sorry." Jon replied.

"That…..is what I want to talk about! The way he rolls his eyes when I speak is so annoying. It's condescending and I don't think he listens to me." Carolina said almost wanting to cry.

"Jon, you need to listen to her." Peggy said more sternly this time.

"So what is it that you want to talk about Carolina?" Peggy said encouraging her to start her issue.

"He is just not considerate. He will come home and set his jackets on the bed and not hang them up. Or he will put them on the stairway entrance, or he will just lay them on the floor in the room and I have to come along behind him and pick them up." The words spilled out of Carolina.

"How does this make you feel? Remember we are trying to get you to express how you feel. This is about your feelings and not about how you think Jon David is a bad guy."

"He makes me feel much unappreciated and I get angry. When I get angry, I lash out at him and get really mean. I hate this about myself, so if he would just pick his stuff up and change then we would not be having any problems and issues." Carolina continued.

"So Jon, I want to repeat what Carolina has said so that she understands that you get it and then I want you to make a commitment to change your behavior. Can you do that for her? This woman of your youth, this beautiful woman who has born all of your children, can you do that for her?"

"Yes, Carolina I can do that …I can try and be better about picking up my clothes. But I would like to mention that the other day you got upset at me for leaving my coat on the stairway going upstairs." Jon said.

"Yes, I remember, but what about it? I did get upset and yelled at you." You know I don't like the jackets on the stairway." Carolina looked at Jon with contempt.

"What I am trying to say in my defense, is that my jacket was on the stairway, but that it was covered up by two of her jackets and she could not even see my jacket only hers." Jon said incriminatingly.

"Yes, but I knew it was there." Carolina retorted to Jon's comment.

"Each week you and I have been coming here to talk about the problems and issues we have. The many things apparently that I do wrong in the relationship. Each week I say that only one thing bothers me. I feel like you are just way too negative about any and everything that I do or say." Jon said calmly.

"There is never an end in sight to the things that you want me to do or stop doing or change. My question is when will it stop? When will you just accept who I am? I do not feel that you truly ever just accept me for being me. Instead we come each week and you tell me what I need to do to make you happy and no matter how hard I try you never seem to be happy. Why? When does a person just decide to be happy with their status and position in life? Carolina, when are you just going to accept me, without feeling this need to change everything about me?" Jon said evenly.

"I do accept you!" Carolina protested.

"When; when did you just allow me to just come home and sit on the sofa? Or just to watch a television show without making a snide little comment? When did you go with me to an employee function or event and not make a big argument out of it. Do you realize that not one person at my job has ever seen you?" Jon, who normally never said a word, was getting upset and starting to really let his feelings out about the relationship, starting to not hold back on the frustration that was building.

"When will you ever truly accept me and say, Hey I don't have to keep trying to change him." Jon continued as he was allowing the walls to crack inside the shell he had put around his feelings for so long.

"You know my Mom, tried to warn me that you would never be happy with me, unless you were happy with yourself, and personally I don't think you're happy with yourself."

"You talked to your Mom about me?" Carolina said obviously offended by the comment.

"Yes, I need someone to talk to. I feel like I can talk to anyone else in the world but you." Jon continued, the whole time realizing that he was opening the door on more issues and problems.

"Anyone?" Carolina questioned, raising her eyebrows with a skeptical look.

"I am glad you could make it to party" Angela said to Jon David as he walked into the room. "I will take you around to meet the rest of the people I know." she said with a smile.

Angela went around to the group, consisting mostly of guys, in the bar and introduced Jon David to them.

Jon could see the questioning looks on all of their faces "what is an old white guy doing here in a young Asian group with a beautiful married Asian girl?"

"Jon, I wanted to introduce you to some of my coworkers and colleagues in the real estate business." Angela said as she was pulling his arm over towards several ladies.

"Hi, my name is Ni Lee" said one young beautiful Vietnamese lady.

"Well you don't exactly look Asian." Ni Lee commented.

"Oh well Dad was in Vietnam and met Mom in the early days of the war, I am half Vietnamese and half American." Jon David said with a mischievous look on his face.

"Let me get your name and email and I will start sending you the dates of the meetings." Ni Lee said politely.

"Thanks I would enjoy that." Jon said smiling as Ni Lee took his information and walked away.

"You are so bad; you have to stop teasing my friends like that, half Asian and half American." Angela snorted and punched him on the shoulder.

"I am just trying to blend in." Jon said jokingly. "Do you want something to drink?"

"Sure, a martini" Angela said sweetly.

"Oh, you are a classy girl." Jon said as he turned to the bartender to place the order and handed him his credit card.

"Keep it open?' The bartender questioned.

"Yes, for now" Jon replied. The bartender soon handed him his drinks and Jon returned to Angela's side and handed her the drink.

"You want to go out on the patio?" Angela asked.

"Sure, sounds great" Jon agreed and Angela grabbed his hand as they walked through the crowd and out onto the roof patio of the club. Ten stories up, the Sky Bar was a popular venue on this Thursday night. The band played hip Latin music and some of the best Salsa dancing in town could be seen on the dance floor. The night air was cool. From the 10th floor there was a beautiful view of the downtown area and the galleria. Midtown is now considered a very hip and trendy place.

Standing in the cool night air, in one of the more romantic places in Houston, Angela turned to Jon and said. "You know he will come for me?"

"Let me guess, we must be talking about Donald again." Jon said in an almost total unbelief of her making the comment. He could feel both a feeling of anger and envy swelling up inside of him.

Angela nodded.

"What makes you think he is coming for you?" Jon said calmly.

"I had a dream about him, that he was coming to get me. And

that we would live together. I saw myself in his SUV and daughter was with me as well."

"Angela, I really don't think he is coming for you." Jon replied. "He has a wife, a family, a new company. What makes you think he wants to give that up to be with a crazy Asian girl?" Jon said in a less than kind voice.

"It sounds like you're jealous?" Angela said coolly.

"I wouldn't say jealous. I might be a little envious, but not jealous." Jon replied.

"What is the difference?"

"Jealous denotes that you are in some way a possession to have and hold. My idea of love is not like that. I don't believe you can ever possess another person and force them to love you. I might be a little envious that he has so much of your love and he doesn't deserve it. And yes, maybe I am a little envious that he has seen you naked and had sex with you and that nothing like that has ever happened between us."

"I told you that I don't feel that way about you."

"I have noticed that you get close to me, you can spend 10 hours on a computer a day glued to the screen typing me emails. Or you drive to Dallas and immediately get on the computer to email me. You call or email me every time you go out of town. Yet, you keep telling me that you don't care." Jon said sternly.

"I do love you and I do care about you, just not in the same romantic way that I cared about Donald. I don't know what it was, he got to me. He broke down my barriers. I just fell in love with him hard. And now I have been paying the price. It's been very painful and I am afraid that I cannot get hurt like that again...I want to believe that the love you and I have for each other is very innocent and pure. I don't want to believe anything else. I do love you, just not romantically like I love Donald."

"I personally think that whenever you get close to me, you find yourself using the images of Donald to prevent yourself from falling in love with me. He is your crutch." Jon said harshly.

"You do love me don't you?" Angela said sweetly and gently.

"Yes, I cannot deny that I do love you. But, I have never thought that having sex was a great idea. There is so much pain inside of you that it is evident there is still so much more to learn about you. If we were just getting together and sharing bodies, there would be no way that all those deeper issues could get resolved. I think you have been traumatized. In some ways you are even delusional. I think this disillusioned side of you has affected you most of your adult life." Jon said thoughtfully.

"Pure, I am sorry; I cannot tell you my love is pure…because it's not. There is very much a strong male desire to this whole relationship. Why not, you are an extremely beautiful and mysterious woman. Besides, I am not even sure I would be the best person to be a life time mate for you." Jon interjected.

"What do you mean?" Angela said surprised.

"All the needs you have. I'm not sure I could meet all of them. I am older which means I will die long before you. I am not as financially secure as your husband, and you have children together which counts for a lot. I don't think this issue you created in your mind of your desire for Donald is as much about him as it is with your own internal needs and emotional issues. I think you are going to have to go back to your husband, give him one more try and be completely honest with him."

"I see, you know I do love you and care… and many times wish I could give you more." Angela said sadly.

"Hey, did I tell you that I was putting my house up for sell." Angela said switching the subject.

"No, you didn't…what did Simon have to say about that?" Jon responded, well aware of how she could manipulate the topic.

"He was sad, and I guess he realizes that our marriage is going to end. Once the house is sold we can go our own separate ways."

"Well, it must be a pretty sad feeling, realizing that those days are coming to an end." Jon added.

"Yes, he was pretty sad when I told him that I was going to sell the house. He and I both have a lot of work to do on the house but I think we will get it all done in a month or two. Then I will get it on the market."

"Do you want to go dance?" Jon said, switching the subject.

"Yes, I would love to." Angela smiled.

They returned to the dance area and danced to several songs before Jon got a call from one of his children, who needed him. Jon excused himself. But on the way home, as he stopped for gas, he realized that he had left his credit card with the bartender.

He called Angela's cell phone, "Angela can you go ask the bartender if he has my credit card."

"Oh, I am almost home now." Angela said.

"Really, I thought you planned to stay for several more hours?"

"No, I just decided to come home." She replied.

"Okay, I will call Ni Lee. She gave me her business card." Jon said as he looked for it.

As Jon drove he was pondered the mixed signals Angela was giving him, as she invited him to parties and left when he was no longer there. Now she was selling her house and then spending all her time talking about Donald.

"What a complicated woman!" Jon thought as he headed for his home.

March 30th, 1976 The Party Centre leaders such as Neon Chea, Pol Pot, and Ta Mok, were meeting to decide the fate of several things inside of Cambodia. There was also a discussion on how to push Sihanouk aside and make him less important to the Cambodian's. The Party Centre was also deciding whether to tear down the Catholic Church in Phnom Penh. Other items on the agenda were party history, economic planning, official holidays and overall government organization.

Three days later, grenades exploded near the Royal Palace and shots were fired at the National Museum in Phnom Penh. The Palace and museum were not far from the heavily guarded compound, which was secretly occupied by Neon Chea, Pol Pot, and other senior officials of the Cambodian Khmer Rouge government.

"Brother number one and the other members of the Centre party saw these events not as an isolated incident of resentful soldiers who had to work in the rice fields. The party center saw this general unrest in the military as an early warning sign that there was a military takeover of the government in the works by various military elements.

Up until this point, the focus had been on finding those who had connections to the Central Intelligence Agency and the former government of President Lon Nol. Tens of thousands of individuals had been executed or murdered in the year following the fall of Phnom Penh. The Khmer Rouge army aimed to completely defeat all remnants of the enemy in that city. The Party Centre did not want to let any of them escape, so they could reorganize and fight against the Khmer Rouge Government.

In April, 1976 when the grenades were thrown, the party leaders were forced to change their direction. Now the party would focus on those inside the Khmer Rouge who were really the enemy. Those who had joined the party but did not believe in the ideas or the leadership of the party. Now the focus would be on smashing those inside the party who were not loyal.

"Kim Sombat, you are a coward." One of his unit soldiers said to him. "You are just a little girl who must work in the fields all day planting rice. You are not a soldier."

"I am not afraid of anything. I am not afraid to attack the enemy or die in battle. I am very brave" Kim replied firmly.

"You are a coward; the war was over by the time you joined us here in the 170 Division. We fight hard against the Americans, the Vietnamese and the government of Lon Nol…but you joined us after the battles were already over.

The 170 Military Divisions were formed shortly after the fall of Phnom Penh in the eastern regions of the country. They were then moved closer to Phnom Penh and ordered to plant rice, which many of them resented. Sok Chhan was commander of this unit, which included Kim Sombat.

"I am not afraid to do anything." Kim responded to the taunting of the other soldiers who were now laughing at him.

"Prove it…here are two hand grenades, go throw them at the National Museum. I heard the Big Brothers might be going there and this would be a warning to them to wake up to the things they are making the military forces currently do." As Sok Chhan spoke he took two hand grenades off his ammunition belt and threw them to Kim.

"Or are you just too afraid?" He taunted.

"No" Kim said realizing that he faced real danger in what he was being ask to do. But he knew that he would lose face if he turned away from his laughing friends and refused this order.

"I will be back" Kim said as he took the two grenades and left. The men continued laughing and were sure that Kim would return, any minute, from around corner to admit that he was too afraid to do it. The men continued to laugh until about ten minutes later when they heard the explosions in the distance. Then the laughing turned to fear as they realized that there would be consequences for this.

The reactions to the grenade throwing were swift. The security forces, called the Santabal, swept into the headquarters of the 170 Division and ordered the commanders taken into custody for interrogation. The men in the units were isolated and told that there would be mercy if they told who did it and who had ordered the grenades to be thrown. Believing they might have a chance to survive several of the men told who had thrown the hand grenades and who gave the order. Sok Chhan and Kim Sombat, along with several other men were taken to Tuol Sleng Prison, which was code named S-21.

Tuol Sleng Prison had been a high school in the city of Phnom Penh before the Khmer Rouge take over. There at the entrance to the prison was a red placard with yellow lettering that read "Fortify the spirit of the revolution! Be on your guard against the strategy and tactics of the enemy so as to defend the country, the people and the party!"

When the Vietnamese invaded Cambodia, Thunnysok's oldest sister Botum was at a youth labor camp in northeastern Cambodia. Botum had grown weak from the years of work and lack of adequate food. By now, she was suffering severe malnutrition.

"We must go" the camp leader said to the girls. The three other girls collected their few possessions and got into the truck that was brought to take them back to their districts.

"We need to head West to get away from the Vietnamese"

"Where is Botum?" the team leader ask the girls.

"She is in the hut; she is very sick and cannot move." One of the girls responded.

The team leader walked to the hut and found Botum on her side and curled up in the fetal position on her cot. She was facing the wall.

"Botum we need to go, the Vietnamese have invaded the country. We must leave the camp before they get here. They have been murdering thousands of people in the areas that they have invaded, we need to go now."

She whispered, "I am very sick. I don't think I can move, please just leave me behind."

"I am not leaving you behind Botum" the team leader said as she reached down to pull her up.

Coughing fevered and severely dehydrated, Botum was led to the wagon. Team leader helped her up into the cart and returned to the hut to get her few possessions as Botum curled up on the floor of the wagon.

The journey to the West continued for several days. Botum started to recover, slowly. Still she was nothing but skin and bones from the years of hard work and lack of food. She looked a sight, she was sickly, weak and her hair had been shaved off as well.

The wagon stopped at a village in the district and the girls were unloaded from the wagon. The team leader went to the village chief to see if there was any food or water available. The little girls were unloaded and then allowed to wander to find whatever was left of family or homes. Many were not even sure if this was where they were from or whether there was any family still alive. If their families had not been murdered, many had fled the villages with the threat of the Vietnamese coming. Many of the huts were empty, all of the inhabitants gone.

Botum just started going to every house in the village and asking if anyone knew her or if anyone knew who her family was.

"Do you know me?" Botum asked the family at the hut that she went to.

"No, my little one, I do not know you. Sorry." And the family shut the door.

"Do you know my family or who I am?" again Botum ask the next family at the next hut she went to in the village.

"No. sorry, we do not know you." The next family also said.

This scene continued for Botum until she was drawing weary going from hut to hut. Then she went to a hut where there was an older man and a man in his thirties. The men looked familiar to Botum. Her heart started to race as she again asked the questions.

"Sir, I am looking for my father and the rest of my family." Botum said in a weak and little voice.

She asked again, with a hollow, emotionless expression in her eyes.

"Sir, can you help me find my father." Botum asked.

The older man started to cry; he raced down the steps of the hut and into the arms of the little girl. "This is Botum!" the man said as he turned to his son on the porch of the hut. "This is Botum!"

Frail and weakened by the famine of food shortage and hair shorn off and gone for years, her father at first did not even recognize his daughter.

He jumped off the porch and flew then to the daughter that he had not seen in years. He picked her up and hugged her. It had been three and half years since she was taken from her family. Botum, Thunnysok's sister had miraculously found her father.

"She is very sweet and precious, she follows me around the fields, tries to help at everything. But there are so many times I end up having to go look for her. It's been two weeks; I think we need to take her over to my brother's farm. She can help him in the fields and then maybe we can find out if she is indeed related to us. We cannot be sure the scar is that of Thunnysok. Thunnysok was still very quiet and did not express herself much nor tell much about where she had been the past few years.

That day they got in the boat and headed up closer to the great lake area. The man took her to his brother's farm and introduced her.

"We think that you might be related to this man and his wife. They might be your grandparents." The man said to her.

Thunnysok had become numb by all the years of conflict and death she had witnessed. She took in the information but did not express how she felt about what was going on around her.

The first week they tried to get her to go to school in a small local school, but this did not work and she wandered off and found the Champ Towers.

Grandfather sent her out early in the mornings to water the fields and help feed the animals. The first week Thunnysok was very obedient and helped with all the work. Then one day she decided to go swimming in the river and did not return to the farm for dinner. Grandfather was standing there in the door way as she approached the farm, after it was dark. With a stick in his hand he led her into the house and started to beat her. Thunnysok did not cry but allowed herself to think about floating in the water, relaxed and free from all worries and fears. This would not be the last beating her grandfather would give her. There was much work to be done each day, maybe even more than the work the Khmer Rouge had melted out of her each day.

Many nights Thunnysok would sneak out into the jungle. Thunnysok was never one to lack the courage to go into the jungle. One night she was in the jungle when she heard the Khmer Rouge soldiers and cadres talking around a camp fire.

"We need to root out the evil in the party. There are many in the countryside that hate us and would try to overthrow us. We need to smash them." The cadre continued.

"How do we find them?" another cadre said.

"We will search their hearts and find them guilty. Tomorrow we will go around the villages and tell everyone that we are holding meetings to make improvements in the government and we will be asking for help and suggestions on how to change things in the area."

"Those who have evil in their hearts will come to try and change the revolution and we will smash them. Those that stay home will be those who support us." Everyone agreed.

A Khmer Rouge soldier got up from the campfire and came over closer to where Thunnysok was and relieved himself in the bushes, barely missing Thunnysok, who was hiding behind a log.

Thunnysok just laid there for hours, waiting for them to disappear and eventually fell asleep. Waking up at sunrise, she ran to the farm. Greeted at the door of the farm first by her grandmother who had tears in her eyes and then by her grandfather who had anger in his eyes and a stick in his hand.

"Girl, when will you learn?" Grandfather said as he made her lean against the chair in the kitchen area and started to beat her on her butt and back of her legs.

Thunnysok wanted to tell him and grandmother about the Khmer Rouge's plan, but she did not say a word. After the beating she was sent into the fields to work without any meal.

Late in the afternoon, grandmother came out to the field where Thunnysok was working. As she handed her some food she said "Grandfather and I have to go to meeting tonight in the village. The Khmer Rouge wants our input on improvements in running the villages. "Grandfather has ideas on how things can run better in the village." Grandmother handed Thunnysok a container with water and some rice portage.

Thunnysok suddenly stopped working and looked at her with fear in her eyes.

"What is it girl, you look as through you have seen a ghost?" Grandmother questioned her.

"It's a trick, Grandmother, they have made a trick to see who will come to the meeting then they will kill them. I was in the jungle and sneaked up to the camp and heard them talking about killing the villagers who come to the meeting. If you go, you will die."

"Thunnysok, thank you for telling me, I hope I can convince your Grandfather not to go."

"But how do we convince your Grandfather of their plan?" She said.

"I have been in the fields all day but if the meeting is being held in the clearing just at the edge of the jungle and not in the meeting room in the village church then you know that I heard them talking. But I beg you not to go. They will kill everyone who goes tonight."

Grandfather was reluctant to believe Thunnysok, seeing her as just a little girl and certain that children could not be trusted to make adult observations. But in his heart he had personally seen how evil and deceitful the Khmer Rouge could be. In his heart he knew the truth and not only was not going to go but went to other families to warn them about the meeting.

Seventeen people went to the meeting that night and none returned. When people were missing, it was never wise to ask where they went. They just were never seen again. Occasionally, someone would see a fresh burial place in the jungle, but when they did, they quickly left and never mentioned what they saw unless it was with close family members.

After that day, Thunnysok still got in trouble and would occasionally receive a beating; however they were shorter in duration and much less severe.

"I see hunger in the countryside, everywhere I go" Son Sary said to his new wife as they sat at the table and talked, out of reach of any of the guards at the headquarters. "I fear the country has slipped and is going in the wrong direction. After all the years of fighting now I see those who are in charge as the murderers of the people of Cambodia. Yet I find now that I am a part of their apparatus of death."

"Can you do anything about it?" his wife said.

"I can try and make sure those in my zone are as healthy as possible. I can ensure fewer people are tortured and murdered, but the more I do that, the more likely I am of being accused a traitor." He said sadly.

"There are many in the Khmer Rouge trying to treat the people right and wish well for the government. But I am disappointed now that we have taken over the country, all the decisions being made seem wrong."

"When do you leave?" his wife asks of him.

"Tomorrow, I am going to the Eastern District to meet with the military and look at the defenses. There are becoming more issues with the Vietnamese on the borders."

"Any sign of your brother?" She warmly asked.

"In all the confusion of the exodus, he was lost, but I will find him." Son Sary sighed.

The next morning Son Sary was up and heading for the Eastern District. He traveled in a convoy of three military jeeps. After driving for most of the day; they finally arrived headquarters and was met by So Phim.

Tran looked up from working in the rice fields to see the jeeps passing on the road. Never realizing how close he was to his brother. Quickly Tran looked back down at the rice in the fields, for being caught looking around could bring severe punishment.

That night there was a meeting called in the huge center hut. Everyone gathered in the hut, there were about two hundred men, women and children. The meeting was called to order and the cadre leading the meeting went over all the rules that needed to be enforced and the consequences of breaking the rules. A woman was led to the front of the meeting room. She was obviously several months pregnant. Her hands were tied behind her back and she had her head down in a defeated manner.

"This woman has broken the rules of our great organization. She has been having relationships with other men, maybe some of whom might be even the enemy. She is sleeping with the CIA agents and the Vietnamese and for that there is a price to be paid." The cadre shouted.

"Bring a life that is not authorized into the country and your life will be forfeited." The cadre continued in his high and mighty tone to the group.

"I was raped" the woman protested. "One of your soldiers raped me" she pleaded.

"Shut up woman!" The cadre screamed and released a kick to her head knocking her to the floor.

The cadre pointed at two boys who were eight and nine years old. "You and you, come up here." As they walked forward the cadre handed them an axe and an iron bar.

"Here, you are to give her the punishment for breaking the rules" the cadre said as he pulled the woman back up to her knees.

"I remind you if you do not do as you are ordered, you will take her place. If any of you look away you will take her place." The cadre continued in order to scare all of the assembly.

The boy that was eight years old was the nephew of the woman. He looked over at the cadre, who motioned him to hit the woman. The boy was hesitating when the cadre knocked him across the face. The nine year old knew that he had to hit her. He brought the axe down into her back, not killing her just inflicting a great deal of pain as her back started to spew out blood. The other one picked up the iron bar and started to hit her. He had to hit her twenty to thirty times…again and again as they made him hit her harder and harder, until the woman lay there on the floor, bloody and lifeless. Both boys had been forced to join together to murder and execute the pregnant woman, who had been raped by the Khmer Rouge.

Tran returned to his hut that night, filled with the fear of being in Cambodia and yet with a strong desire to live. Glad he had not been executed and sad that an innocent victim had been so brutally killed. Maybe she did deserve it, Tran tried to tell himself. But the inner part of his heart told him that there was no way any person deserved to die like this, no matter what they did. And he knew that this could happen to him as well.

Chapter Nine- Going Fishing

"Thunnysok, let's go to the great lake and do some fishing." Grandfather said to her one morning.

Thunnysok loved this idea. First she loved being on the water. Second, it took her away from working in the rice fields, it was always hard work.

That morning they walked several miles to where the boat was docked. They got into the boat and paddled to the great lake. As they fished, Thunnysok was very happy that she caught several big fish as she hauled them into the boat. They went to the shore and cooked several of them for lunch. Then they went back out on the boat to fish for the rest of the day.

Late in the day, Thunnysok looked off to the distant horizon and saw a capsized boat with three men yelling for help.

"Grandfather, look those men are in trouble." Thunnysok said. "We must help them."

They paddled their small boat over to them and helped get them one by one out of the water and back to shore. It took about an hour and two more trips, because their own boat was too small to carry all of them at one time. They were able to save all three elder men. One of whom turned out to be the leader of a nearby fishing village.

"You must stay tonight for a big dinner. It's our way of saying thank you for saving us today." The leader said.

That night, they did stay for dinner. The food was good and the men sat around and talked. Thunnysok made friends with about ten of the other kids in the village. It was not long before she had them organized and playing games together.

"Thunnysok, it might be time we head home." Grandpa said with a small smile.

"I think we need to talk when you get home tonight" Carolina said on the phone.

"Sounds serious, by your tone" Jon David replied.

"It's very serious" Carolina replied.

The drive from work was about forty five minutes and, for the entire trip, Jon David wondered what they would be discussing. Normally, Carolina took no interest, whatsoever, in what Jon did. She never seemed curious, never asked questions, and never seemed like she really wanted to know or understand what the issues were.

Carolina had a stone cold look on her face as she walked into the house, grabbed a glass of wine and abruptly said "upstairs".

Dutifully, Jon David followed her up the stairs and into the master bedroom. She closed the door and locked it. As Jon heard the "click" it was as if he were hearing a gun go off, or the click of a land mine exploding.

"I have been doing some investigating and I have gotten into your email account. I have found thousands of emails between you and "Angela". I think you need to tell me now, what exactly is going on between you two."

"She is a very good friend. I care a great deal about her but I can tell you that there hasn't been anything more than that. We talk about almost anything and everything." Jon said honestly.

"That is bullshit; you care about her more than just as a friend." Carolina said, getting more angry and upset.

"You would throw away twenty three years of marriage for someone that you don't really know and doesn't even love you or have any attraction to you?" Carolina kept driving the point home "She doesn't care about you."

"What makes you think she doesn't care?" Jon replied.

"Here! Right here in her emails. She says that she is physically attracted to Donald and had an affair with him and that she isn't interested having an affair with you or anyone else. She says very clearly that she isn't physically attracted to you." Carolina said pulling the copies of the printed emails out from the nightstand beside the king sized bed.

"Read them, its right here in black and white. Are you stupid?" Carolina said rhetorically.

"Even if it's not a physical affair, it's a very deep emotional affair. Even if you're not sleeping with her, you would if she was interested in you. You are in love with this woman." Carolina accused, her voice getting louder as she got angrier.

"Would you have sex with her if she was interested?" Carolina continued.

"I don't know…… probably yes, because I care about her so much mentally." Jon admitted.

"Damn you! You bastard, I hate you so much right now!" Carolina was screaming now.

When a man knows he has done something wrong, he is more willing to accept the negative insults and comments because he knows he deserves them. Yet, because of all of the negative comments he had received from her over the years, Jon had gone numb to them - numb to the countless times he felt like he had disappointed her. Jon did not feel like he could ever make her happy.

There was a knock at the door. The boys wanted to come into the room. Carolina opened it, told them that this was really important and that they needed to go away. The youngest one could see the tears in her eyes and knew that this had to be a serious conversation between Mom and Dad. That was the last time they came to the door during their talk.

"I don't want you to talk to her any more. You are going to have to make a choice between her and me. I will divorce you if you continue talking to her." Carolina said in her demanding teacher tone.

"Also, I want to go back to Peggy and tell her about this. This totally changes everything that we have been going to counseling for, in the first place."

"All these years we have had issues but I felt that the one thing we had going for us was that we were faithful to each other and now I realize it has all been a lie." Carolina said with tears flowing down her face.

"What about this email?" Carolina said pushing a copy of the email into his face.

Jon looked at the email and realized the gravity of what was written in it.

"Is this email true?" Carolina said frankly.

There are things that happen in our lives when we realize that life is changing. That once you walk through that door there will be no turning back. Jon looked at the email and then started to speak.

"Is this true?" Carolina cut him off.

As if in slow motion, Jon just shook his head yes,

"You are telling me flat out that what you wrote in this email is true?" Carolina repeated the question.

"You admit to having had several affairs in the past?" Carolina again said with more anger coming up to the surface.

"Yes, it's true. I did." Jon, for the first time in many years, finally had the courage to be completely honest with her.

"You lying bastard, I can't tell you how much I hate you at this moment." Carolina said her voice level was again rising.

"Yes, six years ago, I had several affairs. I was at a point where I no longer wanted to be married; I was looking for a way to end the marriage. I wanted out and I didn't really care what happened at that point."

"You are telling me that you have not had an affair in six years?" Carolina questioned him. "I just don't know what I can believe anymore."

"Six years ago I thought the issue might be about sex, that you and I had this horrible sex life and that I had come to resent everything about sex with you. That you controlled every aspect of my life both emotionally and physically." But then I came to realize that the issues were much deeper, the real issue was that you and I could not be honest with each other in our thoughts. That in many ways you were always telling me what and how I should think." Jon was almost surprised in himself that he was finding the courage to be completely honest with someone that he was always afraid to be honest with.

"I want to know all the details of these affairs." Carolina said. "Why was I not good enough for you? Why did you feel that you needed something more?"

"At first, I thought it was sex, which you were so unwilling to try new things. That you controlled when, how, where and how. . . You even used sex to even punish me! You were doing all the things that every marriage book tells you not to do."

"But then I came to realize that it had to do more with the resentments that had built up over the years in our relationship. That I stopped caring about your opinion and many times just wanted to run away from you."

"So why didn't you just leave? Why did you let me live my life in ignorance of what was going on around me?" Carolina questioned resentfully.

"There were several reasons. First, I felt the boys still very much needed me. Second, we both have so much debt that it would be a disaster if we divorced at this point. And finally, I wanted to make sure that I did everything possible to make sure that it would not work before ending the marriage. The truth is that I did want it to work out, I have just become more skeptical about it." Jon continued baring his heart for the first time in many years.

"You know the time, when I had the most hope, was after you went on the walk to Emmaus at church" Carolina said reflecting on the past years and slowly feeling the anger disappears.

"Yes, I felt like it was good, but you never once supported me on those things. When I tried to get us into bible studies, you wanted to leave, when I started us going to church, you quickly found some reason not to go."

"Through all of our married years, I have wanted you to be happy. That is what I tried to provide for you. Yet, you always found a reason to not be happy. I would let you travel all over the country. You stayed home from work for fourteen years so you could be happy, but you never were. You have never been happy no matter what you did and no matter what I did. I guess I have just given up on trying making you happy.

"So you have completely given up? Do you want a divorce now?" Carolina questioned him.

"No, but I am very close, I realize that things cannot continue to go the way they have."

"What about Angela?"

"What you have to realize is that either you need to talk to me as open and honestly as we are speaking right now or you should let me talk to whomever I want to talk to." Jon said.

"I am not sure I can do that." Carolina said.

"You know how, over the last fifteen years, you have complained that I don't open up and share. Well, what I have come to realize is that I can be open and honest; you just have to be receptive to hearing the truth. People pick up how receptive one is to hearing the truth, and the less receptive they are the less likely they are to be sharing what they really believe. This happened to me. I stopped sharing. I am not that head in the clouds person that you think I am. I will talk and share. You just have to be open to hearing it." He pleaded.

Three hours had passed. Finally, Carolina and Jon decided to go out and get some food and a Margarita and continue the conversation. In leaving the room, they realized that the younger men of the house were concerned about what was happening. With ears to the door, as children will do, they realized that the marriage of their parents might be coming to an end.

"Tell the Cambodian's we will return all those who have fled their government" the Premier of Vietnam said to the emissary.

"But you know if they are returned they will all be killed by the government." The emissary responded.

"Yes, but it is for them to treat their own as they see fit" the Premier replied gravely.

"I hear that our people are being slaughtered inside of the Cambodia" said a general at the meeting.

"Yes, yes, I have also heard those reports" said Vo Nguyen Giap, the Vietnam defense minister.

"This situation with Cambodia is getting worse by the day. They rely on the Chinese to defend them and seem to think that they are some big, powerful country. Who could have imagined that they would treat us like this after all the years we helped them come to power?" Hoang Van Loi said. He had been going to Phnom Penh on secret missions to try to improve relationships between the two countries.

"They promise that things will get better, but Pol Pot, and the rest of his government, cannot be trusted to keep their word. They are nothing but uneducated murderers. They speak politely while they plot to slit your throat" Said Vo Nguyen Giap, shaking his head in the disbelieving behavior of the Cambodians.

A military officer walked into the meeting and handed a new report to the general.

"What is it now?" Vo Nguyen Giap was asked by a member of the group.

"The Khmer Rouge has destroyed several villages inside of our country. Two Eastern Divisions of the Cambodian Army have crossed, as far as four to five miles inside of our country, to raid and destroy the villages." Vo Nguyen Giap replied.

"Do we have any idea how many casualties?" One of the officers asks the general.

"Yes, the report says that they have murdered at least a thousand of our people. They've cut off their heads and they even murdered the women and children, and set fire to the villages." Vo Nguyen Giap said grimly.

"What do you want to do?" A junior officer inquired of him.

"Order the military to relocate the other villages back a few miles, for now. Then I want you to send the military into districts along the Cambodian borders. While the bodies from the raid are still rotting, I want you to get some newspaper media into that region with a military escort and have them report to the world what happened there. This is also a battle that needs to be fought on the world stage and not just on a local level. The Russians will give us aid and money but the Cambodians are being supported by the Chinese. This could change if we can show the world who they really are." Vo Nguyen Giap continued.

"General, I want you and your staff to start drawing up military plans for an invasion; we are going to add that little nuisance of a country to our domain" said the Premier of Vietnam.

"Look Son, we were able to raid their country, steal their cattle and burn their villages. We killed many of the enemy as well." The cadre said as he entered Son Sary's command tent.

"You think this is a great victory?" Son Sary asked the cadre.

"We have defeated the Vietnamese. This is a victory for the Party and for Cambodia. They will not interfere with our country any longer." The cadre said proudly.

"The Vietnamese will come to avenge their defeat here today. They will invade the country. They will kill many for each one they that was lost. Mark my words; the beginning of the end is coming for our government." Son Sary said in a resigned tone.

"Don't speak of such things Son. You will be branded a traitor and right now the Party Centre is looking for enemies in the military." The cadre warned his commander.

Several months later, the Vietnamese invaded Cambodia. First they bombed the Air Force Bases, destroying all the planes that were sitting on the tarmacs and in the hangars. Then they invaded the Eastern Region of Cambodia. The Cambodian troops turned and ran in the face of the advancing Vietnamese Army. The Vietnamese knew how to be just as cruel as the Cambodians. They destroyed the villages, murdered their citizens, butchered the cattle and burned their crops. Evil for evil was paid by each side in this war between Cambodia and Vietnam.

The Vietnamese were able to take over most of the Eastern Districts before being hauled by reinforcements from the other military districts in Cambodia. International pressure forced the Vietnamese to retreat after capturing so much of the Cambodia territory. The Party Centre was embarrassed that they had suffered such a military defeat. But they had won a diplomatic victory, at the expense of Vietnam. This diplomatic victory made Pol Pot as bellicose as before. He felt that they could not do wrong in the running of the country. Yet, the failure of the military convinced the Party Centre and Pol Pot of the need to cleanse their own military forces of traitors.

"You seem a little bit distracted." Angela said to Jon as they sat at the Canyon Café in the Galleria area of Houston.

"Yes, I had a very serious talk with Carolina on Friday and I have been thinking about it a lot." Jon said.

"What did she have to say?" Angela inquired.

"She wants me to stop talking to you." Jon replied.

"And what did you say to her?"

"I told her that either she needed to learn to talk to me or that she shouldn't mind if I talked to you. That I had a need to be able to share with someone and maybe she should be more open to talking about anything." Jon explained to her.

"You realize you are going to end up divorced?" Angela said.

"Maybe I will, but it was nice, for the first time in many years, to be truly honest with her about how I felt." Jon said in a resigned tone.

"I am not making you any promises as far as what happens between you and me." Angela felt inclined to mention at this moment to Jon David.

"Look, I have never asked you for any sex or guarantees of a relationship. In fact, you're the one who normally spends all your time telling me about how you're not interested in me and how you're crazy about some guy who wasn't ever crazy about you." Jon sighed.

"Seems like you and I only have one major difference in opinion, whether Donald loved you or not. Personally, I don't think he ever planned on leaving his wife and family and that you were just some mysterious Asian novelty for him to play with." Jon continued candidly.

"Why do you always get a bit nasty when I say anything about Donald?" Angela questioned.

"Look my idea of love is two people who spend a great deal of time talking and sharing every aspect of their lives and growing deeper and deeper in loving each other. I don't think you can be married to someone and say you're in love with the person you're having an affair with." He continued.

"Even you?" Angela quipped back.

"Even me, I don't think I can be in love with someone while I am still married." Jon said truthfully.

"So you would have to be divorced and then, and only then, could you let it develop into a relationship where you fell in love with someone else. I can't promise you anything if you get a divorce." Angela insisted again.

"I never have asked you for promises and I would never put that type of expectation or burden on anyone. I would resolve my own issues….and move on. If someday you are there. It is only because you have resolved your own issues in your marriage and that whatever happens with Donald is resolved as well." Jon answered.

"I read something the other day and it said that a woman who has an affair, falls for the guy she thinks is her "soul mate". Whereas a guy has an affair with someone who he thinks is very sexually attractive and offers him something that is different from what he is getting at home." Jon said.

"So you're still just saying that Donald never really cared about me? But you realize that he once mentioned that he wanted to get an apartment together." She bragged.

"Oh, really?" Jon said, not without some sarcasm.

"Yes. We had just had sex and he said that this was nice and that maybe we could get an apartment together and do this all the time." Angela said, working really hard to convince Jon and possibly her, how much Donald really cared about her.

"You really seem to want to convince me that this guy loved you and that you were not just duped by some guy who showed an interest in having sex with you. Why is it so important for you to try and convince me that he loved you?"

"Why is it so important that you try and convince me that he didn't love me?" Angela shot back.

"Because Donald doesn't deserve the credit or the love you have given whereas perhaps others who truly care for you deserve your affection." Jon responded quickly.

"You mean like you?" Angela said.

"I didn't say that. I think my idea of love and happiness is a far better model than Donald's. I don't want to blame him, because I have had women approach me just like you did to him. I just think you have to call it what it is…lust and not love. Love is something much deeper and more meaningful." Jon said sincerely.

"Yes, I guess I really do agree with you now." Angela nodded.

"Besides, trust me, the last thing you ever want to do if you're interested in a guy is to talk about another guy or how much you love him. Men don't mind if you are complaining about other guys, but no man wants to hear about what a great guy some other guy is whom you are banging." Jon chided her.

"Oh, hush you don't have to be so crude all the time." Angela said reeling him in a bit.

"Besides I still think you are missing the point, you have to find the answers to your relationship with Simon, not Donald. You can't go back to Donald and be happy. Sometimes you are just so frustrating" Jon groaned.

"The one thing I ask you not to do is just don't keep bringing this guy up time and time again, but you seem like you have to keep telling me over and over again how much you loved him. Yet, you never tell me, not even in the slightest way, how you feel about me." Jon said, getting a little upset.

"I want to believe that the love you and I have for each other is pure." Angela quickly said.

"I don't know who is crazier, you for loving Donald or me for loving you." Jon added.

"You love me?" Angela asked.

"Yes, I do love you. I can't say that I am in love with you…but yes, I do love you. For whatever that means right now." Jon admitted.

The waiter kept coming by, filling the drinks and offering deserts.

This time he said, "Maybe you would both like some coffee or cappuccino?"

"Yes, that would be great" Jon and Angela agreed. They were both trying to find some excuse for not leaving because neither was ready to leave the conversation.

"What do you mean?" Angela wanted to know more about how Jon really felt.

"Well, I said I would never ask you for sex unless I was in love with you. And I don't think I can be in love with anyone else as long as I am married. Men approach relationships much like cars. If they find a better car, they want to trade up. Women approach the same situation differently; if they think their car is broken they just want to get rid of it. They don't care if they have to walk or take the bus. They just want to get rid of their car." He said.

"As a man, I don't want to do that. I truly want to only be making love to the woman I am in love with. Since we are both married to someone else, how can I truly be in love with you under these circumstances? And to do anything else would mean I am no different than Donald or any other scum bag man in the world."

"I was that exact same scum bag that Donald is once in my life and I didn't like it." Jon confessed.

"So where does this leave us?" Angela said.

"Look, there are much deeper issues going on inside of you. Maybe we should just focus on those and let the path of life just unfold in front of us." Jon continued "Sometimes it is best to look at life as a leaf floating down a river. You fall into the river at a certain point and you start floating downstream. We come into contact with other leafs as we float down the river. We have to learn to enjoy the ones we come into contact with, because we never really know how long we will have them in our lives. Each day we have to learn to notice the river we float down. Each day we can only see one section of the river. For, tomorrow we can't go back up the river. Sometimes we are pushed to the bank of the river and are no longer floating. Sometimes we just need a little help to get back to the center of the river again. Maybe this is how I see us. Sometimes we are floating this river of life without knowing the outcome or results. I can tell you that I appreciate you being a part of my life and you are very important to me. I cannot deny that I care about you very much." Jon continued in his philosophical way.

"Thank you, you have always been very sweet to me." Angela squeezed his hand, comforted by his words.

"Do you think it's about time that you told me more about growing up in Cambodia? I have been researching it and realize that it had to have been very horrible. I can't help but believe that you must have suffered some very traumatic things there." Jon approached cautiously.

"We Cambodian's do not like to talk about the things that happened there. We fear it will bring all the evil spirits back to us and its very bad luck to talk about the dead. We just don't normally do it." Angela said, once again shutting Jon down about the past.

"Besides there is just so much that I have forgotten and cannot remember. I felt like I remember much up until that time I was in the hospital for the overdose. Then I just seem to have lost many of those memories."

"Have you talked to your Mom and Dad about their memories and how they all fit together?" Jon continued.

"No, my Mother does not want to talk about Cambodia and the time of the Khmer Rouge at all." Angela continued.

"Well, for all those people that want to forget they are doing a very good job helping all of the next generations forget as well" Jon said grimly.

"What do you mean?" Angela said in a puzzled expression.

"I read an article that said that 25% of those under 21 in Cambodia do not even believe that there was a Cambodian genocide during the reign of Pol Pot. This was a massive slaughter of the people. So the Cambodian's are doing a great job of letting the story of what happened go to the graves with those who do remember, those who survived." Jon stated.

"Wow that is scary how easy it is to get people to forget." Angela responded.

"Maybe if more people talked about what happened, maybe it would prevent it from ever happening again in Cambodia or any other place in the world." Jon said in a serious tone.

"Maybe" Angela simply said.

After throwing the hand grenades and implicating his commander in the incident, Yim Sombat and his commander Sok Chhan were both taken to the prison at Tuol Sleng. The guards removed their blindfolds so they could see the Rules of Regulation as they walked into the Tuol Sleng prison gate with their hands tied behind them.

1. You must answer according to my questions - do not turn them away.

2. Do not try to find the facts by making pretext about this or that. You are strictly prohibited to contest me.

3. Do not be a fool for you are chap that has already tried to thwart the revolution.

4. You must immediately answer my questions without taking time to reflect on them.

5. Don't tell me about your immoralities or the essence of the revolution.

6. When getting lashes or electrification you must not cry out at all.

7. Do nothing, sit still, wait for my orders. If there are no orders, keep quiet. When I tell you to do something you must do it immediately without protesting.

8. Do not make pretexts about Kampuchea Krom in order to hide secrets or traitors.

9. If you do not follow the above rules you will get many lashes or the electric wire.

10. If you disobey any of the regulation you will get either ten lashes or five shocks of electrical discharge.

The reputation of this scary, dark and evil prison is that whoever goes into it will never come out again. They disappear into oblivion - never to be seen again.

Yim Sombat briefly glanced over at his commander and wished that he could have just admitted that day that he was afraid - afraid of what other soldiers would think of him. Yim had let his male ego throw the hand grenades that day. Looking at the rules of regulation as he walked into to the prison, he was afraid of what was coming next. He was already beaten badly from the interrogations at the military base.

Yim and Sok were photographed first. Later, they were required to give detailed biographies, beginning with their childhood and ending with their arrest. Yim and Sok were forced to strip down to their underwear. Their possessions were confiscated, although neither really had many possessions. Sok had a few pictures of his wife and children, not realizing that these pictures could be sealing the fate of his family. They were taken to their cells. Those taken to the smaller cells were shackled to the walls or the concrete floor. They slept on the floor without mats, mosquito nets, or blankets.

"You are forbidden to talk to each other."

Yim's and Sok's day in the prison began at 4:30 a.m.

"Strip" came the order that morning. "I must make sure the shackles are not too loose and that you have not hidden something. We do not allow you to commit suicide here. We decide when you are going to die." The guard said.

Over the years, several prisoners had managed to kill themselves. The guards were very careful in checking the shackles and cells.

Then the guard gave Yim four small spoonful's of rice porridge and watery soup of leaves "You will get fed again at 4pm."

"Water?" You are thinking?" The guard said with an evil smile on his face. "Ask, all water you drink, you must ask for permission." The guard sneered.

Drinking water without asking the guards for permission resulted in serious beatings.

Yim was actually thinking about how nice these men seemed. They did not seem like the evil monsters they had imagined them to be.

The door to the cell closed and there was an eerie silence in most of the prison. But Kim could hear the sound of a baby crying - small whimpering sounds. Kim wondered why a baby would also be here in the prison.

The prison had a staff of 1,700 people. About 300 of these were office staff, internal workforce and interrogators. The other 1,400 were general workers, including people who grew food for the prison in nearby areas of Phnom Penh. Many of these were children of the other workers who were at the Tuol Sleng Prison. The chief of the prison was Khang Khek Leu, Duch, a former mathematics teacher who worked closely with the Khmer Rouge leader, Pol Pot.

The documentation unit was responsible for transcribing tape recorded confessions, typing the handwritten notes from prisoner's confessions, preparing summaries of confessions, and maintaining files. The guards in this unit were mostly teenagers, but they represented the largest group of people at S-21. Most of the guards were terrified of making mistakes and feared being tortured and killed themselves.

There were actually more rules for the guards to follow than there were for the prisoners. Guards were not allowed to talk to prisoners, to learn their names, or to beat them. They were also forbidden to observe or eavesdrop on interrogations, and they were expected to obey 30 regulations, which barred them from such things as taking naps, sitting down or leaning against a wall while on duty. They had to walk, guard, and examine everything carefully.

Guards who made serious mistakes were arrested, interrogated, jailed and put to death.

The interrogation unit was split into three separate groups: A "political" unit, "hot" unit and "chewing" unit. The hot unit, sometimes called the cruel unit, was allowed to use torture.

In contrast, the "chewing" unit or cold unit, sometimes called the gentle unit, was prohibited from using torture to obtain confessions. If they could not make prisoners confess, they would transfer them to the hot unit. The chewing unit dealt with tough and important cases. Those who worked as interrogators were semi-literate and usually in their 20s.

Sok Chhan implicated his company commander Chan Chakrei in a conspiracy to kill members of the Centre Party Leadership. Chan Chakrei was imprisoned in the Tuol Sleng Prison, his confession ended up being 849 pages. In his confession he implicated the Eastern Party Secretary, So Phim. Chan Chakrei claimed, in his confessions, that the artillery was set up to bombard the Party Headquarters and kill Pol Pot.

Jean Amery wrote in his book "At The Minds Limits" that "Anyone who has been tortured will never again be at ease in the world. The abomination of the annihilation is never extinguished. Faith in humanity, already cracked by the first slap of face and then demolished by the torture that follows is never again acquired."

There were only twelve people who survived at Tuol Sleng prison. There were over 14,000 people who entered the prison during the four year span, from 1975 to the Vietnam invasion of 1979. Vietnamese soldiers entered the prison to the smell of rotting flesh.

Once a prisoner entered the prison they were already assumed to be guilty and death was an inevitable conclusion, even though a prisoner might not have committed any crime. "Confess" The interrogator would begin to demand of each and every prisoner.

Prisoners were not told what they had done wrong. They were expected to come up with what their crime was on their own. The interrogators did not even know what the prisoners were accused of. They just needed to get the confession out of them. "But I have done nothing wrong." the prisoner said. But this does not bring sympathy, because it is assumed that they must have done something, in order to be here. Therefore, in not doing anything one is seen as not confessing and not giving up information, which brings the harder and crueler torturing of the prisoner.

The ability to endure pain is an individualized ability to deal with the limits of one's own levels of the endurance. One person sees the tools of pain and confesses immediately to whatsoever he is asked to confess. With others, it takes a slight degree of the infliction of pain before confessing to what someone wants us to say in a confession.

Pain was best inflicted at Tuol Sleng. Prisoners were routinely beaten and tortured with electric shocks, with searing hot metal instruments, with hangings, knife cuttings and suffocation with plastic bags. Other methods for generating confessions included pulling out fingernails while pouring alcohol on the wounds or holding prisoners' heads under water. Some prisoners would be forced to eat human excrement and drink human urine.

Female prisoners were often raped by the interrogators.

Each prisoner must produce the names of the "strings" of those they helped in the conspiracy. Each person had to list the names of those above or below him. Each person pointed the finger at someone else and there was no saving any one person. Death was a forgone conclusion. The naming of the names was merely to prolong their own life. They were prolonging their life in the hope that there would be a way out of the prison, a way for them to survive.

The Vietnamese first invaded the country of Cambodia in December of 1977. Then the 50,000 Vietnamese troops invaded 14 to 15 miles inside the borders of the country. Though the international pressure forced them to withdraw shortly after they had invaded, the Cambodian government became concerned about the Eastern Zone and its combat effectiveness during war.

So Phim was the popular Eastern Party Secretary. He was a member of the Khmer Rouge group who decided who would be sent to Tuol Sleng Prison. He becomes sick in April, and in the first part of May, he was in the hospital. During his absence he was named in additional conspiracies that were now causing the entire country to look within for enemies and imploding upon its self.

"This is not good, Son Sary" So Phim told him.

"What is that comrade?" Son Sary questioned him.

"I received an order requesting my presence at a meeting in Phnom Penh with Pauk." sternly and solemnly responded So Phim, realizing the danger of the situation and the probability of a trap.

"That's not good. Remember what happened in the Central Zone. Ta Mok brought his entire cadre's into the district, and they wiped out and smashed all of the cadres in that district, starting at the top of the administration. No one was safe, no one was spared.

"Maybe General Pauk is trying to overthrow the Central Party. Surely, Pol Pot and everyone else know how loyal I am to the revolution. I cannot imagine they think I would be a traitor." So Phim said shaking his head in disbelieve at what was happening.

"These are not logical times. One does not know friends from enemies - the allies from the traitors. How can one trust anything they see or know?" Son Sary continued "Everyone is confessing on everyone else even though they have done nothing. Men confess lies to spare their own lives!"

"What do you recommend?" So Phim said seeking his advice.

"Send your military attaché to the meeting. He'll report on what they need and what is going on. You can claim that you are busy preparing the defenses against an impeding Vietnamese attack.

"Good idea" So Phim said.

So Phim summoned his attaché and sent him, in his jeep, to the Phnom Penh. The journey was only about 7 hours. He was instructed to find out what was happening and report back.

The seven hours had come and gone.

"There's no word from the attaché yet?" So Phim asked Son Sary.

"No Sir, we've had no word yet." Son replied.

"That cannot be good, but maybe the jeep broke down?" So Phim seemed to be grasping at straws as to why the mission was not complete. Avoiding the one obvious answer, he did not want to admit to himself.

"Send someone else to see if the jeep has broken down. They may find them along the way. Make sure they have a radio and can get word back to us."

Another message, a second courier in a second jeep was sent on the way to Pauk's headquarters in Phnom Penh. And again, the driver and message went silent. No word came back to So Phim's headquarters.

Time passed as both Son Sary and So Phim waited.

The next day they were still waiting. But the men were starting to realize that something was seriously wrong.

The next day came and went, urgently So Phim and Son Sary discussed their next move.

"Send someone that you really trust, a family member." Son Sary said.

"I trust you." So Phim said.

"Sir, I would be honored to go for you." Son Sary said realizing that this might be his last mission.

"No, Son, I am honored that you would go for me. But there might be more battles ahead and you are needed here. Besides if something happens to me, you need to try and take care of as many of the men as possible." So Phim said patting him on his shoulder as he stood behind him.

"Then who do we send there?" Son Sary questioned.

"My nephew will go. I will have him on the radio the whole time and we will see where the link is failing. I suspect that Pauk is attempting a coup and if that is the case I will need you to help me fight him." So Phim surmised.

The nephew left shortly after their conversation. As he parted Son Sary could see the fear in his face. Knowing that maybe he might not be coming back.

His nephew stayed on the radio most of the trip. Once he arrived at Phnom Penh, the last sounds were the guards shouting orders to him to sign off the radio to go into the Headquarters of General Pauk. His nephew was never heard from again.

"It's been too long, again." So Phim said to Son Sary as the situation seemed to be escalating.

"I have decided that I must get to Pol Pot and warn him. I am taking an escort of men, my entire family and we are going directly to Phnom Penh. I will bypass the route that takes me into the district of General Pauk. I will head a bit more south and then go to the Centre Party Headquarters and warn them about this military takeover of general Pauk."

"But what if it's not a military takeover by Pauk?" Son Sary said skeptically.

"Then pray Buddha protects our men and families in this district for they will kill not only all troops but all of our families as well."

So Phim stoically said.

"Let me help map out a route." Son Sary said.

The two men went over their plan; So Phim packed his family into the cars and jeeps, his wife, her family, the children and relatives. He also traveled with 30 of his best men with him in the convoy to Phnom Penh.

Taking a longer route and coming closer to the city late at night. The convoy made good time, until they hit a road block – a Khmer Rouge checkpoint, at the bridge over the Mekong River. They hit So Phim and several of his men approached the cadre and the twelve men who were there at the roadblock.

"Do you not know me? I am So Phim. I demand that you let me through the roadblock." So Phim demanded in his most demanding and authoritative voice and tone.

"I have orders, Comrade. I must call my commander." The officer at the roadblock said in total disregard of So Phim's orders.

The cadre, after several minutes on the phone, returned to the small group of men and said "You are under arrest, Comrade So Phim" and with that, grabbed his arm to pull him towards the other guards.

One of So Phim's bodyguards instantly responded, raised his pistol and shot the cadre in the head. Releasing his grip on So Phim they all started to retreat towards the cars as a firefight commenced between the border guards and the bodyguards.

Many shots fired and several men were killed and wounded. So Phim received two wounds. One of his wounds was a serious abdominal wound to his stomach and one to his leg. So Phim was hobbling back to cars. The firing continued and the rest of his men got back into the trailing cars leaving the first couple of lead cars there in the road.

They drove several miles heading into the countryside to hide. They had several days' worth of food and water supplies with them. After six days, So Phim realized that he would not survive his wounds and that he had been abandoned by the party.

Putting a gun to his temple, he ended his life in a field. All of their body guards had already abandoned them. His family was observing the Buddhist rites of dying and funeral rituals when the forces that were sent out to capture them marched in during the ceremony. The family was gathered around his body. "Kill them all" the cadre said. "Leave no survivors."

With those simple orders the entire Phim family was executed. One's enemies are never allowed to live and come back to avenge a death.

War and death make strange bedfellows. Son Sary had returned to his headquarters that night to make love to his wife. Yes, she had been forced to marry him after the death of her own fiancée by the Khmer Rouge, but she had been a good woman and had treated him good. Son Sary told her that, in the morning, she have to flee the camp and headquarters.

"What are you going to do?" Son's wife asked.

"I am going back and get as many men to follow me as possible. We will fight as long as possible, but we will lose." Son Sary said sadly.

"What about our daughter?" his wife questioned.

"They will kill her if they know she is my child, they will kill you as my wife. You need to pose as a widow with an orphan child. I think it would be best if you just got her away from the camp and dropped her in the woods. She needs to tell people she is an orphan. Her only chance of survival is to be alone." Son Sary said.

Son went into were his little girl was sleeping, how sweet and cute she was. Then he turned around he walked away. Her fate was being cast to the dangerous Cambodian winds of chance.

"Stop work, stop work" the guards yelled at the workers in the rice fields. The guards motioned for them to come closer.

'Gather your things; only what you can carry, we are going to a new location, Angkar has decided that we need more fish. You are going back to your province to fish for Angkar. No more working in the fields. It is time to fish for Angkar." The cadre kept yelling at the people. The news was very welcome for them. Most of them were Chams and had been working in the fields since being relocated from the Great Lake area of the country. They hated working in the rice fields, as they had always been fishermen.

Tran was surprised and happy as well. He thought the change would be good. He had been in the Eastern District for the last two and half years. He had missed his family, his brother. He had lost his wife and child. There were times of huge depression when Tran wished to die and join his wife. Yet, he had survived. He worked the fields, faced the starvation that he and the provinces all faced as the food portions were cut back and people perished of malnutrition.

Tran had seen many people murdered. Some right beside him. Men who were working the rice paddy fields were sometimes called aside to have a plastic bag placed over their heads until they suffocated. Tran, like all the others with him, had learned to follow the smallest of rules while pretending to be semi illiterate to keep it simple.

He had come so close to death when he had accidentally stopped on the path and read a sign warning of the minefield they were going to close. How can a man forget so quickly to remember that a simple task of reading a sign could bring him so close to death? Luckily he had used the name that his brother had given him and the cadre's passed on him each time they checked on his background. Lucky he thought to himself, or just another form of torture to meet his death somewhere down the line. The name his brother had told him to use saved him from death but it never brought his brother to rescue him.

Within twenty minutes, the huts were emptied; the people finished packing and were now forming small groups that would turn into longer lines as they were herded out of the work area. They felt hopeful, but they also feared that this may be just another Khmer Rouge trick and they were being led to their deaths. It is the lies before death that keep many a person freely walking a path to their final outcome. The slightest hope that death is not the real course of action. People had no other alternative but to believe the lies - to cling to the belief, the hope, that life will be better and not worse.

Watching the group form, Tran realized that the soldier's did not have any extra food packed. Yet, often there was hardly any food available. One looks for the slightest clues to figure out what is happening in such grave situations of life and death.

This was a group of over one hundred and fifty individuals. Marching in the group were men, women, children and a few babies being carried by either their mothers or helpers.

They walked along the road for several miles. Then they came to a halt, the column of people stopping and given a short rest and some water. Then after forty five minutes rest, the march continued. Instead of continuing on the road, the column took a different route that headed through the jungle. This was not uncommon but there was always more danger in going through the jungle.

There were only sixteen guards watching the group. The Khmer Rouge soldiers were far too few to be able to handle the situation should the whole group decide to try and escape or overpower the guards. But this did not happen. Each person docilely continued on the path.

That night they gathered around building fires, eating dinner, talking and speculating on exactly where they would end up. But no one tried to escape, many slept well that night in anticipation of the continued journey.

The next morning they all gathered up their things and continued the walk.

"Surely, they would have more guards if they were going to hurt us." Tran thought to himself.

The walk through the jungle continued. Then the sun started to go down in the distance sky. Their bodies cast long shadows on the jungle paths.

"Halt!" the loud voice of the cadre came ringing out.

"We need the men to help build a camp and improve the path ahead." The cadre continued.

"We cannot afford to have many guards back here watching you women and children so we are going to tie you up." The cadre offered an explanation of what was happening to reassure the women and children.

"Men, forward" the cadre yelled.

Tran was starting to feel very uneasy about the situation. He wanted to run but was afraid to commit to that grand plan. Better to wait and see what happens, he reassured himself.

The men had gone about a quarter mile up the path when another 20 Khmer Rouge soldiers stepped out from the jungle. Now all the men were ordered to sit down and the soldiers came behind them and bound their arms behind their back. Then they came and put blindfolds over their eyes. Tran really wanted to run, but the idea now of so many soldiers and machine guns convinced him to take his chances and continue the journey, even if he was blindfolded.

The men followed the path another quarter of a mile. Then they were told to stop. The men were lined up and then Tran could hear the "whack of a bamboo stick and the yell of the men beside him being hit and murdered.

Then he passed out. Tran was hit on the back of the head and fell over presumably dead. Several hours passed before Tran woke realizing that he was still alive. He had a horrible headache. There was blood on this body and he could not see out of one eye.

He could not hear anyone. But realized that it would not be long before someone would come back to bury the dead and check them closer to ensure they were all dead. Tran was able to untie his hands from behind his back and crawl to a nearby bush. There he rested. He was so thirsty and his head was throbbing. How had he survived and the other men were all dead.

Hearing sounds of movement around him in the jungle, Tran crawled farther away from the site. He could see the women and children being lead into the same clearing, all had their hands tied behind their backs and were also blindfolded. He knew what fate awaited them.

Tran could not watch as the women and children were smashed and pummeled. He could not however block out their screams. The sun fell as the Khmer Rouge checked to ensure that everyone was dead and that their possessions had been collected from their dead bodies.

Tran was able to crawl farther away. Once a sufficient distance away he stood upright and traveled through the jungle's dense overgrowth, not fearing any animals of the jungle except the Khmer Rouge.

"Do you even want to go with us on the vacation to Jackson Hole?" Carolina questioned as they both sat at the bar at Ninfa's Restaurant, in Clear Lake.

"Yes, of course I want to go. The time away from everything will be good for us to see how we both feel." Jon David continued in an honest look at what was happening in his marriage to Carolina.

"I will go up then, a week early, and spend time with my family in Oklahoma City and then you can fly up and join us on the long trip to Wyoming. I guess I can use the help driving." Carolina said.

"You mean, I can drive the jeep?" Jon said smiling.

"Yes, you can drive." Carolina repeated. "I thought that is what I just said."

The following week, Carolina and the boys left for Oklahoma City. The following week, they picked Jon David up at the Will Rogers Airport before driving to Colorado Springs. From there they continued the long journey through Cheyenne and Casper to the mountain range surrounding Jackson Hole.

"The trip has been really nice during the past two days. I am glad everyone is getting along so well. I am glad we came." Carolina said.

"Well we did already have the deposit for the whole week and how many years has it been since you were here last?" Jon David asked.

"Well, how many years have we been married… and that is how long it's been." Carolina said in a joking way. "I'm glad to be back after all those years."

Each summer she had lived on a small dude ranch in the foothills of the Grand Tetons. After her family's death, the land went back to the national park service. The dude ranch was still there but the cabins are dilapidated and old. You could wander into the cabins and imagine the years of history – if the walls could talk, oh the stories they could tell.

"How much farther?" the boys wanted to know.

"Just about 16 miles, Then we will come to a small village called Moose".

"What's there?" The boys wanted to know.

"Twelve cabins, a teepee restaurant, a bar, and seven gift shops." Carolina responded.

"The mountains are just beautiful beyond belief." Jon said looking over at Carolina.

"Yes, this is probably one of the most beautiful and peaceful places on earth"

Getting there late, they were still able to check into an old wood cabin along the Snake River.

The cabins sat right behind the Snake River and looked into the Grand Teton National Park. The majestic mountains were blocking out the sun as it set in the Western sky.

That night, Jon and Carolina sat on the bench looking at the river and the mountains, relaxing and quietly thinking, neither one really expressing their feelings of fear or hope. They just sat quietly, observing the mountains and river - peaceful for the moment.

What do you want to do today?" Jon asked Carolina and the rest of the family.

"I want to go into Jackson Hole and do some shopping" Carolina requested in a way that everyone else had to agree.

"Sure I would love to go into Jackson Hole and shop, my dear." Jon replied.

That day they went to Jackson Hole to shop. Carolina went her own way and picked up souvenirs for the rest of the family and relatives.

The boys and Jon David went to the bookstore to wait out the long hours of shopping.

While in the book store, Jon browsed the shelves, and a book caught his eye.

"Understanding Trauma and Those Who Have Experienced Serious Trauma" Jon quickly picked up the book and started to read. He wrote down the title and put it in his pocket so he could purchase the book on his return to Houston. He returned to quickly reading and was realizing why Angela had been so strange about certain things and some of her actions and reactions.

"You ready to go?" Carolina said finally returning to the book store.

"Yes, dear" Jon said as he put the book away, for now.

The week flew by, as the family played cards, walked, hiked the mountains. They rafted Snake River, toured Jackson Hole and embraced the whole easy and peaceful lifestyle of the mountains. How could everything seem so simple and easy here and yet so hard back in Houston? Jon questioned himself as they packed and headed back home, a week later. Carolina and Jon were quiet as they headed back to the city.

"You okay?" Jon said looking over at Carolina.

"Yes, I had a great week and I think it helped us both." She continued.

"I do too…I love you." Jon David said as he reached over and kissed her.

Chapter 10- Finding Her Family

Thunnysok worked hard in the rice paddies for her grandfather. Whatever he ask her to do she'd do. She worked long, hard hours, sometimes even more late night hours than the Khmer Rouge. However, there were times when Thunnysok could play with a few of the children from the nearby farms, when the work was done. Irene was one of the girls who had lost all of her family. Some of them had worked for the government in very low level positions and were murdered the first day of the takeover. Then later, her mother and sisters became ill from malnutrition died.

Thunnysok and Irene became great friends - talking, sharing and playing whenever there was no work to do. Irene was taken in by a nearby family, who had lost some of their own children. Cambodia was experiencing a time when family units were destroyed. Where people totally unrelated were thrown together as husbands and wives, were children were taken in by parents or adults they did not know. The Khmer Rouge tried to destroy the roots of all families and yet in the resilience of mankind, families began to form again.

"Thunnysok you are going to take a long journey with your uncle. He is going to take you to meet some people. He will arrive tonight and then tomorrow you will start your journey."

Thunnysok's grandfather said as both girls stood there in yard near the house.

Irene immediately looked very sad. Tears started to flow down her cheeks. Thunnysok immediately said "I am not going without

Irene, I am her only family and I will not leave her." The petite, yet determined, little girl said as she stomped her defiant foot down emphasizing her decision.

Thunnysok saw the smile come quickly back to the face of Irene. Grandfather thought about it and told the girls to go and ask the foster parents. Thunny and Irene were a force to be reckoned with when they teamed up. An hour later, Irene had packed her few possessions and was back at Thunnysok's grandparent's house. That night, Thunnysok saw her uncle for the first time. She did not remember him from her early years, but he was a nice, friendly man.

That night, the girls slept at the house together. Before the dawning of the sun they were all up and eating breakfast before starting the journey. The two girls were loaded onto a bike, which was walked by the men. They would not be going on any major path or road. The girls would make the journey through the thickest parts of the jungle, with two other men.

Traveling in this manner would be less dangerous. Since the Vietnamese Army had invaded the country, the Khmer Rouge had scattered. Initially, they had retreated from the Eastern District. Many of the Khmer Rouge had hidden in the jungle to regroup after the invasion.

After a long day of walking and peddling the bike, they curled up in their bed rolls. They did not light a fire for fear of attracting either the Vietnamese or the Khmer Rouge. Speaking in hushed tones the girls curled up together and excitedly talked about what they might find when they reached their destination.

The next two days, were slow and tiring. The trip was taking longer than expected. The girls were strapped to the bike, one in front of the other and pushed through the jungle as the men cut a path.

"Bang, Bang, Bang" came the loud cracking sounds of the machine guns. No one could be seen, but they clearly heard the firing of machine guns from somewhere nearby. Then from another direction came more machine gun fire. The men all jumped into the bushes and stayed low to the ground behind some trees.

When the first "bang" was heard, it startled Thunnysok and she dropped her back pack on the ground. The two girls we strapped onto the bike and could not easily dismount the bike to hide. Thunnysok reached down to grab her back pack. Just then she felt the warm wet oozing of blood soaking her back. A stray bullet had killed Irene. Thunnysok slowly turned around to see the glassy open eyes of her dead friend.

The fighting between the Vietnamese and Khmer Rouge lasted only a few minutes. Thunnysok was covered in blood and desperately wanted to cry, but there were no tears.

The jungle was too dense and noisy to see much or know exactly where the soldiers were. But everyone remained silent and completely motionless. After several hours of silence, the gunfire having ceased, the men took the body of Irene and laid her on a grassy patch of earth. There was no time to bury her, or to perform any burial rites. They just laid her on the ground and the group continued their journey.

"Why had she survived again? Why did her friend have to die like this? Why had she let her come on the journey? Why had she killed her own best friend?" Thunnysok's sadness burrowed deeper into her young soul.

The food was gone; they looked for something to eat as they

continued through the jungle. Suddenly, a huge boa constrictor snake fell from a tree onto one of the men who was cutting the path. The snake weighted over 160 lbs. and was 18 feet long. It quickly wrapped itself around the man and had started to squeeze, but Thunnysok's uncle reacted very quickly. Using his machete, he hacked into the huge snake until he was finally able to chop off its head. The man gasped for breath as he was released. This shocked everyone to see how quickly a snake could kill its prey.

That night they all ate their fill. Risking a small fire, the small group cooked the huge snake and what a feast it was.

"So where do you want to go to lunch, today?" Angela questioned Jon David.

"Why don't you just join me here at the hotel?" Jon

"You feel comfortable doing that?" Angela responded.

"Sure, why not, I am allowed to have female friends. It's just that most of them are not so attractive." Jon said playfully.

"Oh stop. You're not getting anything from me, so you can stop trying to butter me up." Angela giggled.

"Oh, good point, Crazy Asian" he quipped back to her.

Two hours later at the hotel restaurant, they sat in the far corner away for the other working employees and hotel guests and talked.

"So you had a good vacation trip?" Angela questioned.

"Yes, it was very beautiful and we had a great time. Things have been much better at home. I have taken the approach to try and talk to Carolina just like I talk to you. I am trying to be completely honest and see how she deals with the openness." Jon replied.

"So, what is this I saw in an email - that you went to see Donald?" Jon changed the subject.

"I was close to Sugar Land one day and I decided to go to his office. I sat in the car in the parking lot for almost 30 minutes before I got up the nerve to go in and ask to see him. The receptionist gave me a funny look but I told her who I was and she buzzed him." She said in a matter of fact tone.

"I had to wait about twenty minutes for him to finish a meeting and then he came out. He gave me a kiss on the cheek, and invited me into his office. We talked for about 25 minutes and then he had other meetings and ushered me out of the office." She finished calmly.

"So let me get this straight, you have not seen him for months, and the week I go out of town, you run back to see him?" Jon David said.

"Oh hush, that has nothing to do with it. I didn't run back to Donald, I just happened to be in the area and wanted to see how he was doing." Angela replied innocently.

"And how is he doing?" Jon David questioned further.

"His business is doing great. They have a good team of guys building a business and they are looking to hire all kinds of people. You can look on his website, they are doing very well." She said.

"So I have a question for you going back to the time when you were seeing him on a more intimate basis. What would you have done, for a plan of action, to be together?" Jon David asked.

"Well, I guess we would have divorced our spouses, dated for a while, then moved in together, and maybe someday have a baby." Angela said somewhat reflectively, yet logically at the same time.

"Hmmm so you would have wanted to have another child?" Jon said "And what did he have to say about his, or did you ever mention it to him."

"Yes, I did mention it to him. I'd started dreaming about having a baby and the baby looked like Donald." I got so freaked out about it that I called him and told him about it."

"And what did he say about it?"

"He said, 'that figures', but he didn't say much else." She said glumly.

"I am sure he was thinking, "Damn, how did I get messed up with this crazy beautiful Asian" Jon said a little sarcastically?

"Oh hush." She replied.

"Well, you know what they say; a man can get over an affair in weeks and a woman may take a year or two to get over it." He said solemnly.

"Great, that is just what I needed to hear." Angela groaned.

"Well, trust me, I hate hearing you talk about Donald. There is probably nothing that sets you and me off like a good conversation about Donald - your obsession." Jon David said resentfully.

Lon, the General Manager of the hotel came into the restaurant and came over to the table. Jon introduced him to Angela.

"Sorry to interrupt but I need to talk to you when you finish lunch." Lon said sternly.

"Sure. I will be there soon." Jon replied.

"Not really the friendliest guy in the world." Angela noticed.

"No, he and I don't really get along that well. It's a long story…but he wanted me to take an aggressive financial approach on an issue and I did. Once the company found out, there was hell to pay for doing it the way he wanted me to do the accounting. My boss was so mad and pissed off; I heard her swearing for the first time."

"He said if the issues slapped us in the face, he would take the blame. He did for about five minutes and then gave it all to me. There is a bit of resentment on some other issues as well. You can say that he's not the friendliest guy in the world." Jon said bitterly.

"I have another question for you. I know you said that your mom was separated from your father, and that they were fighting over custody of your youngest sister. But how and when did your step father go from being a guy renting a room in a house to being married to your mom? Seems like a strange way the Cambodian's do this marrying thing…you move them into your house and then just marry them." Jon David said.

"Well I guess you just are around them and get to know them

better when love develops. But not everything was great at first. There was the whole deal with him trying to marry me off to the guy who had actually raped me. There was a time when I was so upset about him breaking up my relationship with the guy I really loved. And then once there was serious issue with my mother."

"You have to understand he is not the same man he was fifteen years ago. He had a lot of anger and would get upset and angry much more. But he had a traffic accident and it hurt him. That injury calmed him down and he suddenly became more spiritual. There was a huge change in him. Once he was beating my mother, I got a knife out of the kitchen and jumped on him while he had her down on the floor. I threaten that I would kill him if he hurt her." Angela said.

"Wow, you actually put the knife to this throat?' Jon questioned.

"Yes, I would have killed him, if he had hurt her. But that was then and now is now…He is a much different person. To me, he is and was my father. I call him that out of respect now. He tried much harder to be a good father to me."

"Interesting" Jon David said softly.

"Let's not talk about it anymore. It's not something I like to think about. I am not proud of what happened." Angela said remorsefully.

Tran Sary's head was splitting with pain. He was unable to focus his eyes and felt very thirsty. He realized he needed to put some distance between himself and the area. The Khmer Rouge would do one final body count and realize that someone was missing. They did not do many things right, but in the area of killing, the Khmer Rouge were experts.

Traveling for a day and a night, Tran finally found a river and was able to drink. He was still thinking about all the people who had been murdered in the jungle. It's hard to image such mass murder. Many times for the smallest of reasons people's lives were taken.

On the second day, Tran could hear noises as he came closer to a road. He stopped before walking out into the open. There was a long line of people being herded from the East to the West. There were Khmer Rouge soldiers guarding them. Yet, the number of people compared to the guards was very small. It would have been easy for Tran to just have joined the column of refugees and walk with them. However, after his experience in the jungle, Tran thought it better to trail far behind them, remaining hidden. It took him longer to walk and make his way through the jungle but refugees were moving slowly.

Tran wanted to join the group. He especially wished he could join them when they stopped for meals. Tran could hear his stomach growling with hunger. Tran recognized part of the group as being Chams. Yet, there were too many of them to tell exactly who they were. On the third day, the group came to a clearing in the road and made camp. The next day they did not start off in any direction. Tran decided to circle the camp and get closer to see if he could find out more what was happening.

Creeping closer the camp, he heard some noises coming from a rice field. At one end of the rice field it appeared there were men digging. They were prisoners digging huge trenches. Tran realized there were only two purposes for huge trenches, bunkers for battle against the Vietnamese or graves to bury bodies.

There was a likelihood of a Vietnam invasion. They had all heard the jets flying overhead and occasional bombing. Tran was not convinced.

But, that night people were led to the site and the executions began. Tran saw the first group of twenty led to the site and murdered. Then a group of thirty people were next, followed every fifteen minutes by another group. The soldier's got so tired of killing they had to start executing them in shifts. The soldiers were taking turns delivering beatings with the bamboo sticks and iron bars through the night. Most people went to their deaths very quietly. Cambodian's had almost become used to so many years of brutality and death, people were resigned to their own fates. Maybe they had become numb to it.

The next morning the Khmer Rouge seemed to be in more of a rush to finish their massacre. They lead groups to the field and just started to shoot them in the back of the head, letting them fall into the trench. Their plan was to use the dead bodies to fertilize the rice fields. How cheap does life become when one's decaying body is used to fertilize fields? The night before they were murdered, the prisoners were blindfolded and their hands were tied behind their backs. Then the next morning, when they were lead into the area, they meekly sat down on the edge of the trench – knowing there was no way to survive.

Tran sat and watched, estimating that by the end of the day, fifteen thousand individuals, almost a whole nation of people, were lying in the trenches.

The next day, the soldiers left. And Tran was able to rummage through the area and find some food.

"If I am going to die, at least let me return to the land of my family. There, I will die." Tran decided as he headed in the direction of province.

After returning from Wyoming, Jon had opened the mail and found an invitation to a wedding. The wedding was the daughter of one of Jon David's friends, Jenny Wu. Jon had gotten to know her and her fiancé very well, as their international trading company was in the office building attached to the Hotel he worked at.

Jenny's daughter had been a former Miss Asia in Houston and she was marrying a man fifteen years older than her. The groom was ranked as the top trial lawyer in Houston. He recently won millions in lawsuits against large corporations based in Houston. The wedding was one of the largest and most popular Asian events in the city.

The reception was held at the Intercontinental Hotel in the Houston Galleria, where five to six hundred guests attended. Jon tried hard to get Carolina to attend but she kept finding reasons not to. Jon went to the wedding reception alone, and had a delightful time, talking to people at his table from around the world and drinking wine. He drank more than usual, because the stress of the events at work and home made him want to forget his emotional pain. Jon noticed that when he and Carolina got into arguments he just wanted to escape the emotional pain and drink, dance and forget that he was married to someone so difficult.

That night in a very dangerous move, Jon drove home even though he was pretty intoxicated. Jon had vowed that he would never drink and drive again after crashing his car at 75 mph into a highway lamp post. Nearly cheating death once again and now realizing how even marriage could cause death and dying.

Carolina walked into the master bedroom where Jon David was

lying down watching television partly out of one eye, while the other one was spinning in sync with the ceiling fan.

"What is this I found in your wallet?" Carolina demanded to know as she walked into the master bedroom.

"That is just Angela's new real estate business card." Jon David replied. He'd put the card in his wallet several weeks ago when he'd had lunch with her she'd given him the card to show him.

"Well, for all I know you have been with her all night - that your girlfriend was at the wedding or that you skipped the wedding to be with her. I am just not going to put up with this anymore. I have talked to all of my girlfriends and they all say the same thing. "Why, am I putting up with this?" I am a beautiful woman and there are lots of men out there who would like to go out with me. I am going to take off tomorrow and see my divorce attorney. I am going to go ahead and file for divorce. I want a divorce if for no other reason than to show respect for myself." Carolina continued.

This was the final straw for Carolina. She could not wonder, every time Jon David went somewhere, if he might be sneaking to see some other woman. It was better for her to cut her loses than to have to worry every day and every night.

Even though Jon David had not been with Angela or anyone else, the years of conflict between himself and Carolina had taken an emotional toll. In a way, Jon David was ready to have the finally conflict come to an end.

Several weeks later, Carolina did file the divorce papers. She asked for temporary child support and many other things. Jon David found a two bedroom apartment, a mile from the house, and moved his possessions out of the house on a chilly winter night. His possessions were all of one brown chair, a dining room table without any chairs, and two thousand books.

"Not really hard to move when there isn't much that your mother wants me to take out of the house." Jon David joked to his son as he was helping him move the boxes out to the car.

"Mom is not even giving you one of the beds or a television?" Jordan, his 14 year old son asked. He was the youngest of the kids but the closest to his father.

"No, no beds. I guess I will just sleep on the floor. This will be kind of like camping indoors." Jon David again joked.

"Mom said I made my own bed and now I had to lie in it." Jon said, hoping some wise cracks would relieve the tension of the moment.

"Dad, are you going to be okay?" his son asks him. "And are you going to still take us to school every morning?"

"Yes, son, I will be okay. I would not let the distance grow between us. I will be over every day, to see you." With that Jon David reached out his hand to shake hands with his son. His 5 foot 8 inch son stepped forward and gave his dad a huge hug. Jon David turned quickly to hide his tears as he went to his car.

As much as Jon David wanted to get away from the conflict with Carolina, he was beginning to realize how painful each day was going to be not coming home to his sons and daughters. Jon David realized he would no longer say good night to his son before going to bed.

That night Jon went to his bare apartment, he lay down on the blankets and cried harder than he had ever cried in his life. The pain was much greater than he'd ever imagined it was going to be, not only because he was finally admitting to defeat in the marriage, but also the pain that his children had to endure as they struggled to understand.

Jon felt painfully alone.

Yim Sombat could not sleep. Sleep was impossible in S-21. Mosquitoes were a problem all night. Crying could be heard in the cells down the hall from where Yim was shackled by his feet to the cold, hard concrete floor. Noises of the night were the quiet walking of the guards outside the cells and the moans of the other prisoners. There were about fifty people in the long narrow open cell. When Yim was not being eaten by the mosquitoes, he was pestered by flies landing in his body.

The smell of urine and feces penetrated the senses even more than the sounds. One could not escape the terrible odors of the human waste that was spread around the room. Yim tried to close his eyes and pretend he was back in the farms fields, working in the bright sunlight. In his mind he tried to escape into his memories of being with his family and times they spent together. Yim tried to take his mind back to the time when all he thought about was the girl in his village who was so pretty. How he would sneak peeks of her working in the fields by hiding up in a nearby tree. How this young girl made him nervous when he saw her. All he really wanted was for her to be proud of him. Yim thought back to the days when all he wanted was to come back from the war with Lon Nol's men, a hero. He wanted to be someone she could be proud of so that he could ask her family to let her marry him.

The harder Yim tried to remember these pleasant visions in the recesses of his mind, the more difficult it became to see them.

His mind was trying to hold onto good memories, in the face of his greatest fear, but he was losing them. He suddenly heard noises coming down the hall towards the door.

"Up you traitors and dirt of the soil" the soldier yelled as several of the guards unlocked the door. Yim heard the soldiers coming into the room to wake everyone.

"I have a list of names of the guests who will have the privilege of being questioned today, for it is your honor that you will have a chance to share your crimes, to confess what you have done to this great country - how you have betrayed Angkar?" the soldier continued speaking to the room in general.

Yim had heard rumors of this place. Not one prisoner had ever come out alive. But, maybe he would be the lucky one who would find a way to survive. There was hope even if it was only slight. Maybe Yim could make them realize how they had mistreated the soldier's and he could help explain the real situation with the moral of the soldiers. Maybe the Khmer Rouge leaders would even be grateful and promote him.

First the soldiers went to several other prisoners in the cell block. He could see them unlocking them and the dread in the faces of the men as they realized what was going to be happening next.

Turning around the men then looked in his direction and then looked again at the list that one of them had in his hand. Yim caught the eyes of one of the soldiers who spoke to the other men softly. His heart sank as he realized they would be coming for Yim next.

The Khmer Rouge prison guards could not have been any older than Yim, unlocked the shackles on his feet. They tied his hands behind his back. Suddenly everything went dark, Yim realized they had placed a sack over his head "traitor" was the only word they spoke to him as they prepared him for interrogation.

Several minutes passed and Yim was walked into another room and ordered to sit down in a chair. The hood came off his head. Yim was now in a much smaller room with a three man interrogation team. They were only slightly older than Yim. These men might have been from the same village as Yim, they might have been comrades in the military, had his luck not gone badly. But now he was their prisoner.

"Confess all your crimes, we will write down the history of where you have been and all the agents you have associated with in these crimes." The interrogator began.

The men were smiling, a common Cambodian trait, smiling as if they were your friend as they prepared to inflict pain.

"Confess quickly" the interrogator said. "Spare your body the pain that is coming. We fear that we may kill you in our eagerness to complete a successful interrogation."

Yim let those words soak in. "Fear you will kill me!" So they did not want to kill him. He was facing a life and death situation now.

The men took his arms from behind his back and hooked them up to the chains that hung from a hook in the ceiling. Pulling the chains, the men lifted Yim higher from the floor. Yim started feeling the sharp pain in his arms and back.

"Confess everything save your pitiful body the pain that is to come." The interrogator shouted.

His body was lifted off the concrete floor and dangled higher by the chains around his arms.

Yim was starting to understand pain. He felt deep physical pain, which made it harder to focus his mind on what was going on in the room. Focus! Yim admonished himself. Take one minute at a time; one second at a time; surely he could make it through the moment.

Yim's mind was rapidly absorbing the details of his surroundings. Yim observed the soldiers, the room, Yim the few furnishings and torture devices in the room. The men were smiling at Yim as if they were having fun and were entertained by him hanging there.

Seconds, one just thinks of the next seconds during torture. Will my mind escape this pain? Yim thought to himself. And he was barely able to hear the words that caused even greater concern. "We have a tool here to make you more cooperative." The man standing in front of him said.

One interrogator approached him with the electrical shock machine. He attached two pronged clamps to his nipples, and then stepping back with that same indifferent smile on his face.

"Go" he said, as he turned to one of the other men.

Yim's body jolted to one side and then another as he received five blasts of electric shock, each one with increasing power. The mind loses all lucidity during moments of intense, prolonged pain. Yim's mind was running wild with imagines of the present and past. Yim wanted to share everything he knew, even make up things, anything to stop this pain.

"Please just stop!" Yim wanted to scream.

Later that night the interrogation stopped. Yim had survived the day. After hours and hours of intense pain, he was still alive. Now his mind turned to what he could tell the men to get them to stop from torturing him. He started to think of anything interesting and made up lies to convince the men of a greater conspiracy that the military was plotting.

Yes, this would be the only way that he would stop the next round of torture. Yim thought as he was being walked back to his cell that night.

Before he was taken back to his cell to be shackled to the floor, Yim could hear the sound of a baby crying in one of the prison cells down the hallway. Yim could not imagine the pain that could and might be inflicted on a helpless baby.

"I hope you are right about what you saying, Jon David." Lon said solemnly as Jon sat in his office.

"I am right." Jon replied to Lon.

"You said that about the way we booked the audio visual and we ended up getting our asses in a sling." Lon retorted.

"I told you we had a basis for making that decision. That doesn't mean the company is going to agree with our decision. You told me, you were going to check with Deborah and you didn't." Jon said accusingly, knowing that he probably could not win this battle.

"Well, Deborah said you should have given me better financial advice." Lon continued

"I gave you excellent advice. I told you they would be pissed off if they realized we were booking it that way and they were.

Remember, they were pissed off, but they didn't think it was worth going back to correct what we did. The bottom line is they knew I was right in my decision. I still think corporate is wrong, they just cannot go back and admit that as a company we are booking the numbers wrong."

Then Jon David's cell phone went off and Lon gave Jon that shitty look.

"I thought I told you to put that damn cell phone on silent." He shot at Jon.

"You did. Sorry. I forgot." Jon groped for the correct reply.

Jon looked at the caller ID, as he left the office. It was Angela, but he didn't dare reply until he got well out of Lon's hearing.

"Hi, want to go to lunch. I am in the area." Angela said as Jon answered.

"It's pretty hectic here at the hotel...but yes. What the hell. Let's go get a bite to eat. Why don't you just pull up in the valet lot to pick me up?" Jon replied.

Several minutes later, Angela and Jon were on their way to a nearby restaurant. The restaurants were busy at the Galleria during lunch, but today they decided to try a new restaurant inside the Galleria Mall.

"You realize that people are talking about you and me." Jon said to Angela.

"I don't really care what people say about me or what they think." Angela responded.

"So how is life being a single white man with lots of money?" Angela said jokingly.

"Well, I think I am closer to being single. I have gone out on a couple dates. I guess you are close to being really divorced when you've moved out of the house and are paying child support and temporary alimony." Jon David continued saying but with a slight smile.

"Yes, sounds like you are close to really being divorced." Angela smiled back.

"No thanks to you." Jon said.

"Don't blame me! It was your decision, not mine. I am still trying to make my own decisions, independent of anything you are doing." Angela continued.

"Funny how you said rich white boy. I think this divorce is going to leave me broke and poor. My ex is asking for everything. Texas says she will get half and she wants it all. Texas says she doesn't get alimony and she wants it anyway." Jon David grimaced.

"So I kept her on my medical, pay her cell phone, kept her as the beneficiary on my life insurance and you know what she did?" Jon said laughingly.

"What?" Angela

"She transferred all of the money out of my personal account to one in her name. Then she changed the password for my account and closed it."

"Wow…Sounds like one angry woman." Angela responded.

"Funny, that is exactly what the bank officer said when I was there trying to figure out what was going on…she said "What did you do to piss this woman off?" Jon tried to chuckle.

"So are you dating anyone, now that you are an eligible, single man?" Angela pried.

"Yes, I have been dating. It's a little strange going out after all these years. And I am really lost as to all the new rules about dating. I don't believe you wait on anyone to look for happiness. You have to live your life and walk down the path and just see if anyone shows up to join you along the way." Jon said somewhat philosophically.

"Well I hope you are not waiting on me." Angela said. "As long as I still feel the same way about Donald I don't know if I can ever really move on with my life. Every time I log into my computer it still reminds me of him." She sighed wistfully.

"Wait! Don't tell me you use his name as one of your passwords?" Jon said incredulously.

"Well, yes. I still do. I have just never gotten around to changing them." Angela said.

"You know, that really does bother me." Jon said, disgusted at her comment.

"Why?" She seemed genuinely surprised.

"You tell me how much you loved him. That is hard enough, then you tell me how thankful you are that I came into your life. That I helped you to get rid of the pain of Donald, so you could get over him. You tell me how his love almost ruined you and everything in your life. Yet you cannot even bring yourself to change your passwords that are his name? You can't do that one little thing to get your damn mind off him?" Jon said as he was getting more and more upset.

"I am sorry; I guess maybe I do see your point. You really don't think I appreciate all you have done to help me or how much you have care for me, even though I have not been able give you more." Angela explained.

"The other day I was watching a movie it reminded me of you. There was a woman who, after suffering some truly traumatic events in her life, began to believe that she lived in two different places and started to lose the ability to know which one was real and which one was imaginary. In one version she lived in a French Château, as a writer and editor. And in the other, she was an editor in New York City." Jon David said.

"So what is your point?" Angela cut in.

"The woman in the movie had a hard time distinguishing between the reality of her own life and what she created in her own mind." Jon said pausing to take a deep breath before continuing "That is what you did with Donald. You created this man who was perfect and had everything you wanted in life. He was worldly, knowledgeable, confident and older. Maybe he was a father figure because you didn't really have a dad. You think you fell head over heels over him as you had a sexual encounter or two. Yet in your mind, there are many disconnected facts that you don't really want to see. You were just some naïve Asian woman who had an affair with some married white guy. You made a mistake and you don't even want to face that as a possibility." Jon David said evenly.

"So you're just throwing it in my face." Angela responded.

"No, I am not throwing anything in your face! I am, and have always, just tried to get you to see the relationship as it is. There is no judgment in me about what you did. I think your real issue is to find out what you are missing in life. The love you feel like you are missing and the reality of how and what you think. You are delusional in some ways. There must have been some really bad things that happened to you in your childhood. And I know that I have tried to respect the fact that you don't want to talk about the past. But the past, those early years, is the real key to understanding you - to understanding what happened to you. I have been reading book after book of what happened during that period of time in Cambodia. I am totally amazed at how cruel your world was." Jon was getting louder and more passionate as he spoke each word to her. "Don't you realize I have been researching all the issues that you must have faced as a little girl?" I know that your life must have been a nightmare - you had to have seen people murdered or worked to death or starved." Jon continued passionately and empathically.

"You have no idea." Angela responded.

"Yes, Angela, I have a very good idea." Jon David said, reaching across the table to cover his hand with hers.

Botum had overheard the elders saying that their uncle had gone on a mission to see if this girl might be her lost sister, whom she had not seen for over four years.

Botum was excited when she realized that her sister might still be alive. Each person and child in Cambodia during the time of the Khmer Rouge had seen many people murdered. Sometimes it seemed like there was no reason or rhyme to who survived and who died.

Botum gave him a little gift necklace to give to her sister. "Tell her this will bring her safely back to me and bring her good luck."

Then Botum went back to the chores she had to do in the village. She could not wait to see her sister. Her two brothers were missing. There had been rumors that they had been killed but no one could be sure. How easy it was for children, parents, even whole families to just disappear.

"Mother, how much time will pass before uncle returns?" Botum kept asking her mother.

"Botum, it will be at least a week and maybe more. We can never tell in times like this, the journey is very dangerous" Mother replied to her eldest daughter who had grown much in the last four years.

"Mother, can I wait on the path for her?" Botum questioned her mother.

"Yes, once you have gotten all your work done, you can wait." Mother replied.

"I want to be the first person to see her. I want to be the first person that she sees when she returns." Botum shared with her mother.

"Yes Botum, you can be the first." Mother replied with a huge smile.

Mother was in the circle of women talking.

"I have sent out messages around to different villages looking for my children. Then I hear that Thunnysok might actually be living close to father's relatives. They say she has a scar on her chin but does not have any memory of who she is or where it's from. It's as if her memory has all been wiped away." Mother said to her sister.

"We have all suffered during these years, many have not survived and few want to remember anything that has happened. So maybe her memory will return once she sees you." Her sister consoled her in a very loving way.

"I pray she does remember at least me or even Botum, at least someone. What a cruel fate if it is not her. Then I will have some orphan child here and I will not be able to send her back. She will have to be my daughter, but then how do I tell her she is not really my daughter." Mother fretted.

"You will learn to love her if this is not Thunnysok, you will love her as if she was Thunnysok." Sister said wisely.

"This trip was only to take a week, but now it is close to two weeks. I grow more concerned each day that they have been captured or killed by the Vietnamese or the Khmer Rouge. These are dangerous times to be traveling anywhere in the country. Even if this is not her, I will tell her that she is my daughter. I could never do anything to hurt any other child in the world. Whether this is Thunnysok or not, this will be Thunnysok." Mother said with determination.

For the next several days, Botum would get her chores done and then go to a spot on the path leading into the village to wait and watch for her sister. The first couple of days turned into a week, and then the week turned into two weeks. Each day Botum was becoming quieter and quieter as she started to lose hope that she would ever see her sister again.

Botum was playing with a stick and in the dirt, making a little village of her own. Botum looked up and saw several men coming up the path. Her heart started to pound as she recognized one of the men as her uncle but then as quickly losing heart when she realized that there were no little girls with them.

Botum hung her head in sadness. As she looked back up, she saw the little girl on the bicycle. One of the men was walking beside the bicycle, hiding the little girl from view.

Botum ran to her sister, who looked sad and worn out by the journey. "My sister, I love you and have missed you." Botum told her.

"Come with me." Botum said to her sister who jumped off the bicycle and ran with her to a tent.

Botum really had not remembered her sister. The years had flown by without seeing her, but to her, this was her sister. She knew it had to be her sister. Taking her into her tent she started to put necklaces around her neck and picking out cloths for her to wear. This had to be her sister.

"She is here! They have returned!" her sister said sticking her head inside the tent.

"Where is she now?" Mother Chim questioned.

"Botum took her to her tent, and she is putting cloths and jewelry on her. She cannot stop talking to her and playing with her. I think the little girl is a bit in shock and does not know what to think about what is going on. Botum keeps telling her that she is glad to see her sister."

Thunnysok had a difficult couple of weeks. Not that she minded leaving her relatives by Tonle Sap Lake. She would not miss them, but she would miss the water and the lake. For the past several weeks she had been walking through the jungle where her best friend was killed. She was still feeling like it should have been her. She could not understand why the bullet killed her friend and missed her.

Hungry and tired, Thunnysok headed up the path with her escorts. To her surprise a girl came running up to her with a huge smile and yelling quickly how happy she was to see her.

Thunnysok had no idea who she was. Gone were the memories of her older sister. In the sea of bad memories, all of the good memories of her family had been completely erased or blocked out. Her sister was too happy to notice to how quiet Thunnysok was and not sharing the same enthusiasm over the reunion. Yet, Botum did not mind. Within minutes Thunnysok was in her sister's tent and showered with love and gifts bestowed on her.

Thunnysok was overwhelmed and surprised by what all she was hearing. Family, she had no memory of family. Her first memory of life was the first day in the Khmer Rouge camp. There were children and adults being in single file lines as they were yelled at by the Khmer Rouge soldiers. This was as far back as Thunnysok could remember. She had no other memories. No brothers, no sisters, no mother and no father. Her life began at 4 years old in a work camp.

A woman walked into the tent as they were putting on clothes and jewelry. "You need to come with me." The woman said to Thunnysok and she reached down to extend her hand to her. Thunnysok stopped what she was doing and took the woman's hand. They turned and started to head out the tent. Botum started to follow them.

"No, you need to stay for a few moments. You mother has requested it."

"Tell Botum to stay in her tent, I want to see if Thunnysok remembers me. Have all the other relatives come to this tent as well." Mother Chim said to her sister.

"What if she does not even remember me?" Mother Chim said with her worst fears coming to the surface. Her sister gave her a hug and went out to get the girl. The other relatives came to the tent to see the reunion. There were twelve people standing now in the tent, this was all that was left of the total Chin extended family. They were huddled in the tent when the little girl was led in by the hand. There was just silence as she looked around the room. Each person looked at her intently and then they would slightly turn to look at Mother Chim to see the expression on her face.

Mother Chim looked at this little girl. She was hoping that she would recognize her. Hoping the child would have some memory from her early years, before the Khmer Rouge. Four was not so long ago to remember. But Mother Chim could see by the little girl's blank expression that she did not remember her.

"She doesn't remember" Thunnysok could hear someone say.

The beautiful woman then stepped forward and bends down and hugged her. There were tears in her eyes, but not of sadness but joy.

"I am your mother." She said to Thunnysok.

Son Sary walked into the house. He looked tired and deeply concerned.

"You are going to need to leave the camp and flee to the north." Son Sary sighed. "I am ordering everyone to leave the camp. Take the route to the north."

"What is happening?" Met Maih questioned.

"The central committee is going to try to kill all the cadres and people in the Eastern District. They are coming for me and my men as well. They have killed So Phim and now are coming with soldiers to try and capture me." Son Sary explained.

"I will order everyone out of the camps and then I want you to get lost in the countryside. I will give you papers and if you go soon then there is a good chance you will make it to safer places." Son Sary said to his wife.

"Thank you, Son. You have been a good husband to me thank you for watching over me through all these years. I know God brought you into my life to help save me during these terrible years." Met Maih said tearfully.

"Someday they will speak of the Khmer Rouge and think that all of us were evil. I am afraid that history will forget all the men who tried to fight against this government." Son Sary said.

"Son, you are a good man, you have saved many lives in your district by providing better food rations and work rules. You were compassionate in ordering lesser punishments for violations. Fate will help you. God has used you in this country." Met Mai said with tears flowing down her face.

"What are you planning to do?" Met Mai questioned.

"I am going to take some of my men and fight for as long as possible. This should give the column time to get into a safer area." Son replied.

"What about the little one?" Met Mai

"Thunnysok, my sweet Thunnysok" Son Sary said.

"Her best chance for survival is to be left as an orphan with no parents. There are some remote huts and houses along the road. I know of one that has a family that was once the family of one of the Cambodian generals. Drop her close to the house; maybe the lady will help her. You both stand a better chance of survival if you separate." Son said grimly.

"Do you want to say good bye to her?" Met Mai said.

They both walked to the room where Thunnysok was asleep and stood there for a moment looking at her. Standing there they could not help but think how beautiful and sweet this little girl, Thunnysok was.

"I pray that God will protect her and you." Son Sary said, giving his wife a kiss good bye.

"Thank you, Son. You have been my hero. I pray as well that God will protect you and your men." Tears were still flowing down her face.

"Tonight, pack and get ready. The orders will come early and you will need to go quickly."

That night, they made love, knowing that it was there last night together. In their last moments, the closeness of their bodies and hearts reassured them. But, the sun does rise in the morning and what will come, will come, regardless.

Before the sun was up, Son was gone. He gathered several of his loyal troops and headed down the road to the bridge. Son allowed the advance troops of Mok to cross the river and when the lead column started across, he blew it up with the explosives he'd wired it with. His men were able to kill the ones who had already crossed. The first skirmish went well but Son Sary knew they were only buying time for others to get away.

"Damn! Damn!" Jon David said loudly in his office that day. Edina, Lea and Doris all came running to find out what was wrong. Rare was the day that Jon David Conner cursed. There must be something really wrong.

As they came to the door of his office, they saw him sit back with a huge smile on his face. Obviously he was very pleased.

"What's wrong? " Edina said to Jon. "Or should I say, what's right?"

"I found it!!" Jon exclaimed.

"Found what?" Edina questioned.

"I found the answer to this whole dispute between the owners of the office complex and the hotel. I found the answer to the problem."

"What did you find?" Edina continued to ask knowing full well she would probably not understand anyway.

"Embedded in a spreadsheet from 8 years ago... I found the place where the office building changed the formula in the billing to the hotel - where they started charging the hotel more money but added back in all the wages to the distribution."

"Jon, you know I don't really understand what you're saying, and probably no one else is going to understand, so tell me in very simple terms, boss. What does this mean?"

"It means that I can prove we were overcharged and that this battle is going to be over. For every dollar we owe them, they owe us two. And I'm sure they are going to want to settle the whole dispute and give up. Then I can write the settlement issues that will make it easier for the new owners who are buying the hotel to manage the relationship in the future."

"That is great." Edina clapped her hands together.

Jon took the news to his boss and his boss called the Asset Manager over the hotel. The Asset Manager requested that Jon call the Chief Financial Officer of the building complex and explain the hotels position. Within 24 hours of finding the error, the dispute between the two companies was resolved. Within a week emails and letters were circulating around the company praising the efforts of Jon David.

"Congratulations!" Lon said. "You did a great job and the whole company has taken notice. Congratulations"

"You do realize, however, that you might have just put yourself out of a job. When the new owners come in they normally don't keep the Director of Finance. They bring in their own people."

The good news is that the new company has asked you to interview with them as well as all the other managers to stay on when the new company takes over the hotel, but it could just be out of respect and there might not really be a job for you after the interview.

Several weeks later, Jon did interview with the nationally recognized new hotel company. The date for the sale was finally set, after Jon David was able to resolve the conflicts between the office building and the hotel ownership. Then the managers and employees just had to wait to find out who would receive offers and who would receive "turn down letters."

The day finally arrived.

"Well are you feeling good or bad about the chances of you having a job?" Terry Manson the Director of Engineering asks Jon, as he stood in the doorway of Jon's office.

"Well, I woke up at 3:00am this morning with the word, "seven" in my head." responded Jon.

"What does that mean?" Terry said.

"Well, I took it to mean that there would be seven managers who did not get offer letters and one of them would be me." Jon responded.

"I am a little nervous" Terry said "you know being sixty one years old and the fact that the new company does not operate with Directors of Engineering at properties this size, I don't think they will offer me a job either."

"Well good luck" Jon said, somewhat realizing that Terry was probably right, they probably would not keep him. And it would be harder for him to find a job.

Terry dropped by several hours later and said "well I'm out. They gave me walking papers. I leave in two weeks."

"Did you hear what happened?" Terry went on to explain "They told Chris that he didn't have a job, after seventeen years of working here and doing a great job they didn't pick him up! And to make it worse, they tried to make him feel better by telling him that Sergio, the Executive Chef, was not going to be picked up either. Well, Sergio's dad died several days ago and now everyone in the hotel is going to know that he doesn't have a job before he does! You would have thought a big company like that would have been a little better at taking over new properties."

"Yes, well sometimes things don't always go as planned." Jon responded to Terry.

"When you going?" Terry questioned.

"I just got the call, I am next."

"Good luck" Terry offered words of encouragement to Jon. Yet, in the back of Jon's mind he already knew that they were not going to offer him the job but he felt like he still had to go through the motions.

"Come on in" Mrs. Matthews said as he walked into the meeting room, which had been set up to handle the job and exit interviews."

"Well, are you going to keep me or send me packing?" Jon asked.

"I am afraid we are not going to offer you the job. We normally don't run our operations with such high dollar financial people. It's just not economically feasible for us to keep you." Mrs. Matthews said with a very pleasant smile on her face.

Jon could not help but think back to what he had recently read about the Cambodian's Khmer Rouge. They had a saying to the workers. "To keep you is no gain and to lose you is no loss" and how when even getting ready to murder someone the Khmer Rouge would be polite and smiling.

"Funny isn't it?" Jon remarked.

"What?" Mrs. Matthews said seeming surprised at how well all the managers who were not offered jobs, instead they just accepted their fate as if they were sheep being lead to the slaughter.

"Well, I have already saved the new company coming in over hundred and seventy thousand dollars a year. And for every year in the future, additionally, I saved the last company close to a million dollars of money. Saying that my salary is not "economically feasible" seems utterly absurd. Jon got up, turned sharply on his heel and left the room.

His last day on the job was now only now barely over a month away. And he was now realizing that he had actually helped make the sale possible. He had inadvertently hurt some of the same people he had only wanted to help.

Chapter Eleven - Leaving Cambodia

Thunnysok looked at the long line of people in the field and thought how it resembled a line of ants. Thousands of refugees strung out in an absolute perfect line, each one stepping into the steps of the person in front of him. People lined up as far as the eye could see, each one taking their turn to walk through the mine fields.

Thunnysok and the group had been traveling for days. Thunnysok had not slept or eaten much in the past several days. The line of humans going through the mine field had started at daybreak. First to enter the mine field were the men who had once been soldiers. They went into the fields to mark the location of known mines. Then they would instruct all of those behind them to walk only in their footsteps. "Ants" Thunnysok said. "Be quiet, Thunnysok" her mother quickly scolded. "Be quiet and concentrate on where you are stepping."

The line of people had been moving for the past four hours. There was no resting while going through the mine field. There was no place to stop the line, lest someone be pushed into an uncharted section of the mine field. One could only go forward. There was no turning back.

Thunnysok shifted her weight adjusting the backpack she was carrying. Inadvertently, she had stepped off the path and into the uncharted mine field. "Thunnysok!" Mother Chim scolded. "Sorry Mother" Thunnysok replied "Thunnysok there is no 'sorry' in these situations, there is only life or death. There is no room for sorry."

"I will do better." Thunnysok promised and then lowered her head and looked away. "Little one, hand me your backpack and

I will carry it" came a voice from behind her.

With that, the Thunnysok slowly handed the man, who was in his 60's her back pack. "Thank you" Thunnysok said as she handed him the pack. The man looked at her and smiled. "I wish my grandfather had been more like this man, kind and gentle." Thunnysok thought as she turned back around and kept moving in the long line of humans.

"Click"

Several minutes had passed since Thunnysok had handed the older man her back pack. He was less than 3 feet from her when Thunnysok heard the "click" of his foot stepping on the mine. The mine exploded and the man's body was thrown forward in a protective manner that shielded Thunnysok from the full blast of the mine's explosion. Thunnysok could see parts of his body fly past her and there was the deafening sound of the blast. Most of his body landed about 12 feet away from the line. Everyone seemed relieved that there was one less mine for them to worry about and they continued as if nothing had happened. Death came quickly and frequently in Cambodia.

Three years, eight months and twenty days after the Khmer Rouge had won power, the slave state came to an abrupt end. On December 25th, 1978 the Vietnamese launched an all out invasion into Cambodia from several different sections. In what had been a failed theory, on how to defend the country against invasion, the Khmer Rouge had put most of the best men along the borders of Vietnam. The Vietnamese quickly broke through these static defenses and there were not enough Khmer Rouge soldiers behind the front lines to stop the Vietnamese Army from advancing. Within several days they had taken the greater part of eastern Cambodia. The Central Party Leadership packed up in their Mercedes and large Town Cars and quickly headed to the west, towards Thailand. Phnom Penh, a city which had contained 1.8 million people in 1975, was now occupied by less than 40,000 people. By January 7th 1979, the city had been abandoned by all the top leadership. Defenses were hastily set up around the city by men who ended up fleeing their positions. The Vietnam Army entered the city less than two weeks after the military offensive had started.

Between January and March of 1979, the struggle continued between Khmer Rouge forces and the Vietnamese. The Khmer Rouge launched important attacks from their bases, which were not far removed from the rice-producing central plain. The Khmer Rouge forces persisted in frontal assaults. However, Vietnamese tactical flexibility and greater firepower soon forced them to retreat into the mountain ranges along the Thai frontier. Some fled into the dense forests in the southwest, where there was a shortage of food. There were many military units collapsing from hunger, because no new supplies were arriving from China.

April and May brought the beginnings of a flood of refugees, coming out of Cambodia, and into camps in Thailand. The numbers swelled noticeably after September, when people in Cambodia realized that not enough rice had been planted for harvesting in November and December.

"We must move closer to the Thai border" Mother Chim said to the girls. "You need to pack your things so we can go to Battambang. It will be safer there, and we are more likely to be able to get food assistance from that government." She continued talking to the girls and others in the tent. They were leaving the region of the Great Lake and moving north along Highway 5 towards Battambang.

The Chim family started the walk toward Battambang. At first, they were with a large other group of people. But, Botum was ill and her illness slowed down the family down. Finally they were separated from the larger group. After several miles they had to carry Botum, Thunnysok's sister. Even though she was two years old than Thunnysok she did not have the energy to walk. They would be walking and she would get slower and slower until someone had to carry her. Nobody really understood why she has having problems walking or what was going on inside of her young and fragile body.

A journey that should have taken less than a week was now stretching into two weeks.

Botum sat down on a log in the jungle.

"Sister, we must keep moving." Thunnysok said to her sister.

"I cannot go anymore, I do not have the energy to walk, and I just want to lie down here on the ground and die." Botum said to her sister.

"I have been sick for a long time, and I know that I am slowing you and mother down. I am increasing the chances of you and mother dying as well by having to wait on me." She continued.

Mother Chim and Thunnysok were both now beside Botum

"Mother, just leave me here." Botum said to her. Her mother picked her up again.

"Mother, you cannot carry me the whole way. Leave me. I am ready to die." Botum in her weakened state argued.

"Botum, I have already lost too many of my family. I will die with you before I would leave you again." Mother said with a great deal of fortitude. Then she picked up her daughter and continued the journey to Battambang, arriving there three weeks later, from what should have only been a week long journey.

After being in Battambang for several months, Mother Chim and the rest of the family decided they had to move closer to the border of Thailand. Maybe they should cross over into the Thailand and enter a refugee camp some were suggesting. Food was becoming a serious issue. They moved to a place called Preah Vihear in Cambodia.

Cambodia became the most heavily bombed country in the world from the aerial attacks by the US. Now it was also the most heavily land mined country, per square mile.

Landmines were used around the borders of bases, to protect roads, paths, fields and any other areas that needed protection. There were over 10 million land mines scattered throughout the country.

Even today, there are still approximately 50 people a day who are injured or killed by the landmines. Yet, at no time was it greater than during the Khmer Rouge years.

The columns of refugees heading into Thailand were protected by the Freedom Fighters. Most of the Freedom Fighters had once been Khmer Rouge soldiers, but now fought against Pol Pot and his cronies. Among the refugees were the Chim family as well as many other families and children who had survived the Khmer Rouge work camps.

Thunnysok herself had barely survived the mine fields, the day before she had one go off within three feet of her, killing a kind man who had offered to carry her backpack. The process of going through minefields was horrible. The tedious concentration required as one watched each step through the field to make sure they stepped in the footprint of the person in front of them. There were long lines of people crossing fields and forest area to get to the refugee camps along the border.

There were areas along the paths and roads, which were cleared of mines, so that people could gather and camp for the night before starting out again, the next day.

The Cheng family was also making the trek to Thailand. The children, given the absence of war and pain, found a way to talk and play with each other.

"This is horrible. I wish we could find something else to eat." Pakchan Cheng said to her older brother, Phuong. "Would you see if you can find me something else to eat?" She said sweetly. He was now the man of the family, since there was no father.

"Sister, I will go look for you." Phuong said, getting up from the ground where he had been resting.

"Be careful there are many mines around." She said to Phuong.

"Don't go!" the other sister said.

"It's too dangerous to be looking for food out there! Many people died on the mines today!"

"Sister, I am always careful. I can see where the mines were placed and go around them." He said with a small confident smile, almost skipping off in the direction of the jungle clearing.

Fifteen minutes later. Pakchan Cheng heard a mine explosion. She knew in her heart and an overwhelming sickening feeling that the mine had killed her brother.

Pakchan's sister came running and crying to her younger sister and Pakchan knew without any question, her brother was dead. Pakchan was remorseful every day for the rest of her life. She had asked her brother to go find her more food. Pakchan blamed herself that she had caused his death. Phuong's body was left where it fell in the blown out land mine hole. One of his arms and one leg had been blown off of the trunk of his body.

Pakchan Cheng cried through the night and the next morning as they left the place where Phuong had died. Guilt often dwelled in the minds of those who survived. They felt guilt for the things they had done or guilt for surviving when others had not.

The next morning they were all near the camp at Preah Vihear, a huge Cambodian refugee camp with well over 42,000 people who had stopped right before crossing over into the Thailand. The normal border crossing, several miles down the road, was closed and heavily protected by guards and Thai soldiers. They were not letting any more refugees from Cambodia cross the border.

There were Vietnamese soldiers trying to track down and

eliminate the Khmer Rouge. And there were Khmer Rouge fighters who were fighting to control the camp. This battle for the camp began on June 8th, 1979. A group of Vietnamese soldiers approached and the Freedom Fighters, who were guarding the camp, opened fire. The camp was spread out. On its southern end, the Khmer Rouge was also trying to break into it. There was fighting on three sides of it. The people in the camp decided it was time to cross one more mine field and try to get across the Thai border. There was a large mountain fronting the Thailand side of the border. This would be the best spot to cross.

There were sounds of machine guns firing in the distance and more from the southern end of the camp. The refugees started spreading out to climb up the mountainside.

Thunnysok could see the fighting going on outside the camp as her mother, sister and she got higher and higher up the side of the mountain. They had been going up the mountain slowly. Several hours had passed since they started the climb; Thunnysok became very thirsty and was starting to feel hungry. Yet, Mother Chim kept Thunnysok and Botum moving.

There were thousands of refugees going up the mountain. Before reaching the top, troops from Thailand appeared on the mountain ridge and started firing down at the refugee's, killing many of them. The refugees were forced to turn, running back down the mountain.

"RUN!" Mother Chim frantically yelled to Botum and Thunnysok "RUN!" Thunnysok turned around and started back down the mountain side, running, tumbling and getting back up to run more.

Thunnysok was running when the woman beside her tripped on

a land mine and blew her leg away from her body. She fell to the ground but no one stopped to help her. Everyone was fleeing, running down the mountain and away from the gunfire. But having escaped the Thai Army, they found themselves forced back into mine fields where more would die before reaching the safety of the camp again.

Then an even worse sound filled the air, the loud boom was unmistakable. The Thai Army was shelling the refugee's.

At the bottom of the mountain they stopped to rest and catch their breath. They had managed to put some distance between themselves and the soldiers.

The two girls and Mother Chim hid behind a small cluster of trees. They were resting when they heard overhead a whistling sound overhead in the sky. They had heard the sound many times in the past. An artillery shell was coming in their direction. But there was only a couple of seconds between the sound of the shell dropping and the shell actually hit the ground. The reflexes of the girls and mother seemed to be in slow motion each certain they were facing their last moments on earth.

The 75 mm artillery shell hit the ground the ground only several feet away. Mother Chim and the girls looked at each other. The shell had stuck in the ground and it was a dud!

The shooting and bombing chased them off the mountain and back across the mine field to the camp, where they were trapped in the midst of the fighting between the Vietnamese, Khmer Rouge and now the Thailand military.

The fighting went on for four days before the International Red Cross and United Nations got involved and they were able to organize a cease fire between the three groups.

Leaving Cambodia and crossing into Thailand would have to wait just a little bit longer.

Tran Sary had been wandering in the jungle for weeks. He was now seriously malnourished. Finally he wandered back into the district where he had grown up. At first, he didn't seem to recognize the countryside. But, when he finally did, he was glad to be back in a familiar place.

Tran found his house in complete ruins. There was nothing left to salvage. He was able to find the graves of his mother and rest of the family, even his fathers' grave was there. They appeared to have been hastily made, Son Sary, he thought. Son must have come back and buried them that day they had said goodbye at the cave.

Tran, standing beside the graves, trying to decide what to do, thought about the safety of the secret cave. It was harder to find than Tran had imagined that it might be. There was a lot of overgrowth in the jungle area, maybe his memories had faded more than he ever realized. Tran found the entrance and went into the cave. He knew that it would provide shelter and a safe hiding place, but not much in the way of food or other supplies. Sometimes the mind can be a powerful weapon and also a dangerous one. Memories were becoming a Cambodian tragedy. It was a country that was losing entire families, and trying to forget it.

To Tran's surprise, once he got inside the cave, he saw that there were many boxes there. There were containers of water and food. There was also a machine gun and ammunition. There was everything that one would need to hide out and even protect himself. There was only one person who could have supplied the cave - his brother, Son Sary. Tran knew that no matter what happened over the years, Son was trying to help him.

During the Khmer Rouge days, in the work fields and through the many murders Tran had witnessed he had found himself wanting to curse the memories of his brother. Why had his brother not found him? Why had he not been able to save him and his family? Yet deep in his heart, Tran knew his brother loved him and was trying to help him. The supplies were proof that he brother was still looking out for him and loved him.

Tran decided that he would rest, eat and nourish himself before again heading out to the dangers of the surrounding countryside. Occasionally, he could still hear the fighting, in the distance, between the Khmer Rouge and the Vietnamese.

One day he was looking inside one of the boxes and noticed a letter. There was a small folded note at the bottom of the box of food. Tran opened the letter and it read:

"I am probably already dead as you read this letter. I thought I would do my country some good and instead I just became an instrument of evil. There were many good Khmer Rouge soldiers and those who cared about the people and tried to find ways to help them. Remember the good in me and the love I had for you and our family.

Make your way to Thailand.

Love, your brother _ SS

Tran was very sad thinking about his brother. He would always remember him.

Two months later, Tran felt well enough to make the journey and the food supplies were now running very low. Tran left the cave and headed out looking for neighbors that might still be alive. Finding some neighbor's from the past, Tran was able to get a better idea of the situation in the country. The Vietnamese had taken over most of the central farmlands. The Khmer Rouge counter attacked and had done very badly in a head to head combat with the Vietnamese military.

The neighbors were able to tell him where he could meet up with a column of refugees heading to Thailand. The group had the protection of Freedom Fighters and it would be safer to go with them. He gave the neighbors some of his supplies before he headed out.

Several weeks later, he ended up at Preah Vihear, in a large refugee camp. Earlier in the day he had seen a little girl that looked familiar, Thunnysok. There was the little girl that he had known in the city of Phnom Penh before the fall.

"Thunnysok" Tran said to her. She turned around, but she did not recognize Tran.

"Tran" Mother Chim said as she realized who had called out Thunnysok's name. Tran and Mother Chim smiled and hugged. They were glad to see each other again. After all this time, it was nice to see someone from her former life had survived.

That night, they talked about things that happened and how life had changed so much over the years. It was nice having someone that knew your history and who you were and where you had lived and worked before the fall of the capital.

The phone rang in Jon David's office.

"Accounting, this is Jon David." Jon answered the phone.

"Hi, this is Angela…I am going to be in the area and was hoping you would want to grab a bite to eat." Angela said.

"Sure," Jon responded, he always looked forward to seeing her. "Hey also, I was going to tell you that there is a meeting next Thursday of the Asian Association and I was wondering if you wanted to go." She continued.

"Yes, that would be great. I don't have any plans that night." Jon replied.

"You never do, what's the deal, a single guy and no plans?" Angela said joking with him.

"You, dear, I am holding out for someone like you and those just don't come along every day." Jon said jokingly.

"Yeah, yeah, whatever." Was her normal sarcastic response, when she didn't know what else to say.

An hour later they were eating at a Thai restaurant that was close to the hotel.

"I have something I want to share with you." Jon said. Angela could tell he was tense about whatever he was going to say.

"What is it?" She asked cautiously.

"I told you once that I wanted to find out more about what happened to your father. So I decided to do a background check on you and some of the things I was curious about, concerning you. Some things that you did and said did not make much sense." Jon continued.

"Like you told me that your birthday was in July and when I checked all the records they have your birthday listed in December." Jon said slowly.

"So you have been really checking on me?" Surprised but not really offended as Jon thought she might be.

"Well, I don't know whether to be offended that you checked or flattered that you care enough to get to the truth about my life." Angela said with a smile.

"When we were applying to come to the United States, my uncle who was filling out the forms did not know our birthdays. So he just decided to put December 16th on all the application forms.

"So you are not really sure when your birthday is?" Jon responded.

"Well, I think it's in the middle of July, maybe the second week, but no I am not totally sure." She said slowly.

"Okay, I have another question; the marriage records list your name not as Chim but rather as "Kimson".

"When I was going through the immigration process, the lady told me I could pick any name I wanted, that many of the people pick names to reflect a more American sounding name. I just picked it out of the air." She explained easily.

"Why Kimson?' Jon said as he become more puzzled.

"Why not, I was only 11 eleven years old and I had a chance to pick any name. Don't be so surprised. I have already had five different names in my lifetime already. The Khmer Rouge was always changing their names to protect themselves." She said.

"Oh, so what is your real Cambodian name?" Jon David questioned further.

"Well, the first year my mother called me Kontaknika, but that was the Queens' real name and my mother thought the name might cause problems with others, so she changed my name to Thunnysok."

"Well, Thunnysok it's a pleasure to finally meet you after all the emails, lunch dates, and time together." Jon David said somewhat jokingly and somewhat sarcastically.

"Oh hush. It's just me" She said smiling.

"I have some more questions. I was trying to research what happened to your dad. I am pretty good about going through old newspapers articles, and I could not find anything on your dad. There were no stories in the Houston Chronicle about your dad's death. So I decided to write to the City of Houston, under the freedom of information act and see what I could find out about the murder of your father."

"Here is the letter they sent me last month." Jon David said as he pulled out the letter from the City of Houston assistant district attorney handing it to Angela (Thunnysok).

Angela read the letter which confirmed that her father had been murdered on that date but that it was a closed case file, which meant that they had appealed to the State Attorney General's Office to keep it sealed from the public.

"So the City of Houston doesn't want to share any details of the murder with you?" She was puzzled.

"The City appealed to the State Attorney General to keep them sealed and I got this letter this week ago from the State saying that they were agreeing with the City of Houston to keep the records sealed."

"It looks like your father's murder investigation is still open." Jon continued.

"I am surprised you went to all that effort to find out about me and my father. I feel honored that you cared enough to get to the truth about me rather than just trying to get down my pants." She said bowing her head slightly.

"Oh great, 20,000 emails later and you still think I am trying to get down your pants!" Jon said laughing.

"Well, you are persistent" She chuckled.

"There are some other things that don't add up. You told me that you thought your step mother might have ordered his death for insurance money. But I found her address and the value of her house and she lives very modestly. Her house is not worth very much at all, there is no sign that she has all this money that you claim she has." He continued.

"Well, many Asians do not show they have money, because they keep it hidden." Angela replied.

"She has done a very good job of keeping it hidden." Jon David responded.

"You don't think she got all that insurance money?" Angela

questioned.

"No, I don't. Which means your idea of her putting a hit on your dad really doesn't make sense. Also, the fact that your dad was wearing a bullet proof vest for the weeks leading up to his murder leads me to believe that it was someone close enough to know him and yet not in his immediate house, like your step mother. One doesn't wear a bullet proof vest if the person is in the same house." Continuing Jon added. "They get the hell out of the house because they have to sleep at night and not worry about the person killing them!" Jon David continued with his theory.

"You don't think she was behind the murder do you?" Angela said.

"No. I don't. I think the murderer had to be someone who knew him and was extremely angry at him, and did not care about the money at all. I think this was a "Kum" murder." Jon David said quietly.

"I am very impressed that you know our culture so well" Angela said surprised.

"I've read many books about your culture and history. One conclusion I came to was that it's a miracle you survived those early years in Cambodia - you should have been marked for death and there has to be some incredible stories of how you survived. You should not be sitting in this chair right now. You should be dead." Jon David said.

"What do you want to hear?" Angela said, almost beaten down, but feeling ready to release her past to him. She felt that Jon David deserved to know the truth. He had taken the time, made such effort, and never wavered in trying to understand who she was in her soul and heart.

"I want you to start at the first memory of your childhood and then walk me forward to how you got out of Cambodia. I want to hear all you know - all memories you have." Jon David prodded.

"There are many things I have forgotten and many that are too painful to remember." She answered her eyes glistening with tears.

"Give me that pain. Give me those memories. The only way to truly be free of those painful, sleepless nights filled with bad memories is to give them to someone else who cares and loves you and can validate them." Jon David coaxed.

"Okay… I was standing in the courtyard of the headquarters in line with everyone else and the Khmer Rouge cadre was yelling at us…." Angela started to share her first memory of her life in Cambodia.

That day Jon did not go back to work. They stayed at the restaurant and talked all afternoon. She shared the stories and memories of the many painful things she had endured during the years of the Khmer Rouge.

Son Sary gathered the Eastern District soldiers around the camp fire. Standing up and pacing around it as he spoke.

"We had some success today in attacking and slowing down the column of men from those bastards Mok and Pauk. They will be back. They will strike in greater numbers and they will smash those of us who stay. Those of you who chose to go to Vietnam and form a resistance force should go. Bring back the Vietnamese army and defeat this evil Khmer Rouge Regime.

They have destroyed our lands and destroyed so many people's lives.

"I will go to Vietnam, I will form a resistance force and I will take some of the men with me." Heng Samrin said.

"I will go as well." Hun Sen said.

"You will need to leave tonight, to make it there before Mok and Pauk close all the escape routes out of the country. They will try to kill all of us and destroy as many people as possible in the Eastern District. We will need to spread word for the people to flee to Vietnam or at least get out of the Eastern District. I will stay to help them get out. I will try and slow down the military operations" continued Son Sary.

"They will eventually kill you." Heng said to Son Sary.

"Everyone dies, but not everyone dies well." Son replied. "I helped this monster of a government come to power. Now, I must help destroy the beast."

The next morning, the soldiers said goodbye to each other and those who were heading to Vietnam started the journey east. Those who were staying to fight and die alongside Son Sary headed north. Over the next two months, Son Sary and his men were able to save many lives by helping villagers escape the wrath of Pol Pot. However, over 100,000 people died in the eastern district, at the hands of the Pol Pot.

At first, Son Sary was successful, using his excellent military tactics to strike and run guerrilla operations against Mok and Pauk. Then the more fire fights they got into, the less ammunition they had to work with. Casualties among his men were increasing. Food was becoming very scarce.

"Shoot me" the wounded soldier begged Son Sary.

"You know if they capture me, they will torture me. With this leg wound I will never be able to keep up with the men. I will only slow you down." The captain in his small army pleaded. He had fought closely with Son Sary, through many years.

"You know that the enemy is too close. I cannot shoot you." Son Sary whispered.

"Then cut off my head. Do not let them have my head, take my head and bury it in a place they will not find it." The captain pleaded with Son Sary.

Son knew the man was right. To leave him, meant torture and a much more painful death.

"Yes my friend. I can do at least that for you." Son Sary said with the firm resolve of a man who had killed many men and had witnessed the worst that war had had to offer. But to kill a loyal man, a good man, a longtime friend! That is difficult, even for a man like Son Sary.

Taking a machete from his belt, the captain took off his helmet and handed the machete to Son Sary.

"Here use mine; I just sharpened it last night. My machete will cut much better than yours. You have been using your machete cutting thru the jungle all day." He said with a small smile on his face.

"Be quick, waiting on death is the worse part of dying." He said as he turned over and put his neck out on a log to make it easier for Son to cut off his head.

Son struck swiftly and head rolled to the ground, landing face up with eyes open, looking at Son, with what seemed like a smile.

Son wanted to cry, but being a leader of men, this was never an option. In the leading men, one had to hide their emotions. Son pushed on, deeper into the jungle.

Son's men had been pushed back into a small area of jungle and were now surrounded on several sides by the troops who were sent to capture him and his remaining men. Several days later, Son was trying to make his way out of the jungle at night when he tripped on a landmine. Both of his feet were blown off. Bleeding and trapped on the ground, Son struggled to get his own weapon to kill himself.

Troops from Mok's army soon appeared and captured the remaining men who were with him. They kicked away Son Sary's weapons.

"Is this the end of the great Son Sary?" One of Mok's soldiers' questioned.

"Son Sary's fate will be to die a painful death in a dense jungle with no family, friends and no proper burial funeral. No one will remember you or what you did." The soldier spit on him as he bled on the ground.

Son Sary knew he was dying as he faded in and out of consciousness. His mind went back to the days of his youth, to those pleasant memories of his family, thoughts of the girl he had planned to marry. Life before the Khmer Rouge days, before his life and history had gone so wrong in Cambodia.

After bleeding to death, Son's head was severed and taken to Mok, Pauk, and Pol Pot as proof that the resistance in the Eastern District was over and that Son Sary was dead.

The rest of Son Sary's men were shipped off to S-21 to face the horrors of torturous deaths.

"Do you want me to pick you up tonight, so we can go together?" Angela asked.

"Sure that would be great, but it's supposed to be heavy rain tonight. So the weather might not be cooperative." Jon continued.

"It's okay; I will be by after work to get you." Angela continued.

"I look forward to seeing you later then." Jon replied.

  The last couple of days had been really good, with Angela. Not that any day was bad, but the emotional barriers that had existed were all gone. She was now open to sharing the memories of her past. Emotionally, Jon was feeling closer to Angela. The stories of her survival only made him respect and love her more. She had become a living hero who had survived the worst that the world had to offer. Yet, whether by the hand of God, or just plain stupid luck, she was still alive, although she carried the emotional scars from the trauma suffered during childhood.

"I am realizing more how one's childhood affects a person's future." Jon David said to Angela after she showed up at the hotel and they went into the bar to have a drink.

"What do you mean?" Angela said taking off her coat. The rain had just started to pour down as she had walked into the lobby to get Jon David.

"Well, we come out of our childhoods with deep emotional needs and then I think we spend the rest of our lives either trying to fix them or trying to feed them." Jon explained his theory.

"What needs do I have?" Angela questioned.

"Your needs have been many. The fact that you were alone for so long, that you lost so many people in your life, has left you with a fear of people leaving. And you find it hard to trust the words and actions of others. You're afraid to love and care deeply. But those are just a few of the many things I see you need. Want something to drink?" Jon asked.

"That rain is really coming down now. I don't think in Houston is a good place to be when it rains like this. There's a chance of flash flooding. You know, once I was on my way home on I-45 and there was this massive traffic jam on the side road. When I got home, I found out that two ladies had driven into the water and their car stalled and that within an hour they were dead. Imagine two women drowning in that intersection? Now, when I pass it I think about how quickly things can change in life in general." Jon said.

Jon and Angela had drinks, talked more about the past and relaxed as the rain continued. After several hours, Angela suddenly asked, "Are you trying to seduce me tonight?"

"Well, I never start out to trying to seduce you. But I think that, if it ever happens, I would be very open to it." Jon replied.

"That is a very honest statement. But it's never going to happen." Angela responded.

"I know you think I might be shy and that I would not make the first move, but that is not the case, if I wanted to have you physically, I would make the first move. I would seduce you. It's just that I have never been physically attracted to you like I was to Donald." Angela said.

"With Donald I made the first move to kiss him. I was very open to going to his warehouse to have sex. It was easy for me to get naked and have sex with him because I was so physically attracted to him and so in love with him." Angela continued.

"Yes, you have told me many times how much you were in love with him. Your ideas of love, and mine, do not line up. I believe that you can be attracted to someone and love what is on the outside and the inside both. Donald was only making you his little Asian play toy. He was never serious about a relationship. And if you had bothered to take the time to really get to know him, before having sex with him, you would have realized the errors of your actions and not be here a year and half later, wishing you were still with him." Jon responded realizing that he was starting to get upset with her after having such a wonderful night.

"Why are you getting so jealous of him?" Angela inquired.

"I am sick of hearing about him! I am sick of being compared to him! I am sick of his name. And mostly, I resent that you still yearn to be with a guy who used you, and how confused you are about love and the meaning of love." Jon said with exasperation.

"You probably have 4 other guys who want to have sex with you, Ernesto, just being one and several more you go to lunch with and talk to. Sometimes I just feel like you have been using me to help you heal, to get over Donald and occupy your time." Jon continued.

"Sorry, I didn't mean to hurt your feelings. It's just that I want the complete package. The deep emotional connection I have with you and the deep physical connection I had with Donald." Angela said apologetically.

"Let me just recap this. We have talked and shared everything for a year and half. You have told me, through that whole time, what an angel I have been helping you to get over Donald, helping you to grow and change and cope with Simon better. But now, you are telling me that what you are really looking for is that sexual connection you had during an affair while you were married?" Jon paused to take a breath, and then continued "and that you love what you have with me emotionally, but that it will always be just a plutonic friendship?" Jon finished.

"Yes," Angela interjected.

"Well, what you really need to do is figure out why the two men you want do not include your husband. I think you need to go work on your marriage. You know, tonight, I realize something about myself. I want the same thing you do. I want the "total package" too, the deep emotional love of someone else and the deep physical touch that comes with that loving another person so deeply." Jon expressed.

"I need to be going" Jon said as he ushered Angela up getting ready to leave. Jon was ending the conversation, something he rarely wanted to do in the past. But, he could no longer talk about Donald. This was it. He'd had enough.

Jon walked Angela to the car and then drove to Clear Lake and his apartment. Jon David had an apartment that he had ended up in when his marriage ended, because he was not willing to give up communications between Angela and himself. And now he was wondering if he had made a huge mistake.

While driving to the apartment Jon's cell phone rang. It was Angela.

"Are you mad?" Angela questioned Jon.

"Yes, mad and hurt." Jon truthfully responded.

"I am very sorry that I can't give you more. I find that I still want Donald, as crazy as it seems. I don't know what is wrong with me." Angela continued.

"Maybe we need to stop talking for a while and see how things go. You need to find a woman that can give you more, and I need to figure out my life. Sorry, I have to go, it's still raining here and Simon is coming to the car door with an umbrella to help me get into the house." Angela said.

"Okay" Jon replied.

"I am sorry." Angela said and then the connection went dead.

The International Red Cross and United Nations were successful at getting the Thai government to open their borders to Cambodian Refugees. Several camps were established in the southeastern sections of Thailand.

It took a great deal of effort from the world bodies to bring about a cease fire at the camp where Thunnysok's family and Tran Sary were. But after a month, they were allowed to cross over into Thailand. Thunnysok and her sister had been allowed to play like normal little girls around the camp. They were not allowed to get too far away or get too close to the Thai guards. They made crude remarks to the refugees and treated them very badly, sometimes even assaulting and raping the girls.

Thunnysok's father was nowhere around. Vichem had left the village where he had seen Thunny but then disappeared from the village when he ran off with a local woman.

This was before Thunnysok had seen him. And it had been over half a year since he had been with the family. Then he suddenly showed up in camp, one day, out of the blue, looking for his family.

The reunion of husband and wife was cool at best. Even Tran, who was 10 years younger than Mother Chim, was disgusted with her husband for showing up to take care of his family after the worse was over to him.

Several weeks passed as Mr. & Mrs. Chim worked at reuniting together. Finally Mother Chim gave in and allowed her spouse to sleep in the same bed. Not long afterward, she became pregnant with another child. Mother Chim probably decided that after living through seeing so much death and dying, one finds bad human behavior easier to deal with. Mother Chim had lost two boys, and knew in her heart, that they had perished during the years of the Khmer Rouge.

After six weeks at the camp. Father Chim came running into the hut and said that everyone needed to hurry up and pack to get out of the camp. How quickly their lives changed again. They quickly packed and headed out through the gate that leads down into the jungle. The Chim family walked for several weeks before they were able to get into another camp. This camp had more guards and was a much safer place. Slowly Thunnysok was able to piece together what had happened in the camp. Apparently,

Father had married a female Khmer Rouge commander. When he ran off with the woman from the local village he had been captured by the Khmer Rouge. Slowly over time he was able to win the heart of the female commander and even married her, never telling her that he was already married to Mother Chim.

After Father had married the commander and lived with her for a time, he escaped. He went to the refugee camp and eventually found Mother Chim, who was still very much in love with him, even though she was bitter about what had happened.

The Khmer Rouge commander came to the refugee camp looking for Vichem Chim. She brought several of her soldiers with her and Vichem heard that she was there and asking for him. With that little head start he was able to get the family packed up and out the gate before she realized he had been there.

Vichem Chim was not a faithful man. He was a lover of many women. Mother Chim was elegant and graceful and stood by him through many of his exploits. Even in the new camp, Vichem's' eye had wandered and he found a woman who intrigued him. She had a family of her own as well. When the Chim family finally was sponsored by Mother Chim uncle to come to the United States Vichem would later sponsor this women to come to the United States to live in the same house as Mother Chim.

Tran was almost a year behind and finally was allowed to immigrate to the United States and also ended up in Houston, Texas.

Thunnysok did not remember much about coming to the United States except when they were flying over Houston she could not believe all the lights on the ground. Her ears were hurting so badly by the change in the cabin pressure that she was in a great deal of pain when the jet finally landed.

Their family migration party consisted of Mother and Father Chim, Botum and Thunnysok with her Aunt and Uncle. The processing through immigrations was slow. They were allowed to go to government housing for six days while waiting for their sponsoring uncle to pick them up and take them to his home.

It was six months before the Chims' were able to find a small apartment to live in as a family and then within the year, Tinnyka was born and they were able to move to a small house.

One day, the family was at the house when Vichem Chim brought home another woman along with her family. Vichem had sponsored another woman to the United States and wanted them to all live there in the house together.

Eventually, the insult that Mother Chim felt was so great that she moved out with Botum and eventually Thunnysok moved in with her as well. She was able to rent a house and decided to rent out the rooms to other Cambodians who were in need of a place to stay.

Tran Sary ended up renting one of these rooms.

The sale of the hotel did go through. There ended up being some issues and the new owners had asked Jon David to stay on for several more weeks. Jon was glad that he had been really busy, because every time he was idle he thought about Angela.

Since their last argument about Donald, there had been no more emails. Previously, Angela had emailed him every morning, midday, afternoon, night and middle of the night. Now there was nothing. No calls. No emails. No dropping in on him, at work to see what was going on. She had just disappeared.

Jon knew what was really going on; that they had been pulling at each other; and that Jon had finally had enough of hearing about Donald and what a wonderful guy he was. The truth was something so totally different. This was a test of wills, to see which of them could survive without the other. When you get used to sharing every day of your life with someone, and then suddenly pull away, the question is who will miss the other most. Jon David felt like he was going through another divorce. And, in a way, this one was more painful and depressing.

This last month at the hotel was difficult. There was so much work to do and so many details occupying Jon's thoughts. People like to refer to forgetting things as being absentminded. However, the truth of the matter is that one gets so much on their mind that details get missed because they are thinking too much. They don't forget them. They just get crowded out.

"Did you double check those prorating entries, like I had asked you to?" Deborah Sharp called to ask.

"I was in hurry and juggling 5 things at once. But yes, I looked at them and forwarded you a copy." Jon responded. "Why"

"I think they might be wrong." Deborah responded

"The numbers on the guest ledger looked out of balance and I checked them against the other reports which confirmed it." Deborah continued.

Jon pulled out the packet of information and, sure enough, the numbers for selling the hotel had an error in them.

"It looks like we screwed the pooch on this one." Jon calmly said.

"Yes, you did!" Deborah said and hung up.

"Is Deborah mad?" Enedina said standing at the door.

"Yes, she is mad but she is normally pretty good about forgiving and getting over things." Jon replied. "I don't blame her; sometimes it's hard to admit we make mistakes." Jon David's mind started to wonder about Angela and maybe, in her mind, she knew she had made a terrible mistake, but was finding it difficult to admit it to her.

"I am going to miss you." Enedina said to Jon David. "We don't say goodbye in the hotel business." Jon responded.

"Jon, I have worked with you for five years, and I always knew you were there, protecting me and making sure that I was doing okay. I just want you to know how much I appreciate it. I am going to miss you very much." Enedina started to tear up at the realization that her boss would no longer be a part of her day to day life.

"Thank you. I am going to miss you as well." Jon replied.

Yim Sombat woke that morning with throbbing pain in his whole body. One does not really sleep in s-21, but lies in a constant state of pain. There was also the moaning of other prisoners in pain from that day's torture. Yim had endured some incredible torture in the two weeks he was there. His head and arms were tied behind him and he was dunked into a water bucket until he'd almost drowned. He'd been beaten repeatedly. He'd had electrical shocks applied to his body, causing uncontrollable spasms as each bolt permeated his body.

There were days when Yim was brought into the quiet room, where the interrogators would be nice and smile as they offered him cigarettes to smoke and talk. Then days when he would be taken into the pain rooms, to be tortured within an inch of his life.

Yim was not taken first thing this morning, as he had been during the two preceding weeks. Instead he was left to lie on the floor. He did not mind that he was given the day off from the pain. It was a welcome relief. Late in the afternoon they came to get him. He was taken into the quiet room, the interrogators were waiting.

"We wanted to read your confession to you to make sure it is exactly correct." The interrogator said to him.

The interrogator read the twenty pages of confession back to Yim. It was only about five percent of true. The rest of it he made up to stop them from torturing him. The more information he could give them, the less likely they were to continue the torture. He felt badly that he had mentioned anyone's name in his confession he realized that they might end up here as well.

Yim tried to tell himself that they would find a way to escape this place, or they would find a way to talk their way out of being here. But deep inside he knew he had sentenced every person he had mentioned in his confession to death.

"If this is true, please sign your confession. This is your confession of your life."

Yim could no longer sign his name. He could only place a simple mark on the page, because his wrists and hands had been so badly damaged.

"Take him back to the cell" the chief interrogator said to the soldier.

"Sir, we are out of hoods right now." He apologetically said to the officer.

"Then let him see where he has been all this time." The officer replied. Normally, the prisoners had their heads covered, as they were walked to and from the cells. But on this day, Yim got to see his way back to the holding cell. He saw the walls of the building, bleeding red. The cells were washed down once every few days and the blood stained water ran out, causing an appearance of the building bleeding. Yim also saw a white prisoner coming down the hall, but he did not look up.

Several American's who had been classmates in California had traveled to Thailand to obtain a load of marijuana. They planned on sailing the cargo to Hawaii. But their boat got too close to the Cambodian coast, and they were picked up by the Khmer Rouge navy. They were taken to S-21 where they were tortured as CIA agents. They even confessed to being CIA agents since the young age of 12. Men will confess to anything given enough pain and pressure.

Yim was placed back into his cell and was not given any food. Several hours went by and the night had arrived. After dark, the cell doors opened. There was a sound of the guards entering the large cell block and the unlocking of the shackles that held the prisoners to the floor. There was not much talking among the guards, they normally talked more. The prisoners taken that night never came back.

This night they came and got Yim.

Yim's head was covered in a canvas bag and he had difficulty breathing. They tied his arms behind his back and led him down the hallway toward the interrogation room. But then the guards turned to the left and headed down a flight of stairs, they had to help Yim negotiate down the stairs since his face was covered.

Then Yim could feel the breeze on his face and he realized that he was outside of the building. He could hear sounds of other guards and prisoners nearby. Then he heard the word "lift" and he was hoisted up onto a truck. He could tell that the truck was filled with other people. When one prisoner said something, he was smacked in the face. Yim could hear the loud groan from the man. He also heard the sound of the baby in the mother's arms, crying, and wondered if this was the same baby that he had been hearing since he'd gotten to the prison.

After another half hour, the trucks started to move. Yim thought they were moving through the city and heading south, but he was not sure, because his head was still covered. But he could tell that they had turned left, coming out of the prison, and occasionally, he saw the dim lights of the city shinning in through the mask.

After about half an hour, the road got bumpier and Yim could tell that they were out in the country. The lights no longer shined through the canvas mask. And still, the baby cried.

Another half hour and the trucks pulled into a grassy area with less bumps and stopped. Then there was a voice calling numbers, someone was checking names on a list of who was on the trucks. Checking and double checking to make sure they had the correct people. Once this task was completed they were unloaded and walked across the field and up a small slope. Yim knew what was happening, he knew that was going to his death but still, he held onto a small hope that maybe the outcome will be different - maybe they are just taking us to another prison site. Maybe they are taking us somewhere else to interrogate us. Maybe they are going to release us into the countryside. Hope exists right up to the last second.

Yim was forced to kneel down. Then he heard the woman beside him say "Please do not kill me, I have done nothing!" in a small voice. The soldier beside him leaned down and said to her "If I do not kill you, then they will kill me." Then Yim heard the iron bar hit the back of her skull with a loud "crack" and she fell into the pit the prisoners were kneeling in front of.

Yim still heard that baby crying nearby and wondered what was going to happen to the baby?

Then the baby suddenly stopped crying.

Several days before leaving the hotel, the new owners came down to make sure they had a clear understanding of the shared service agreement between the hotel and the office complex.

Ross Adams, the acquisitions manager, stopped Jon David in the lobby.

"Jon, I just wanted to personally thank you for your help with the shared service agreement. Also, I wanted to introduce you to our Chief Operating Officer, Larry Blankstein and Zack Murrey, who will be the asset manager for the hotel."

"We heard that maybe you would not have a job once the sale goes through. I wanted to know if you might be interested in flying up to Dallas to discuss working for us directly - maybe supervise the accounting department of the hotel for the new ownership group." Larry, a shrewd businessman, said to Jon David.

Jon, surprised, but elated, said, "I would be very interested in talking more about the prospect of a job with your company."

"Well, here is the business card for Deborah Jones, the Director of Human Resources. Give her a call to make arrangements. I was thinking maybe next week, on Thursday, you could fly up." Larry continued.

"Yes, I will be available then. " Jon replied.

"Kismet" Jon thought to himself as he walked away. A word, that expresses the idea that sometimes fate plays a role in the way things work out. In this case the company, who had rejected him, would now be asking him questions about how to operate the hotel.

Jon left the conversation, feeling surprised, but glad.

This was a weekend that Angela had looked forward to. She was going sky diving. She was going no matter what her husband or anyone else said about it. Simon who had no desire to fly to 10,000 foot altitude in an airplane and then jump out, still he went with her.

Traveling to East Texas, Angela and Simon took classes on how to sky dive. Angela went up into the plane and did a tandem jump with her instructor. She felt the rush of falling to the earth. Maybe she liked facing the prospect of death. Having seen so much of it growing up, it held no fear for her. Death was an inevitable consequence of living. The parachute opened and she landed safety.

That weekend Angela found herself feeling closer to Simon than she had in a very long time. Thinking to herself "He did jump out of an airplane just to be closer to me."

Jon was in his office packing his belongings. He stopped to look at the portrait he had of Angela. It was a pencil drawing, which was done from a picture that Jon had received from her. Costing several hundred dollars, Jon had planned to give it to her as a gift for the grand opening of her new real estate office.

"I guess I should go ahead and send it to her" Jon thought to himself. Then reaching down to pick up the phone he dialed the purchasing agent for the hotel.

"Katherine" do you think you can do me a favor and drop off a portrait to someone?"

"Sure. Just print out the directions and I will take it by later tonight on my way home."

"Thanks Katherine, I'll drop it off in your office." Jon said.

The next day, Katherine with portrait in hand came walking back into Jon David's office.

"What happened? You weren't able to deliver it?" Jon seemed puzzled.

"Well I have some good news and some bad news" Katherine said with a smile on her face "The bad news as you can see I wasn't able to deliver the portrait."

"Okay" Jon responded

"So ask me the good news?" Katherine said again smiling with a huge smile. "Okay, what is the good news?" Jon played along.

"I got lost on my way there. So I called her and we talked for about ten minutes. She was so nice; she said she was going to a meeting and that she would come by later today to get it in person. Aren't you happy? She seemed like such a sweet person on the phone and you could tell she was excited." Katherine smiled.

"Yes, it will be good to see her, but I guess I am a little nervous too." Jon said.

"Why?" Katherine seemed puzzled by his comment.

"Oh, long story" Jon responded.

"I thought you would be happy" She repeated.

"I am." Jon said "I am."

About 3:45 Katherine came walking into Jon's office. "Look what I found down in the lobby" Katherine said with a smile

Getting up from his desk Jon David walked around to the door. There was Angela with a huge smile. She reached for him and gave him slight hug. There beside her was her daughter, with pigtails and radiant smile.

"Hi Angela and hi Meredith" Jon greeted them.

"Hi Jon," Angela said "I brought my helper with me. She has been helping me all week at work."

"Mommy, look it's a picture of you." Meredith said walking over to the portrait.

"Yes, Meredith" Angela said "That is what we came to pick up from Mr. Conner."

"Oh Mommy, it's a very pretty picture of you." A child's innocence comes out at moments like this.

Jon waited for any clues whether or not Angela wanted to stay and talk.

"Jon, would you like to go upstairs and talk for a few minutes? I think I have some explaining to do." Angela asked.

"Yes, I would appreciate that. I think you do owe me at least an explanation of what happened." Jon said politely but maybe still a little hurt by all that had happened.

The three of them went up to the restaurant. There were slow moving cars driving by. The sun was out, with small rolling clouds in the distance.

"I am pregnant." Angela said as they sat down on at the table.

"Wow, I guess there have been some changes in the last two months." Jon was completely shocked.

"I guess I do need to sit down" Jon said with a smile on his face.

"I guess I kind of wigged out when I found out. And it took a long time to adjust to the idea of having another child. It was not planned, at all." Angela admitted.

"I guess Simon is happy?" Jon continued.

"Yes, Simon is very happy. He has his wife back and will have another child. He is relieved the worst is behind us. Hopefully we can move forward with our lives together. I have been sick for the past couple of months. And only started feeling better in the past couple of days." Angela continued.

"Congratulations. I am happy for you." Jon politely said.

"Thank you, Jon. I was a bit concerned that you would not understand." Angela said with some regret.

"So catch me up from the night you and I were on a way to the Asian Association event…" Jon said, trying to put together the pieces of the puzzle since Angela had disappeared.

"I went to the event and then decided not to stay…I wanted to leave and did. I was just feeling very emotional about everything that was happening. So I decided to leave." Angela explained.

"And you didn't think I deserved an explanation, but instead left me to wonder if you were alive or dead, or hurt?" Jon questioned her.

"Jon we both know if you had really thought something had happened to me, you would have knocked down walls to find out what happened. You would have called or come to my house, or came by the office to see me. You would have found me any time you wanted to find me. I think you need to focus on dating and allow more people into your life, I figured you were better off without me in your life" Angela continued.

"Didn't you think I deserved an explanation?" Jon pressed her.

"Yes, you did, I am sorry. The best I can tell you is that I have had a really hard time the past couple of months, and yes, I have missed you very much." Angela said.

"I wrote Donald a letter. I sent my company information and told him I was pregnant and that I was doing really well and then mailed it to him. Knowing Donald, he probably just threw it in the trash. But, after I sent the letter, I have not thought about him again. He is gone from my memories. I don't care anymore." She said.

"I am happy for you Angela. Personally I think you allowed the man to exist in your mind more than in your life." Jon said reflecting back on the battles Angela had suffered over Donald.

"Yes, Jon, I feel like I am healed and I know that you were there, helping me, the whole time. I am sorry for the way I hurt you. I wish I could have given you more." She continued.

"I never asked you for anything more Angela, not then, not now." Jon said with a stern voice.

"I know. I am just trying to tell you that I see myself, and maybe the rest of the world, more clearly now. I am trying to tell you that I care about you and really do appreciate all that you have done to help me." Angela sounded genuine.

Meredith was climbing over the chairs and eating the ice cream they'd ordered for her, all the while, vying for mom's attention.

"She looks so much like you Angela." Jon changed the subject.

"My mother says she is exactly like me." Angela reflected.

"Yes, I can see the resemblance. I look at her and think of your childhood in Cambodia. It could have been her instead of you. It's really amazing that you survived." Jon sighed.

"Yes, I guess you are right. Amazing I survived and then ended up experiencing so much pain and then the death of my father here in America as well." She elaborated.

"You know, Angela, I have thought about your father's murder. And I know that you hated him and think that you don't really care. But I've come to the conclusion that there were only one or two people who had the motive to kill your father. I don't buy the idea that it was a robbery, because the three thousand dollars, was found with his body." Jon said.

"Yes, I have always felt that was the case." Angela agreed.

"So the murderer had to be someone with a motive for killing him." Jon continued.

"Yes, I told you that I have always believed the murderer was my step mother. She was starting to have an affair with some other man and took out a huge life insurance policy on my father." Angela began.

"Well, that was one suspect but you realize that there was one other person, on your side of the family, who has to be a suspect as well…your step- father, Tran Sary." Jon announced.

"Why?" Angela was shocked.

Well, if the police were checking your trash cans, and looking around your house, then they must have felt like maybe someone in your family had murdered him." Jon said.

"But why?" Angela questioned.

"Many men in the world have been killed by rivals. If your dad still loved your mother and wanted to come back into her life, he would have been threatened by the man who now loves her. There would have been a rivalry between the two men. So yes, I think your step father might have killed your real father. "

"I just don't think he did it." Angela stuttered.

"No, of course you wouldn't. Angela, no one wants to believe that someone they are close to would do something like that…but the truth is someone did." Jon pointed out the obvious.

"I chose to believe that he was murdered by his ex-wife. She was very evil. This is one Jon, you are just going to have to let go of. This is one mystery that maybe just needs to stay a mystery." Angela sighed.

"I have always believed the dead call out for justice, even now. Whether in Cambodia or in America, the dead seek peace and justice." Jon said solemnly.

"Maybe…" She agreed.

Jon and Angela spent another 45 minutes talking, until they could both feel time winding down.

"I guess I should be going now." Angela said looking at him sadly, it seemed like a part of her wanted to stay just a little bit longer."

"Come on, I will help you with the portrait to your car." Jon offered.

Jon led Angela and Meredith to the parking garage. Just before getting to the car, Meredith looked at Jon and said "Do you mind if I carry the portrait of my mommy?"

"Sure, here you go." Jon said handing her the portrait. The portrait was almost the same size as Meredith. Angela got the door and Jon started to help Meredith put it in the car.

"My mommy is really pretty" Meredith said to Jon David.

"Yes, Meredith. Your mother is a very pretty woman." Jon said.

Meredith took the portrait and gave her mommy's picture a kiss on the cheek.

The doors to the SUV closed and Jon looked into Angela's eyes. There was no sign of any emotions there. After all her years in the Cambodia Killing Fields, Jon wasn't surprised that it was impossible to tell what she was truly thinking or feeling.

Heading back to his office, Jon finished packing the small box, picked it up and looked around the office, one last time, before he closed the door.

Jon headed to his car, through the laundry area of the hotel, stopping briefly to say good bye to the many employees he had gotten to know through the years. Then Jon David walked through the kitchen area, walking briskly to avoid good byes to others. He was starting to feel teary as he walked through the kitchen and out the back banquet hallway.

Jon almost always parked in the same spot in the parking garage. It was dimly lit, and Jon never really liked the parking garage since the day he had happened across a local street gang breaking into one of the cars in the garage and instead of running away from him. They boldly started toward him. Jon took a step backwards but did not run. Then the thugs, realizing that he did not want to harm them and nor did he wish to run calmly walked away from the failed crime. He was still defiant.

Jon was nearing his car in the dark garage with boxes in his arms when he realized that someone was approaching quickly behind him. Startled Jon turned his head to see a man coming towards him with what looked like a gun pointed at his head.

"Click" said the man. "That is how easy it would have been to have killed you." The stranger said.

Jon's heart was racing as he realized what the man had just said was true. He could have just killed him and Jon would have been to slow in responding. Instead he had just pointed his finger at his head and now placed his hand back into his jacket pocket.

"So this is what happened to Angela's dad?" Jon asked.

"Yes, actually it was easier; it was raining that night which covered my footsteps and any evidence that I might have accidently left there. He barely even had time to turn around before he was dead on the ground."

"What do you want?" Jon asked.

"I want you to leave the case alone, let it go; there has not been a day since it happened that I have not regretted what happened. I know that I will pay for the karma I have brought upon myself with this murder. I told myself that I was just protecting the family." He continued.

"Please let this go. I am returning to Cambodia and I do not intend to return to the United States again. I have no desire to harm anyone else in this lifetime. But if I am forced to, I will."

"There is nothing worse than taking the life of another person. It still haunts my dreams at night. His ghost visits me and reminds me of his image and of what happened that night." The man said solemnly.

One of the few times in Jon's life, he was at a loss of what to say or do.

"Remember my words." The killer turned and walked away, this day there was no trace of the anger that had been there that fateful night fifteen years earlier.

In February, Angela gave birth to a little girl, Aubrey Cerrina. The months had passed very slowly and there were several times when Angela had come close to losing the baby. After that day at the hotel, Jon David and Angela went back to spending a great deal of their time together. They would email, meet for lunch or coffee, and occasionally even have dinner together. Angela became so open about Jon David being a part of her life that she invited him to her baby shower the day with her family and friends.

"I am healed. Thanks to you," Angela said to Jon David at the baby shower.

"You are welcome." Jon said a little embarrassed, standing in the kitchen with the other members of her family.

Feelings of confusion and manipulation created by fogs and mists

At times, she felt like it was her beloved Tree she'd been spending so much time with.

However, her real beloved tree would never came forth to deny nor agree

After two years Lady Fox still felt his presence, emotionally and spiritually,

Often peaking and bragging of her beloved Tree to her new found tree friend

As time goes by, this new Tree grew to deeply love Lady Fox.

But Lady Fox could only think and dream of her beloved Tree

With jealousy, hurt, and rage, the new Tree tried and brain wash Lady Fox

Not knowing how much distress he put her through

And a major argument set them onto separate paths

Then, one day the sun came out and cleared away the dark fogs and mists

Through her own instincts and investigations, Lady Fox found her way back to her Beloved Tree

Approaching her beloved tree and his territory and there were both of the Trees

Lady Fox built a truce with both of them.

Needing confessions from either one, Lady Fox would like to see

They come forth to admit their deceptions, manipulations, and lies.

Good intentions with care and love beget scheming by her

Beloved Tree

All and all Lady Fox felt betrayed and played for a fool

But through her insight, wisdom and good heart, she silently forgives both trees.

Angela

Tears rolled down Jon's cheeks as he read the parable but at the same time he was smiling and laughing to himself. In Angela's mind she could not accept the rejection she'd felt after her affair with Donald. Her mind would not allow her to accept the fact that Donald had never loved her. Jon wanted to hate her, but couldn't. He knew her better than anyone else, and he realized that she was still that little, tortured girl - a prisoner of her childhood memories. Her only escape is through her own tortured delusions of love.

"People see the beautiful woman, but they will never understand the places she has been and what she has experienced. They will all see her beauty and sex appeal… but only I had the opportunity to see how tortured and how deep a soul truly exists inside of her." Jon thought to himself as he started to look around his apartment at all the things he would need to pack up before moving.

Update

Brother Number One Pol Pot, died in 1998.

The UN-backed genocide tribunal in Cambodia staged its first historic hearing Kaing Guek Eav, known as Duch. The head of the brutal regime's notorious Toul Sleng torture Centre appeared before the panel of five judges on Phnom Penh's outskirts, accused of war crimes and crimes against humanity.

"My name is Kaing Guek Eav," he said. "I am 66 years old."

But descriptions of the crimes committed on his orders at Toul Sleng prison were also detailed: the people allowed to bleed to death, victims whose toe-nails were pulled out, or those put in pits that filled with water until they drowned.

Prosecutors argue that his freedom could stir anger and unrest. They feared that he might flee justice, and observers believe it highly unlikely the tribunal will grant him bail after refusing an earlier application.

None of the top Khmer Rouge leaders have been brought to justice. Most former Khmer Rouge leaders are in their 60s and 70s, and are still living in Cambodia.

Cambodia
Pablito

A land of beauty that you must see
Majestic mountains and giant trees
Unknown jungles to explore and find
Be careful for the unexploded mine

Traditions go back thousands of years
Millions of families and billions of tears
Tortured memories and fears they forgot
Shallow philosophies the Angkar taught

Contrasts of the land I could see
Simple people living by the sea
Green trees that cover all the hills
Millions of lives lost in the fields

A land of Buddhist monks and temples
Living their lives just plain and simple
Khmer Rouge soldiers came one day
They told the monks they could not stay

Many were taken not too far away
Tortured and murdered the soldiers did slay
Death all around them, during these days
People could not protest, they could not say

Beautiful face, dark eyes and black hair
Her eyes would not, at me, even stare
A mute, not speaking, She did not dare
Her life never seemed to be quiet fair

But out of this Cambodian land of pain
Covered by bones and a bloody stain
Tortured memories inside her refrained
Love was found in two, nothing but gain

www.ingramcontent.com/pod-product-compliance
Lightning Source LLC
LaVergne TN
LVHW051622080426
835511LV00016B/2126